MACBETH

The RSC Shakespeare

Edited by Jonathan Bate and Eric Rasmussen

Chief Associate Editor: Héloïse Sénéchal

Associate Editors: Trey Jansen, Eleanor Lowe, Lucy Munro,
Dee Anna Phares, Jan Sewell

Macbeth

Textual editing: Dee Anna Phares and Eric Rasmussen

Introduction and "Shakespeare's Career in the Theater": Jonathan Bate

Commentary: Héloïse Sénéchal

Scene-by-Scene Analysis: Esme Miskimmin

In Performance: Karin Brown (RSC stagings) and Jan Sewell (overview)

The Director's Cut (interviews by Jonathan Bate and Kevin Wright):
Trevor Nunn, Gregory Doran, Rupert Goold

The RSC Shakespeare

William Shakespeare

MACBETH

Edited by Jonathan Bate and Eric Rasmussen

Introduction by Jonathan Bate

The Modern Library
New York

CONTENTS

INTRODUCTION

WHAT IS TRAGEDY?

Macbeth is Shakespeare's shortest, quickest tragedy. Its colors are black and red. It summons up dusk and midnight and at last a poor player who struts and frets with empty sound and fury, his life a snuffed out candle. But along the way we witness high passion, vaulting ambition, alliances made and broken. Macbeth himself is great in action but not in judgment. Give him a task on the battlefield and he will carry it through with aplomb. But give him words and he will be first easily led, then hesitant. His wife chides him for this but, ironically, as the two of them wade deeper into blood, he becomes more purposeful, she a nightmare-beset shadow of her former self.

Every day you will find some local "tragedy" described in the pages of your newspaper: a child drowns, a car crashes, a woman is murdered. The word is used so frequently, and sometimes with regard to misfortunes that in the overall scale of things are so commonplace, that it has been emptied of its primal force. If the word had been treated with the respect it deserves, kept ready for the truly awesome and the world-historical horrors, then a phrase such as "the tragic events of September 11" might have had genuine force instead of being a mere formula that rolls off every politician's tongue.

"Is this the promised end?" asks the Duke of Albany at the end of Shakespeare's *King Lear*. "Or image of that horror?" replies the Earl of Kent. Every human death is, for those who witness it, an image of our own promised end, but until relatively recently the word "tragedy" had not been applied to the mundane cycle of death, the expirations and silencings that occur every hour, every minute, every second. In Shakespeare's world the term was reserved for two exceptional kinds of disaster. One was the catastrophe that seemed cosmic in its scale and horrific in its particulars, so genuinely seeming to be an image of the apocalypse, the promised end of all things.

When William Caxton, England's first printer, wrote of "tragicall tidings," the sort of thing he had in mind was the fall of ancient Troy—the end of a whole civilization, a turning point in history.

The second traditional sense of the word *tragedy* was shaped less by scale than by structure. "Tragedie," wrote Geoffrey Chaucer, father of English verse, "is to seyn a certeyn storie, / As olde bookes maken us memorie, / Of hym that stood in greet prosperitee, / And is yfallen out of heigh degree / Into myserie, and endeth wrecchedly." The higher they climb, the harder they fall: tragedy is traditionally about heroes and kings, larger-than-life figures who climb to the top of fortune's wheel and are then toppled off. It is a structure saturated with irony: the very quality that is the source of a character's greatness is also the cause of his downfall.

This is why talk of a "tragic flaw" is misleading. The theory of the flaw arises from a misunderstanding of Aristotle's influential account of ancient Greek tragedy. For Aristotle, *hamartia*, the thing that precipitates tragedy, is not a psychological predisposition but an event—not a character trait but a fatal action. In several famous cases in Greek tragedy, the particular mistake is to kill a blood relative in ignorance of their identity. So too in Shakespeare, it is action (or, in Hamlet's case, inaction) that determines character, and not vice versa.

In Shakespearean tragedy, the time is out of joint and the lead character is out of his accustomed role. Hamlet the scholar is happy to be presented with an intellectual puzzle, but unsure how to proceed when presented with a demand to kill. Macbeth the soldier, by contrast, relishes violent action but is restless when it comes to waiting for his reward. Hamlet meditates on the nature of providence, while Macbeth is prompted to take his fate into his own hands. Imagine Macbeth in Hamlet's situation. He would have needed no second prompting. On hearing the Ghost's story, he would have gone straight down from the battlements and "unseamed" King Claudius "from the nave to th'chops." His courage and his capacity to act are without question.

King Lear cannot let go of the past, Macbeth cannot wait for the future, Hamlet cannot stop worrying about the future: none of them is content to live in the moment. This is not so much an individual tragic flaw as a universal human failing. We are creatures bound by time but always longing for another time.

Macbeth is more like Hamlet than he appears to be at first glance. He has a conscience. When his ambition is stirred by the weyard sisters' prophecies, he tries to slap it down: "Stars, hide your fires: / Let not light see my black and deep desires." And when he returns to his castle: he soliloquizes on the afterlife every bit in the manner of the Danish prince. But where Hamlet is profoundly alone, unable to bring himself to confide in Ophelia because Gertrude has destroyed his faith in womankind, Macbeth has a wife to take charge of him. She enters as he is concluding his conscience-ridden soliloquy and with a few brisk exchanges and put-downs ("When you durst do it, then you were a man") she changes his mind and settles him to the terrible feat.

His conscience is still working after the regicide, as he is haunted by the sound of the voice crying "Sleep no more." His wife, on the other hand, is cool and practical ("A little water clears us of this deed"). But as the play progresses, in one of Shakespeare's finest structural movements, a reversal takes place. It is Lady Macbeth who sleeps no more, whose mind is emptied of everything save the night of the murder, who cannot wash away the blood ("All the perfumes of Arabia will not sweeten this little hand"). Macbeth, by contrast, steeps himself so far in blood that it becomes easier to carry on than to turn back. He does not tell his wife about the plan to murder Banquo and Fleance, and by the fourth act, when he massacres the innocent Macduffs, she has temporarily disappeared from the action. By the fifth, he is willing on the final encounter: "Blow wind, come wrack, / At least we'll die with harness on our back." The final thoughts inspired by his wife are fatalistic: she began by spurring him to take his destiny into his own hands, she ends as the provocation to his meditation on the meaninglessness of life.

Bound by time but always longing for another time: in the face of this dilemma, Shakespearean tragedy pulls in two different directions. There is a movement toward acceptance of the moment, which means acceptance of death. Thus Macbeth: "She should have died hereafter. / There would have been a time for such a word." And Hamlet: "If it be now, 'tis not to come: if it be not to come, it will be now: if it be not now, yet it will come: the readiness is all." And Edgar in *King Lear*: "Men must endure / Their going hence, even as their coming hither: / Ripeness is all." This is a kind of tragic knowledge that derives from the classical philosophy of Stoicism. Stoicism meant resignation, fortitude, suppression of emotion.

But Shakespeare was also skeptical about Stoicism. It is the Stoic philosophy that he mocks when a grieving father refuses comfort in *Much Ado About Nothing*: "I will be flesh and blood," says Leonato, "For there was never yet philosopher / That could endure the toothache patiently, / However they have writ the style of gods / And made a pish at chance and sufferance." The trouble with Stoicism is that it neglects the capacity to feel, something which makes us human just as much as the capacity to reason. The counter-movement in Shakespearean tragedy is toward an acknowledgment of the emotions, as they express themselves in the body. Gloucester in *King Lear* has no eyes and yet he sees how the world goes: he sees it feelingly. Before Macduff can act like a man in taking revenge against Macbeth for the murder of his family he must first *feel* his grief as a man—he must let himself be a weeping human before turning himself into an alpha male.

"A play read," mused Dr. Samuel Johnson in his preface to Shakespeare, "affects the mind like a play acted." It doesn't: what you have with a play acted is the actor's body. Shakespeare was not a Stoic because he was a player. A player works with his body as much as with his words. In the theater, the body is a supremely expressive instrument of feeling.

"Words, words, mere words," says Hamlet-like Troilus in Shakespeare's acrid Trojan tragedy *Troilus and Cressida*, "No matter from the heart." In the end, what matters about Shakespearean tragedy are not the fine words of resignation and Stoic comfort, but the raw matter of the heart and the solid presence of the body. The body in pain. The body emptied of life but still available for a farewell kiss or blessing. The bodies of Romeo and Juliet, of Othello and Desdemona, come to rest in an embrace. Horatio, best of friends, is there to bid Hamlet's body goodnight. Lear is allowed to mourn over Cordelia; when he has said goodbye to his daughter he is ready for his own heart to break. *Macbeth* is the loneliest of the tragedies because the

Macbeths, having begun the play as one of the few happily married couples anywhere in Shakespeare, drift apart and each dies profoundly alone. There is no Horatio or Earl of Kent to "Give sorrow words" on behalf of the audience. Only in this play could Shakespeare have described life as a walking shadow, a poor player, a tale "Told by an idiot, full of sound and fury, / Signifying nothing."

THE KING'S PLAY

Macbeth is a play about how dreams may become nightmares, how a castle that by day seems the pleasant seat of nesting birds is transformed by night into hell itself—with a grimly witty Porter at the gate. And how the world may be turned upside down: the sun refuses to rise the morning after Duncan has been killed and other strange phenomena are interpreted as disruptions of the natural order.

The English court, in contrast, is represented as a haven, a place of grace and "healing benediction." Malcolm's stay in England serves as an education into virtue. His conquest of Scotland, with the worthy English Siward in support, is made to seem like a restoration of nature, the moving trees of Birnam symbolic of spring and rebirth. The play was written in the first few years after King James united the thrones of Scotland and England: Macduff's final entrance with the tyrant's head and his announcement that the time is free express hope for an end to the uncertainty about the nation's future which had attended the final years of the Virgin Queen's reign.

Within weeks of James VI of Scotland becoming James I of England in 1603, Shakespeare's acting company were given the title "The King's Men." In return for this honor, they were expected to play at court whenever required. They duly gave more command performances at royal events than any of their rivals: between ten and twenty shows per year for the rest of Shakespeare's career.

Two years after his accession, in the summer of 1605, King James visited Oxford University. At the gates of St. John's College, there emerged from an arbor of ivy three undergraduates cross-dressed in the female garb of prophetesses or "sibyls" from classical antiquity. The first hailed him as King of Scotland, the second as King of England, and the third as King of Ireland. They reminded him that three prophesying sisters had told the ancient Scottish thane Banquo that, though he would not be king himself, his descendants would one day rule an immortal empire. Some time before, James himself had commissioned a family tree that traced the Stuart line back to Banquo and Fleance: the sisters were now reconfirming their prophecy.

Macbeth was almost certainly performed in the king's presence, possibly in the summer of 1606 during a visit from the Danish king. This may explain why Norway is made Scotland's enemy in the opening battle, where it was Denmark in the *Chronicles* that were Shakespeare's source. *Macbeth* is steeped in the preoccupations of the new king: the rights of royal succession, the relationship between England and Scotland, the reality of witchcraft, the sacred powers of the monarch (James revived the ancient custom of "touching" his subjects in order to cure them of scrofula, "the king's evil"). And there was one enduring concern inherited from his predecessor's reign: anxiety about high treason and Roman Catholic plots. The Porter's reference to "equivocation" has often been seen as an allusion to the verbal cunning shown by Father Garnet, leader of the British Jesuit community and confessor to the Gunpowder Plot conspirators, during his trial in the early months of 1606.

"Thou shalt get kings, though thou be none," says the Third Witch to Banquo. When Macbeth returns to the weyard sisters in the second half of the play he sees a vision of the generations begotten by Banquo: "A show of eight kings and *Banquo* last: with a glass in his hand." Some critics have supposed that the glass was a mirror pointed at King James sitting in the audience, creating a reflection of his image onstage as Banquo's ghost walks behind. It is more likely to have been a representation of a magic crystal of the sort that was supposed to contain visions of the future. In dramatic terms, there is perhaps also an echo of the diamond given by Banquo to Macbeth on the night of the murder just before he sees another vision, that of a dagger with its handle toward his hand. Whatever the precise nature of the glass, there can be little doubt that the king imagined within it is James, the "two-fold balls" representing the orbs of Scotland and England, the "treble sceptres" denoting his claim to be King of Great Britain, Ireland, and France.

Are the weyard sisters fair or foul? They are more fair than foul in Holinshed. And in the astrologer Simon Forman's recollection of the performance of *Macbeth* he saw at the Globe Theatre in 1611, they are described as "fairies or nymphs," which also sound more fair than foul. The sense of their foulness derives principally from the Middletonian witch-scenes. Banquo's description in Act 1 Scene 3 suggests physical foulness, but his language is characterized primarily by bafflement as to the sisters' appearance. Could they initially have been fair ladies giving apparently fair but in fact foul prophecies? Whatever their appearance, it is significant that they foretell rather than control. In Shakespeare's original text, the sisters may have been morally ambiguous creatures who do nothing more than give voice to mysterious and equivocal "solicitings," oracular prophecies. Middleton may then have converted them into the kind of overtly evil singing and chanting witches who had appeared in Jonson's *Masque of Queens* and about which he wrote his own *The Witch*. He also doubled their number and brought on Hecate and assorted attendant spirits, including one in the shape of a cat. Crude practitioners of black magic, they are unequivocal almost to the point of comedy. This said, we should not necessarily dismiss Middleton's contributions as "spurious interpolations": they are the product of the play's evolving life in the Jacobean theater.

Shakespeare's sisters are elusive and equivocal. They are more like classical Fates than vernacular witches. The term "weird" at this time referred specifically to the Fates and the power of prophecy. In order to suggest something of this nature, and to avoid the modern vernacular associations of "weird," our text adopts the Folio-based spelling "weyard," suggesting "wayward, marginal." The sisters are women on the edge: between society and wilderness, culture and nature, the realm of the body-politic and the mysteries of the hieratic.

HOW MANY CHILDREN?

Why was King James so interested in witches? The main reason was that his ideology of kingship was closely bound to a cosmology of good and evil. He believed passionately in the idea that the monarch was God's representative on earth. The king was the embodiment of virtue, blessed with the power to heal his people and restore cosmic harmony. The idea that the devil was active in the world through the dark agency of witchcraft was the necessary antithesis of this vision. The imagery of Shakespeare's play creates a pervasive sense of connection between the state and the cosmos: witness those signs of disruption in the order of nature reported by Lennox and Ross on the night of Duncan's murder.

Another consequence of James's theory of kingship was the idea that royal succession was divinely ordained rather than achieved arbitrarily through a struggle between rival candidates or through a popular vote. It is therefore extremely significant that in Holinshed's *Chronicles* Duncan's anointing of his son Malcolm as Prince of Cumberland is a turning point in Scottish history: this is the moment when the principle of primogeniture is established in Scotland. In Holinshed, Macbeth is Duncan's cousin and until this moment he has the right to the succession in the event of Duncan dying before Malcolm comes of age.

In the mid-twentieth century there was a tendency among critics to mock the Victorian scholar A. C. Bradley for treating Shakespeare's characters as if they were real people, with a past and a life beyond that which is seen onstage. The shorthand term for this mockery was Bradley's question, "How many children had Lady Macbeth?" But Bradley has outlasted his critics: to a greater degree than any other writer prior to the flowering of the realist novel, Shakespeare *did* use language to create the illusion that his characters have an interior life and that there is a "backstory" to his plots. The language of *Macbeth* is steeped in images of children, of birth, of inheritance and future generations. The sons of Duncan, Banquo, and Macduff are all crucial to the action, and there is even a telling bit part for the son of the English soldier Siward. No other Shakespearean tragedy has so many significant male children in the cast. Only Macbeth is without a son. Hence his appalled realization that he has a barren sceptre in his hand, that his bloody deeds have been done only "to make them kings, the seeds of Banquo kings."

Shakespeare doesn't usually portray married couples working

together as partners. There are moments of exceptional tenderness between the Macbeths. Yet there is an emptiness at the core of their relationship. The play is scarred by images of sterility and harrowed by glimpses of dead babies. Is power in the end a substitute for love, ambition nothing but compensation for the sorrow of childlessness? It has to be assumed that Lady Macbeth means what she says when she speaks of having "given suck" and of knowing "how tender 'tis to love the babe that milks me": we can only assume that the Macbeths have had a child and lost it. Perhaps that is why they channel the energies of their marriage into the lust for power instead.

Shakespeare is the least autobiographical of great writers, but can it be entirely a coincidence that, a decade before, he too had lost a child, his only son Hamnet, and that in the years since then he had channeled all his creative powers not into a family but into his work, his theater company, and the thrill of those extraordinary occasions when he found himself—a grammar boy from the provinces with no university education—witnessing the King of England and Scotland, with all his court, listening in rapt attention as his words were spoken from the platform of the banqueting hall in the royal palace?

THE WORD INCARNADINE

The forms of Shakespeare's verse loosened and became more flexible as he matured as a writer. His early plays have a higher proportion of rhyme and a greater regularity in rhythm, the essential pattern being that of iambic pentameter (ten syllables, five stresses, the stress on every second syllable). In the early plays, lines are very frequently end-stopped: punctuation marks a pause at the line ending, meaning that the movement of the syntax (the grammatical construction) falls in with that of the meter (the rhythmical construction). In the later plays, there are far fewer rhyming couplets (sometimes rhyme features only as a marker to indicate that a scene is ending) and the rhythmic movement has far greater variety, freedom, and flow. Mature Shakespearean blank (unrhymed) verse is typically not end-stopped but "run on" (a feature known as "enjambment"): instead of pausing heavily at the line ending, the speaker hurries forward, the sense demanded by the grammar working in creative tension against the holding pattern of the meter. The heavier pauses migrate to the middle of the lines (where they are known as the "caesura" and where their placing varies). Much more often than in the early plays, a single line of verse is shared between two speakers. And the pentameter itself becomes a more subtle instrument: the iambic beat is broken up, there is often an extra ("redundant") unstressed eleventh syllable at the end of the line (known as a "feminine ending"). There are more modulations between verse and prose. Occasionally the verse is so loose that neither the original typesetters of the plays when they were first printed nor the modern editors of scholarly texts can be entirely certain whether verse or prose is intended. The iambic pentamenter is the ideal medium for dramatic poetry in English because its rhythm and duration seem to fall in naturally with the speech patterns of the language. In its capacity to combine the ordinary variety of speech with the heightened precision of poetry, the supple, mature Shakespearean "loose pentameter" is perhaps the most expressive vocal instrument ever given to the actor.

Open the text of *Macbeth* at random and you are guaranteed almost immediately to find a strong example of this loose pentameter. In a first test of this claim, the script fell open at the end of Act 5 Scene 5. A messenger brings news of Birnam Wood: "Within this three mile may you see it coming: / I say, a moving grove." The announcement ends on an abrupt half line, so Macbeth speaks the other half:

If thou speak'st false,
Upon the next tree shall thou hang alive
Till famine cling thee . . .

As if in imitation of what is being said, Shakespeare makes the verse "hang alive" at the line ending: instead of a deadening end-stop, there is the most momentary pause before we tumble headlong into the next line. The heavy pause then comes in the very middle of the line (after the fifth syllable, not the more customary fourth or sixth). When he turns away from the messenger, Macbeth goes into meditative mode. He soliloquizes even though he is not alone:

I pull in resolution, and begin
To doubt th'equivocation of the fiend
That lies like truth. . . .

The flow of his thought is enacted in the running on of the lines: "begin / To doubt," "the fiend / That lies."

Always in Shakespeare, metrical innovation goes alongside verbal invention: "cling thee" is what you would expect a lover to do, not starvation. Simile and metaphor are among the key building blocks of his poetry. "Was the hope drunk / Wherein you dressed yourself?" Lady Macbeth chides her husband, "And wakes it now, to look so green and pale?" The waking image is a superbly accurate imagining of a severe hangover. The ingenuity of the comparison comes from the application of something so physical as the bodily symptoms of a hangover to something so psychological as the idea of "hope." We are eased into the physicality by "dressed." Clothing is one of the similes through which the play repeatedly embodies abstractions that denote social status:

New honours come upon him,
Like our strange garments, cleave not to their mould
But with the aid of use.

And:

. . . now does he feel his title
Hang loose about him, like a giant's robe
Upon a dwarfish thief.

Metaphors are usually most powerful when they link things from very different frames of reference; for instance, the amplitude of "life" itself and the confinement of "a poor player / That struts and frets his hour upon the stage / And then is heard no more." Within this metaphor there are further configurations of multiple meaning: "poor" simultaneously suggests "mere," "ill-paid," and "unskillful," while "frets" suggests "wears out," "worries his way through," and "rants." But when Macbeth begins to doubt the "equivocation of the fiend"—at this point he is with his last remaining follower, who rejoices in the name of "Seyton" (a dark pun: the name may be pronounced "Satan")—he comes up with a simile that links things from the *same* frame of reference: "That lies like truth." To lie and to tell the truth at one and the same time: that is true equivocation, literally the vocation—the voicing—of things that are equal but opposite.

The play does it all the time, from the first appearance of the weyard sisters ("When the battle's lost and won," "Fair is foul, and foul is fair") through Macbeth's first entrance ("So foul and fair a day I have not seen") to Ross's moving tribute to old Siward's battle-slain son ("He only lived but till he was a man. . . . But like a man he died"). In this world, even the ornithology palters with us in a double sense: "Light thickens, / And the crow makes wing to the rooky wood." Simultaneously like and unlike: the crow is a large black bird that feeds upon the carcasses of beasts and that lives in pairs (fittingly, in that Macbeth is at this point speaking to Lady Macbeth), while rooks, though closely related to crows, are sociable birds that live in vast colonies. Crow and rook are both similar and different, as Macbeth is both similar to and different from the other thanes. Rooks live in rookeries, but the adjective "rooky" is a Shakespearean coinage that plays brilliantly on an old dialect word "rawky" or "roky": as one dictionary has it, "We say it is a rooky day, when the air is thick and the light of consequence feeble."

Language in *Macbeth* is thickened to a viscous texture. Like that of clotted blood. Another form of what might be called poetic equivocation is the restatement of the same idea in two different idioms:

Will all great Neptune's ocean wash this blood
Clean from my hand? No, this my hand will rather
The multitudinous seas incarnadine,
Making the green one red.

The two latter lines say the same thing twice, first in erudite Latinate polysyllables, then in plain monosyllabic Anglo-Saxon colors. Shakespeare holds together the complex linguistic inheritance of English at the time of his mother tongue's richest expansion. He speaks in one line to his educated and elevated courtly audience, then in the next to the ordinary people, the penny-paying groundlings. *Macbeth* is a play steeped in stage blood, but perhaps its greatest achievement is to incarnate—to incarnadine—the hot blood of life into the evanescent breath of the poetic word.

ABOUT THE TEXT

Shakespeare endures through history. He illuminates later times as well as his own. He helps us to understand the human condition. But he cannot do this without a good text of the plays. Without editions there would be no Shakespeare. That is why every twenty years or so throughout the last three centuries there has been a major new edition of his complete works. One aspect of editing is the process of keeping the texts up to date—modernizing the spelling, punctuation, and typography (though not, of course, the actual words), providing explanatory notes in the light of changing educational practices (a generation ago, most of Shakespeare's classical and biblical allusions could be assumed to be generally understood, but now they can't).

Because Shakespeare did not personally oversee the publication of his plays, with some plays there are major editorial difficulties. Decisions have to be made as to the relative authority of the early printed editions, the pocket format "quartos" published in Shakespeare's lifetime, and the elaborately produced First Folio text of 1623, the original "Complete Works" prepared for the press after his death by Shakespeare's fellow actors, the people who knew the plays better than anyone else. *Macbeth* exists only in a Folio text that is reasonably well printed. However, as explained in the introduction above, the surviving text, which is much shorter than those of the other tragedies, may represent a theatrical adaptation post-dating Shakespeare's retirement, possibly overseen by Thomas Middleton. The extent of Middleton's involvement is debated by scholars: the Hecate scenes have long been attributed to him, but the possibility of detecting his hand elsewhere in the play is hotly debated (the 2007 Oxford edition of Middleton's complete works actually included *Macbeth*). Since our editorial principle in the RSC Shakespeare is to follow the First Folio wherever possible, we print the Hecate scenes as they appear there, giving only the opening words of the songs. The full text of the songs from Middleton's *The Witch* is given at the end of the play, but we cannot know for sure that exactly the same words were used in *Macbeth*.

The following notes highlight various aspects of the editorial process and indicate conventions used in the text of this edition:

Lists of Parts are supplied in the First Folio for only six plays, not including *Macbeth*, so the list here is editorially supplied. Capitals indicate that part of the name which is used for speech headings in the script (thus "King DUNCAN").

Locations are provided by the Folio for only two plays, of which *Macbeth* is not one. Eighteenth-century editors, working in an age of elaborately realistic stage sets, were the first to provide detailed locations ("another part of the palace"). Given that Shakespeare wrote for a bare stage and often an imprecise sense of place, we have relegated locations to the explanatory notes at the foot of the page, where they are given at the beginning of each scene in which the imaginary location is different from the one before.

Act and Scene Divisions were provided in the Folio in a much more thoroughgoing way than in the Quartos. Sometimes, however, they were erroneous or omitted; corrections and additions supplied by editorial tradition are indicated by square brackets. Five-act division is based on a classical model, and act breaks provided the opportunity to replace the candles in the indoor Blackfriars playhouse that the King's Men used after 1608, but Shakespeare did not necessarily think in terms of a five-part structure of dramatic composition. The Folio convention is that a scene ends when the stage is empty. Nowadays, partly under the influence of film, we tend to consider a scene to be a dramatic unit that ends with either a change of imaginary location or a significant passage of time within the narrative. Shakespeare's fluidity of composition accords well with this convention, so in addition to act and scene numbers we provide a *running scene* count in the right margin at the beginning of each new scene, in the typeface used for editorial directions. Where there is a scene break caused by a momentary bare stage, but the location does not change and extra time does not pass, we use the convention *running scene continues.* There is inevitably a degree of editorial judgment in making such calls, but the system is very valuable in suggesting the pace of the plays.

Speakers' Names are often inconsistent in Folio. We have regularized speech headings, but retained an element of deliberate inconsistency in entry directions, in order to give the flavor of Folio.

Verse is indicated by lines that do not run to the right margin and by capitalization of each line. The Folio printers sometimes set verse as prose, and vice versa (either out of misunderstanding or for reasons of space). We have silently corrected in such cases, although in some instances there is ambiguity, in which case we have leaned toward the preservation of Folio layout. Folio sometimes uses contraction ("turnd" rather than "turned") to indicate whether or not the final "-ed" of a past participle is sounded, an area where there is variation for the sake of the five-beat iambic pentameter rhythm. We use the convention of a grave accent to indicate sounding (thus "turnèd" would be two syllables), but would urge actors not to overstress. In cases where one speaker ends with a verse half line and the next begins with the other half of the pentameter, editors since the late eighteenth century have indented the second line. We have abandoned this convention, since the Folio does not use it, and nor did actors' cues in the Shakespearean theater. An exception is made when the second speaker actively interrupts or completes the first speaker's sentence.

Spelling is modernized, but older forms are very occasionally maintained where necessary for rhythm or aural effect.

Punctuation in Shakespeare's time was as much rhetorical as grammatical. "Colon" was originally a term for a unit of thought in an argument. The semicolon was a new unit of punctuation (some of the Quartos lack them altogether). We have modernized punctuation throughout, but have given more weight to Folio punctuation than many editors, since, though not Shakespearean, it reflects the usage of his period. In particular, we have used the colon far more than many editors: it is exceptionally useful as a way of indicating how many Shakespearean speeches unfold clause by clause in a developing argument that gives the illusion of enacting the process of thinking in the moment. We have also kept in mind the origin of punctuation in classical times as a way of assisting the actor and orator: the comma suggests the briefest of pauses for breath, the colon a middling one, and a full stop or period a longer pause. Semicolons, by contrast, belong to an era of punctuation that was only just coming in during Shakespeare's time and that is coming to an end now: we have accordingly used them only where they occur in our copy texts (and not always then). Dashes are sometimes used for parenthetical interjections where the Folio has brackets. They are also used for interruptions and changes in train of thought. Where a change of addressee occurs within a speech, we have used a dash preceded by a full stop (or occasionally another form of punctuation). Often the identity of the respective addressees is obvious from the context. When it is not, this has been indicated in a marginal stage direction.

Entrances and Exits are fairly thorough in Folio, which has accordingly been followed as faithfully as possible. Where characters are omitted or corrections are necessary, this is indicated by square brackets (e.g. "[*and Attendants*]"). *Exit* is sometimes silently normalized to *Exeunt*, and *Manet* anglicized to "remains." We trust Folio positioning of entrances and exits to a greater degree than most editors.

Editorial Stage Directions such as stage business, asides, indications of addressee and of characters' position on the gallery stage are only used sparingly in Folio. Other editions mingle directions of this kind with original Folio and Quarto directions, sometimes marking them by means of square brackets. We have sought to distinguish what could be described as *directorial* interventions of this kind from Folio-style directions (either original or supplied) by placing them in the right margin in a different typeface. There is a degree of subjectivity about which directions are of which kind, but the procedure is intended as a reminder to the reader and the actor that

Shakespearean stage directions are often dependent upon editorial inference alone and are not set in stone. We also depart from editorial tradition in sometimes admitting uncertainty and thus printing permissive stage directions, such as an ***Aside?*** (often a line may be equally effective as an aside or a direct address—it is for each production or reading to make its own decision) or a ***may exit*** or a piece of business placed between arrows to indicate that it may occur at various different moments within a scene.

Line Numbers in the left margin are editorial, for reference and to key the explanatory and textual notes.

Explanatory Notes at the foot of each page explain allusions and gloss obsolete and difficult words, confusing phraseology, occasional major textual cruces, and so on. Particular attention is given to nonstandard usage, bawdy innuendo, and technical terms (e.g. legal and military language). Where more than one sense is given, commas indicate shades of related meaning, slashes alternative or double meanings.

Textual Notes at the end of the play indicate major departures from the Folio. They take the following form: the reading of our text is given in bold and its source given after an equals sign, with "F2" indicating a reading that derives from the Second Folio of 1632, "F3" one that derives from the Third Folio of 1663–64, and "Ed" that it derives from the subsequent editorial tradition. The rejected Folio ("F") reading is then given. Thus for Act 3 Scene 6 line 25: "**son** = Ed. F = Sonnes" means that the Folio text refers to Duncan's two sons, where the context clearly demands one, so we have corrected to the singular. It is possible, of course, in this case that the mistake is Shakespeare's, not the printer's: he might have forgotten that he sent Donalbain to Ireland and only Malcolm to England. The editorial task is a never-ending process of conjecture and debate.

KEY FACTS

AUTHORSHIP: There is no doubt about Shakespeare's authorship of the bulk of the play, but it is probable that the printed text bears the marks of some theatrical revision, possibly by **THOMAS MIDDLETON**. In particular, the scenes involving Hecate seem to be additions by Middleton.

MAJOR PARTS: (*with percentage of lines/number of speeches/scenes onstage*) Macbeth (29%/146/15), Lady Macbeth (11%/59/9), Malcolm (9%/40/8), Macduff (7%/59/7), Ross (6%/39/7), Banquo (5%/33/7), First Witch (3%/23/4), Lennox (3%/21/6), Duncan (3%/18/3), Second Witch (2%/15/3), Third Witch 2%/13/3, Porter (2%/4/1), Wife of Macduff (2%/19/1), Scottish Doctor (2%/19/2).

LINGUISTIC MEDIUM: 95% verse, 5% prose.

DATE: 1606? Certainly Jacobean rather than Elizabethan, to judge from its several compliments to King James. Performed at the Globe in April 1611 and perhaps at court in August or December 1606. References to "equivocation" and other allusions suggest written soon after trial of Gunpowder Plot conspirators (January–March 1606). The ship *Tiger*, mentioned in Act 1 Scene 3, sailed for the east in 1604 and returned after a terrible voyage in the summer of 1606.

SOURCES: Based on account of reigns of Duncan and Makbeth in "The Chronicles of Scotland," from vol. 2 of Raphael Holinshed's *Chronicles of England, Scotland, and Ireland* (1587 edition), with some use of material elsewhere in the Scottish chronicles. Shows awareness of the Stuart dynasty's claim to lineage from Banquo. Some of the imagery is influenced by the language of Seneca's tragedies.

Hecate scenes incorporate material from Thomas Middleton's play *The Witch*.

TEXT: 1623 Folio is the only early printed text. Its brevity suggests possible theatrical cutting. Good quality of printing, though with severe problems of lineation.

THE TRAGEDY OF MACBETH

LIST OF PARTS

King DUNCAN of Scotland

MALCOLM ⎱
DONALBAIN ⎰ his sons

A CAPTAIN in Duncan's army

MACBETH, Thane of Glamis, later Thane of Cawdor, then King of Scotland

LADY MACBETH, his wife

A PORTER at Macbeth's castle

SEYTON, servant to Macbeth

A DOCTOR

A GENTLEWOMAN, attendant upon Lady Macbeth

THREE MURDERERS

BANQUO, a thane

FLEANCE, his son

MACDUFF, Thane of Fife

LADY MACDUFF, his wife

MACDUFF'S SON ⎱
LENNOX
ROSS
ANGUS ⎰ Thanes
CAITHNESS
MENTEITH

AN OLD MAN

SIWARD, Earl of Northumberland

YOUNG SIWARD, his son

DOCTOR at the English court

THREE WITCHES, known as Weyard Sisters

HECATE, Queen of Witches

Lords, Thanes, Attendants, Servants, Torchbearers, Soldiers, Drummers, a Messenger, Apparitions (including an armed head, a bloody child, a child crowned, a show of eight kings)

Act 1 Scene 1

Thunder and lightning. Enter three Witches

FIRST WITCH   When shall we three meet again?
In thunder, lightning, or in rain?
SECOND WITCH   When the hurly-burly's done,
When the battle's lost and won.
5   THIRD WITCH   That will be ere the set of sun.
FIRST WITCH   Where the place?
SECOND WITCH   Upon the heath.
THIRD WITCH   There to meet with Macbeth.
FIRST WITCH   I come, Grey Malkin.
10   SECOND WITCH   Paddock calls.
THIRD WITCH   Anon.
ALL   Fair is foul, and foul is fair:
Hover through the fog and filthy air.   *Exeunt*

Act 1 Scene 2

Alarum within. Enter King [Duncan], Malcolm, Donalbain, Lennox,
with Attendants, meeting a bleeding Captain

DUNCAN   What bloody man is that? He can report,
As seemeth by his plight, of the revolt
The newest state.
MALCOLM   This is the sergeant
5   Who like a good and hardy soldier fought
Gainst my captivity.— Hail, brave friend;   *To the Captain*
Say to the king the knowledge of the broil
As thou didst leave it.
CAPTAIN   Doubtful it stood,
10   As two spent swimmers that do cling together

1.1   *Location: an open place*   3 hurly-burly turmoil, uproar, strife   **5 ere** before   **9 Grey**
Malkin a cat, the First Witch's familiar (a spirit in animal form that carried out evil deeds for
a witch)   **10 Paddock** the Second Witch's familiar, a toad   **11 Anon** soon, in a moment
1.2   *Location: Scotland, outdoors, exact location unspecified   Alarum* a trumpet call
to arms   **2 plight** condition, appearance   **3 newest state** latest state of affairs   **5 hardy** bold/
vigorous   **6 captivity** capture by the enemy   **7 broil** battle, tumult   **10 spent** exhausted

And choke their art. The merciless Macdonald —
Worthy to be a rebel, for to that
The multiplying villainies of nature
Do swarm upon him — from the Western Isles
15   Of kerns and gallowglasses is supplied,
And Fortune on his damnèd quarrel smiling,
Showed like a rebel's whore. But all's too weak,
For brave Macbeth — well he deserves that name —
Disdaining Fortune, with his brandished steel
20   Which smoked with bloody execution,
Like valour's minion carved out his passage
Till he faced the slave,
Which ne'er shook hands nor bade farewell to him
Till he unseamed him from the nave to th'chops
25   And fixed his head upon our battlements.

DUNCAN   O valiant cousin, worthy gentleman!

CAPTAIN   As whence the sun 'gins his reflection,
Shipwrecking storms and direful thunders,
So from that spring whence comfort seemed to come,
30   Discomfort swells. Mark, King of Scotland, mark:
No sooner justice had, with valour armed,
Compelled these skipping kerns to trust their heels,
But the Norwegian lord, surveying vantage,

---

11 choke their art destroy their skill (i.e. weigh one another down and drown)   12 to that to
that end, for that reason   13 multiplying . . . nature increasing numbers of evils within
nature/growing numbers of unnatural rebel soldiers   14 Western Isles the Hebrides (islands
west of Scotland) and possibly Ireland   15 Of kerns with lightly armed foot soldiers
gallowglasses soldiers armed with axes   supplied reinforced   16 quarrel dispute/hostile
cause ("her damnèd quarry" would be an alternative reading)   17 Showed appeared/
sexually displayed herself   19 brandished shining/flourished   21 minion favorite one,
darling   carved . . . passage hacked his way through   22 slave villain (i.e. the rebel
Macdonald)   23 Which who (i.e. Macbeth)   24 unseamed him ripped him in two (clothing
metaphor)   nave to th'chops navel to the jaws   27 As . . . thunders just as destructive
storms and dreadful thunder originate (like the Norwegian invaders) in the east, where the
warming sun rises/just as when the sun begins to return at the spring equinox, it is
accompanied by storms 'gins begins   reflection shining/return   29 spring source (of
water)/springtime   comfort encouraging news   30 swells wells up/becomes swollen   Mark
note, pay attention   32 skipping lightly armed/nervously bounding/absconding   trust their
heels run away   33 Norwegian lord i.e. Sweno (original pronunciation: "Norweyan")
surveying vantage perceiving an advantage

With furbished arms and new supplies of men,

35   Began a fresh assault.

DUNCAN   Dismayed not this our captains, Macbeth and
             Banquo?

CAPTAIN   Yes, as sparrows eagles, or the hare the lion.

If I say sooth, I must report they were

As cannons overcharged with double cracks,

40   So they doubly redoubled strokes upon the foe.

Except they meant to bathe in reeking wounds

Or memorize another Golgotha,

I cannot tell.

But I am faint, my gashes cry for help.

45   DUNCAN   So well thy words become thee as thy wounds:

They smack of honour both.— Go get him surgeons.

                                    [*Exit Captain, attended*]

Enter Ross and Angus

Who comes here?

MALCOLM   The worthy Thane of Ross.

LENNOX   What a haste looks through his eyes!

50   So should he look that seems to speak things strange.

ROSS   God save the king.

DUNCAN   Whence cam'st thou, worthy thane?

ROSS   From Fife, great king,

Where the Norwegian banners flout the sky

55   And fan our people cold.

Norway himself, with terrible numbers,

Assisted by that most disloyal traitor,

---

34 furbished gleaming/revived   **37 Yes . . . lion** i.e. only as much as a weak creature would dismay a powerful predator   **38 sooth** truth   **report** tell (plays on the sense of "noise of a cannon firing")   **39 cracks** charges of gunpowder   **41 Except** unless   **reeking** bloody/steaming (as the hot blood meets the air)   **42 memorize** make memorable   **Golgotha** "place of skulls" where Christ was crucified   **45 become** befit/honor   **46 smack** savor (plays on the sense of "the noise lips make in tasting" and so continues the idea of **gashes** as mouths)   **48 Thane** title of a member of the Scottish nobility (broadly equivalent to an English earl)   **49 looks through** appears in   **50 seems to** seems to be about to   **53 Fife** region on the east coast of Scotland   **54 flout** defy/mock   **56 Norway himself** i.e. Sweno, King of Norway   **terrible numbers** terrifying quantities of soldiers

The Thane of Cawdor, began a dismal conflict
Till that Bellona's bridegroom, lapped in proof,
60　Confronted him with self-comparisons,
Point against point, rebellious arm gainst arm,
Curbing his lavish spirit: and to conclude,
The victory fell on us—

DUNCAN　Great happiness.

65　ROSS　That now Sweno, the Norways' king,
Craves composition:
Nor would we deign him burial of his men
Till he disbursèd at Saint Colme's inch
Ten thousand dollars to our general use.

70　DUNCAN　No more that Thane of Cawdor shall deceive
Our bosom interest: go pronounce his present death,
And with his former title greet Macbeth.

ROSS　I'll see it done.

DUNCAN　What he hath lost, noble Macbeth hath won.

Exeunt

Act 1 Scene 3

running scene 3

Thunder. Enter the three Witches

FIRST WITCH　Where hast thou been, sister?

SECOND WITCH　Killing swine.

THIRD WITCH　Sister, where thou?

FIRST WITCH　A sailor's wife had chestnuts in her lap,
5　And munched and munched and munched.
'Give me', quoth I.

---

58 dismal devastating/ominous　**59 Bellona's bridegroom** i.e. Macbeth　**Bellona** Roman
goddess of war　**lapped in proof** wrapped in armor of tried and tested strength
60 Confronted . . . self-comparisons i.e. matched him in every respect　**61 Point** sword's
point　**arm** weapon　**62 lavish** unrestrained, wild　**65 Norways** Norwegians　**66 Craves
composition** requests a peace treaty　**67 deign** condescend to permit　**68 disbursèd** paid out
Saint Colme's inch Inchcolm, an island in the Firth of Forth (estuary on the east coast of
Scotland)　**69 dollars** English name for the German thaler, as well as for silver coins from
various northern countries　**71 bosom interest** closest, most intimate concerns　**present**
immediate　**1.3** *Location: a heath*　**6 quoth** said

'Aroint thee, witch!' the rump-fed runnion cries.
Her husband's to Aleppo gone, master o'th'*Tiger*:
But in a sieve I'll thither sail,
10 And like a rat without a tail,
I'll do, I'll do and I'll do.
SECOND WITCH   I'll give thee a wind.
FIRST WITCH Thou'rt kind.
THIRD WITCH And I another.
15 FIRST WITCH I myself have all the other,
And the very ports they blow,
All the quarters that they know
I'th'shipman's card.
I'll drain him dry as hay:
20 Sleep shall neither night nor day
Hang upon his penthouse lid:
He shall live a man forbid:
Weary sennights nine times nine
Shall he dwindle, peak and pine.
25 Though his bark cannot be lost,
Yet it shall be tempest-tossed.
Look what I have.
SECOND WITCH   Show me, show me.
FIRST WITCH Here I have a pilot's thumb,
30 Wrecked as homeward he did come.   *Drum within*
THIRD WITCH A drum, a drum:
Macbeth doth come.

---

7 Aroint thee be off with you   **rump-fed** fed on rump (a generous cut of meat), hence
greedy/with a well-fed vagina, hence lecherous   **runnion** abusive term for a woman (possibly
plays on the abusive slang sense of "penis")   **8 Aleppo** trading city in northern Syria
master captain   *Tiger* the ship's name   **10 like** in the guise of   **11 do** act/have sex (it was
thought that witches often seduced their male victims)   **15 other** other winds   **16 ports they
blow** a wind blowing from land would make a port inaccessible to a ship at sea   **17 quarters**
directions/compass points   **18 I'th'shipman's card** in the sailor's chart/card showing the
compass points   **19 drain** exhaust/drain sexually   **21 penthouse lid** eyelid (that projects like
a top-heavy upper floor of a building)   **22 forbid** cursed   **23 sennights** weeks (seven nights)
24 peak and pine waste away and starve (perhaps with connotations of phallic detumescence)
25 bark ship   **26 tempest-tossed** tossed on the sea by storms   **29 pilot** steersman of a ship

ALL   The weyard sisters, hand in hand,   *They dance in a circle*

Posters of the sea and land,

35   Thus do go about, about,

Thrice to thine and thrice to mine

And thrice again, to make up nine.

Peace, the charm's wound up.

Enter Macbeth and Banquo

MACBETH   So foul and fair a day I have not seen.

40   BANQUO   How far is't called to Forres?— What are these,

So withered and so wild in their attire,

That look not like th'inhabitants o'th'earth

And yet are on't?— Live you, or are you aught   *To Witches*

That man may question? You seem to understand me

45   By each at once her choppy finger laying

Upon her skinny lips. You should be women,

And yet your beards forbid me to interpret

That you are so.

MACBETH   Speak if you can: what are you?

50   FIRST WITCH   All hail, Macbeth: hail to thee, Thane of Glamis!

SECOND WITCH   All hail, Macbeth: hail to thee, Thane of Cawdor!

THIRD WITCH   All hail, Macbeth, that shalt be king hereafter!

BANQUO   Good sir, why do you start and seem to fear

Things that do sound so fair?— I'th'name of truth,   *To Witches*

55   Are ye fantastical or that indeed

Which outwardly ye show? My noble partner

You greet with present grace and great prediction

Of noble having and of royal hope,

---

33 weyard wayward; with the power to control or foresee destiny; the fact that there are three witches invites a comparison with the classical Fates (always spelled "weyard" or "weyward" in Folio; never "weird," the spelling in the play's source, Holinshed's "Chronicles of Scotland") **34 Posters** swift travelers **35 Thus . . . nine** the witches perform a ritualized dance or series of movements **38 Peace** be still/be silent **charm** magic spell **wound up** prepared, ready **39 foul and fair** darkly stormy yet bright in terms of military success (the phrase also resonates with the sense of "morally wicked and virtuous") **40 is't called** is it said to be **Forres** town in the northeast of Scotland, east of Inverness **43 on't** on it (the earth) **aught** anything **45 choppy** chapped **46 should be** would appear to be **53 start** flinch/react nervously/recoil **55 fantastical** imaginary **indeed** in truth/in deed **56 show** appear to be **57 present grace** immediate honor **58 having** gain

That he seems rapt withal: to me you speak not.

60 If you can look into the seeds of time
And say which grain will grow and which will not,
Speak then to me, who neither beg nor fear
Your favours nor your hate.

FIRST WITCH   Hail!

65 SECOND WITCH   Hail!

THIRD WITCH   Hail!

FIRST WITCH   Lesser than Macbeth, and greater.

SECOND WITCH   Not so happy, yet much happier.

THIRD WITCH   Thou shalt get kings, though thou be none:

70 So all hail, Macbeth and Banquo!

FIRST WITCH   Banquo and Macbeth, all hail!

MACBETH   Stay, you imperfect speakers: tell me more.
By Sinel's death I know I am Thane of Glamis,
But how of Cawdor? The Thane of Cawdor lives,

75 A prosperous gentleman: and to be king
Stands not within the prospect of belief,
No more than to be Cawdor. Say from whence
You owe this strange intelligence or why
Upon this blasted heath you stop our way

80 With such prophetic greeting? Speak, I charge you.

Witches vanish

BANQUO   The earth hath bubbles, as the water has,
And these are of them. Whither are they vanished?

MACBETH   Into the air: and what seemed corporal
Melted as breath into the wind. Would they had stayed.

85 BANQUO   Were such things here as we do speak about?
Or have we eaten on the insane root
That takes the reason prisoner?

---

59 rapt withal entranced, absorbed by it   **62 neither . . . hate** neither begs your favor
nor fears your hate   **68 happy** favored by fortune/content   **69 get** beget, conceive
72 imperfect unclear/cryptic/incomplete   **73 Sinel** Macbeth's father   **76 prospect** field of
view/anticipation of the future   **77 whence . . . intelligence** where you got this strange
information   **79 blasted** blighted/accursed   **80 charge** command   **83 corporal** physical,
bodily   **84 Would** I wish   **86 on** of   **insane root** root of plant (probably henbane) that was
reputed to cause madness if eaten

	MACBETH	Your children shall be kings.
	BANQUO	You shall be king.
90	MACBETH	And Thane of Cawdor too: went it not so?
	BANQUO	To th'selfsame tune and words. Who's here?

Enter Ross and Angus

ROSS   The king hath happily received, Macbeth,
The news of thy success, and when he reads
Thy personal venture in the rebels' fight,

95   His wonders and his praises do contend
Which should be thine or his: silenced with that,
In viewing o'er the rest o'th'selfsame day,
He finds thee in the stout Norwegian ranks,
Nothing afeard of what thyself didst make,

100   Strange images of death. As thick as tale
Can post with post, and every one did bear
Thy praises in his kingdom's great defence,
And poured them down before him.

ANGUS   We are sent

105   To give thee from our royal master thanks,
Only to herald thee into his sight,
Not pay thee.

ROSS   And for an earnest of a greater honour,
He bade me, from him, call thee Thane of Cawdor:

110   In which addition, hail, most worthy thane,
For it is thine.

BANQUO   What, can the devil speak true?

MACBETH   The Thane of Cawdor lives:
Why do you dress me in borrowed robes?

115   ANGUS   Who was the thane lives yet,

---

91 th'selfsame the very same   **93 reads** perceives, comprehends   **94 venture** risky involvement   **95 His . . . his** i.e. his personal feelings of awe and praises for you are both so great as to compete with one another (the result being that he finds himself **silenced**) **98 stout** brave   **99 Nothing afeard** not at all afraid   **what . . . make** i.e. slaughter on the battlefield (**strange images of death**)   **100 As . . . post** messengers arrived as thick and fast as the tales they had to tell (though some editors emend "tale" to "hail," which fits better with the subsequent **poured down**)   **106 Only . . . thee** only in order to usher you into his presence, not as a means of rewarding you   **108 earnest** pledge, foretaste   **110 addition** title   **115 Who** he who

But under heavy judgement bears that life
Which he deserves to lose.
Whether he was combined with those of Norway,
Or did line the rebel with hidden help
120   And vantage, or that with both he laboured
In his country's wreck, I know not:
But treasons capital, confessed and proved,
Have overthrown him.

MACBETH   Glamis and Thane of Cawdor: *Aside*
125   The greatest is behind.— Thanks for your
        pains.—   *To Ross and Angus*
Do you not hope your children shall be kings   *Aside to Banquo*
When those that gave the Thane of Cawdor to me
Promised no less to them?

BANQUO   That, trusted home,   *Aside to Macbeth*
130   Might yet enkindle you unto the crown,
Besides the Thane of Cawdor. But 'tis strange:
And oftentimes, to win us to our harm,
The instruments of darkness tell us truths,
Win us with honest trifles, to betray's
135   In deepest consequence.—
Cousins, a word, I pray you.   *To Ross and Angus; they*

                                                converse apart

MACBETH   Two truths are told,   *Aside*
As happy prologues to the swelling act
Of the imperial theme.—

                        I thank you, gentlemen.—   *To Ross*

                                                and Angus

140   This supernatural soliciting   *Aside*

---

116 judgement sentence   **118 combined** in league   **119 line** reinforce (metaphorically, "line
the rebel's garment")   **rebel** i.e. Macdonald   **122 capital** deserving of the death penalty
125 behind yet to come   **129 home** fully   **130 enkindle** inflame, provoke   **133 darkness**
i.e. the devil   **134 trifles** insignificant things   **135 deepest consequence** the profoundly
serious outcome   **138 happy** fortunate   **prologues** preliminary actions/lines spoken by an
actor before the beginning of a play   **swelling** growing/exalted   **act** division of a play (plays
on the sense of "deed, action")   **139 imperial theme** royal subject matter (**theme** plays on the
sense of "subject that causes action")   **140 soliciting** incitement

Was heavy on me. Thou art so far before
That swiftest wing of recompense is slow
20   To overtake thee. Would thou hadst less deserved,
That the proportion both of thanks and payment
Might have been mine. Only I have left to say,
More is thy due than more than all can pay.
MACBETH   The service and the loyalty I owe,
25   In doing it, pays itself. Your highness' part
Is to receive our duties, and our duties
Are to your throne and state, children and servants;
Which do but what they should by doing everything
Safe toward your love and honour.
30   DUNCAN   Welcome hither:
I have begun to plant thee and will labour
To make thee full of growing.— Noble Banquo,
That hast no less deserved, nor must be known
No less to have done so, let me enfold thee   *Embraces him*
35   And hold thee to my heart.
BANQUO   There if I grow, the harvest is your own.
DUNCAN   My plenteous joys,
Wanton in fullness, seek to hide themselves
In drops of sorrow.— Sons, kinsmen, thanes,
40   And you whose places are the nearest, know
We will establish our estate upon
Our eldest, Malcolm, whom we name hereafter
The Prince of Cumberland, which honour must
Not unaccompanied invest him only,
45   But signs of nobleness, like stars, shall shine

---

18 before ahead (in terms of merit)   **20 Would . . . mine** I wish that you were less deserving so that I might have had sufficient thanks and payment with which to reward you   **23 all** everything, all my **thanks and payment**   **25 In . . . itself** i.e. being a loyal servant is sufficient reward   **29 Safe toward** to safeguard   **33 nor . . . so** i.e. your equal worth must be recognized   **34 enfold** embrace   **38 Wanton** unrestrained/abundant   **39 drops of sorrow** i.e. tears   **40 nearest** closest to Duncan (i.e. relatives and favored nobles)   **41 establish our estate** settle the succession of the state   **43 Prince of Cumberland** the title given to the heir to the Scottish throne   **which . . . only** an honor that must not be the only one to be bestowed (i.e. other nobles will be favored too)   **44 invest** adorn, clothe

On all deservers.— From hence to Inverness,   *To Macbeth*
And bind us further to you.

MACBETH   The rest is labour which is not used for you:
I'll be myself the harbinger and make joyful
50   The hearing of my wife with your approach:
So humbly take my leave.

DUNCAN   My worthy Cawdor.

MACBETH   The Prince of Cumberland: that is a step   *Aside*
On which I must fall down or else o'erleap,
55   For in my way it lies. Stars, hide your fires:
Let not light see my black and deep desires.
The eye wink at the hand; yet let that be
Which the eye fears when it is done to see.   *Exit*

DUNCAN   True, worthy Banquo, he is full so valiant,
60   And in his commendations I am fed:
It is a banquet to me. Let's after him,
Whose care is gone before to bid us welcome:
It is a peerless kinsman.   *Flourish.   Exeunt.*

Act 1 Scene 5   *running scene 5*

Enter Macbeth's Wife, alone with a letter

LADY MACBETH   'They met me in the day of success: *Reads*
and I have learned by the perfect'st report, they have more in
them than mortal knowledge. When I burned in desire to
question them further, they made themselves air into which
5   they vanished. Whiles I stood rapt in the wonder of it, came
missives from the king, who all-hailed me "Thane of
Cawdor", by which title before, these weyard sisters saluted

---

46 Inverness town in the north of Scotland, location of Macbeth's castle   **47 bind . . . you**
make me more indebted to you (as your guest)   **48 The . . . you** a period of rest that is not
used to serve you seems like hard work/anything that is not done on your behalf is tedious
49 harbinger royal messenger   **57 wink . . . hand** shut itself to the deeds carried out by the
hand   **be** come to pass   **59 he . . . valiant** Macbeth is just as brave (as you say); Duncan and
Banquo have been conversing during Macbeth's aside   **60 his commendations** praises given
to him   **62 care** considerate solicitude   **63 peerless** without equal   **1.5** *Location:*
Macbeth's castle, Inverness   **2 perfect'st report** most accurate testimony   **6 missives**
messengers

60 **MACBETH**   My dearest love,
Duncan comes here tonight.

LADY MACBETH   And when goes hence?

MACBETH   Tomorrow, as he purposes.

LADY MACBETH   O, never

65 Shall sun that morrow see!
Your face, my thane, is as a book where men
May read strange matters. To beguile the time,
Look like the time: bear welcome in your eye,
Your hand, your tongue: look like th'innocent flower,
70 But be the serpent under't. He that's coming
Must be provided for, and you shall put
This night's great business into my dispatch,
Which shall to all our nights and days to come
Give solely sovereign sway and masterdom.

75 **MACBETH**   We will speak further.

LADY MACBETH   Only look up clear:
To alter favour ever is to fear.
Leave all the rest to me.   *Exeunt*

Act 1 Scene 6

*Hautboys and Torches. Enter King [Duncan], Malcolm, Donalbain,
Banquo, Lennox, Macduff, Ross, Angus and Attendants*

DUNCAN   This castle hath a pleasant seat: the air
Nimbly and sweetly recommends itself
Unto our gentle senses.

BANQUO   This guest of summer,
5 The temple-haunting martlet, does approve

---

63 **purposes** intends   67 **strange** mysterious/unnatural/unfamiliar   **beguile** deceive
68 **Look . . . time** look ordinary, appear to be like everyone else   71 **provided for** prepared for,
taken care of (relates to hospitality and to murder)   72 **dispatch** management   74 **solely**
entirely, exclusively   **sway** rule   76 **look up clear** appear to be untroubled and innocent
77 **alter favour** change your accustomed facial expression   **1.6** *Location: outside
Macbeth's castle*   **Hautboys** players of oboe-like instruments   **Torches** torchbearers
1 **seat** setting   3 **gentle** noble/made gentle by the air   5 **temple-haunting** nesting in or
frequenting places of worship   **martlet** swift (type of bird)   **approve** prove, demonstrate

By his loved mansionry that the heaven's breath
Smells wooingly here: no jutty, frieze,
Buttress, nor coign of vantage, but this bird
Hath made his pendent bed and procreant cradle:
10   Where they most breed and haunt, I have observed
The air is delicate.

Enter Lady [Macbeth]

DUNCAN   See, see, our honoured hostess.—
The love that follows us sometime is our trouble,
Which still we thank as love. Herein I teach you
15   How you shall bid God yield us for your pains,
And thank us for your trouble.

LADY MACBETH   All our service
In every point twice done, and then done double
Were poor and single business to contend
20   Against those honours deep and broad wherewith
Your majesty loads our house: for those of old,
And the late dignities heaped up to them,
We rest your hermits.

DUNCAN   Where's the Thane of Cawdor?
25   We coursed him at the heels, and had a purpose
To be his purveyor: but he rides well,
And his great love, sharp as his spur, hath holp him
To his home before us. Fair and noble hostess,
We are your guest tonight.

30   LADY MACBETH   Your servants ever

---

6 **mansionry** mansions, i.e. nests   7 **wooingly** enticingly   **jutty** projecting part of a building
frieze decorative section underneath the cornice of a building   8 **Buttress** support built
against a main wall   **coign of vantage** advantageous corner   9 **pendent** hanging
procreant fertile   11 **delicate** pleasant, delightful   13 **The . . . love** while I am always
appreciative of the love behind it, such devoted service can be troublesome (to me/to you)
14 **Herein . . . pains** by saying this I am encouraging you to ask God to reward me for your
efforts (said in a lighthearted or self-deprecating manner)   15 **yield** reward   18 **point** aspect,
detail   19 **single** weak   **business** affair/effort   **contend Against** compete with
21 **those of old** honors previously bestowed   22 **late** recent   23 **rest your hermits**
remain your beadsmen (i.e. those who pray on behalf of others)   25 **coursed** chased
26 **purveyor** official sent ahead to make arrangements for his master's food, lodging, etc.
27 **holp** helped

Have theirs, themselves and what is theirs, in compt
To make their audit at your highness' pleasure,
Still to return your own.

DUNCAN   Give me your hand,

35   Conduct me to mine host: we love him highly,
And shall continue our graces towards him.
By your leave, hostess.   *Exeunt*

Act 1 Scene 7   *running scene 7*

Hautboys. Torches. Enter a Sewer and divers Servants with dishes and
service over the stage. Then enter Macbeth

MACBETH   If it were done when 'tis done, then 'twere well
It were done quickly: if th'assassination
Could trammel up the consequence and catch
With his surcease success: that but this blow

5   Might be the be-all and the end-all — here,
But here, upon this bank and shoal of time,
We'd jump the life to come. But in these cases
We still have judgement here, that we but teach
Bloody instructions, which, being taught, return

10   To plague th'inventor: this even-handed justice
Commends th'ingredients of our poisoned chalice
To our own lips. He's here in double trust:

---

31 **theirs** i.e. their own servants   **in compt** held in trust (from the king)   32 **audit** account
33 **Still . . . own** always ready to return to you what is yours   36 **graces** favors   37 **By your**
leave with your permission   **1.7**   *Location: within Macbeth's castle*   **Sewer** butlerlike
official in charge of serving meals   **divers** various   **service** portions of food   1 **If . . .**
done if it were truly over and finished with when the action itself has been completed
3 **trammel up** entangle, trap (as in a net; may play on sense of "bind up a corpse")   **catch**
seize/ensnare   4 **surcease** ending, death   **success** a final outcome/good fortune (plays on
sense of "succession of heirs")   **that but** if only   6 **bank and shoal** riverbank and shallow
(though Folio's "Banke and Schoole" could alternatively mean "bench and school," pointing
forward to the court and schoolroom imagery that follows, whereas "shoal," an alternative
spelling of "school," emerges from the preceding fishing nets of "trammel" and "catch")
7 **jump** risk/overleap   8 **still** always   **here** i.e. in this life   **that** in that   9 **instructions**
lessons   10 **th'inventor** the teacher, he who composed the **instructions**   11 **Commends**
presents, offers   **chalice** goblet (perhaps recalling the cup used in Holy Communion;
Macbeth's is **poisoned** because of the unholy nature of murdering a king)

First, as I am his kinsman and his subject,
Strong both against the deed: then, as his host,
15   Who should against his murderer shut the door,
Not bear the knife myself. Besides, this Duncan
Hath borne his faculties so meek, hath been
So clear in his great office, that his virtues
Will plead like angels, trumpet-tongued, against
20   The deep damnation of his taking-off:
And pity, like a naked new-born babe,
Striding the blast, or heaven's cherubin, horsed
Upon the sightless couriers of the air,
Shall blow the horrid deed in every eye,
25   That tears shall drown the wind. I have no spur
To prick the sides of my intent, but only
Vaulting ambition, which o'erleaps itself
And falls on th'other.—

Enter Lady [Macbeth]

How now? What news?

LADY MACBETH   He has almost supped. Why have you left the
chamber?

30   MACBETH   Hath he asked for me?

LADY MACBETH   Know you not he has?

MACBETH   We will proceed no further in this business:
He hath honoured me of late, and I have bought
Golden opinions from all sorts of people,
35   Which would be worn now in their newest gloss,
Not cast aside so soon.

LADY MACBETH   Was the hope drunk
Wherein you dressed yourself? Hath it slept since?

---

14 Strong both i.e. both strong reasons   **17 faculties** kingly powers   **18 clear** faultless
20 taking-off murder   **22 Striding** sitting astride (as on a horse)/standing over to defend
blast storm/gale   **cherubin** cherubs (angels traditionally associated with the winds)   **horsed**
on horseback   **23 sightless couriers** invisible messengers (i.e. the winds)   **25 That** so that
tears . . . wind tears (of sorrow but also a reaction to having the **deed** blown into the **eye**) will
be so plentiful that they will calm the wind   **27 Vaulting . . . th'other** like a rider attempting to
vault into his saddle, ambition leaps too far and crashes to the ground on the other side of the
horse/ambition spurs the horse over an obstacle and horse and rider fall   **33 bought** won
35 would should   **newest gloss** freshest luster

And wakes it now, to look so green and pale
40   At what it did so freely? From this time
Such I account thy love. Art thou afeard
To be the same in thine own act and valour
As thou art in desire? Wouldst thou have that
Which thou esteem'st the ornament of life,
45   And live a coward in thine own esteem,
Letting 'I dare not' wait upon 'I would',
Like the poor cat i'th'adage?

MACBETH   Prithee, peace.
I dare do all that may become a man:
50   Who dares do more is none.

LADY MACBETH   What beast was't, then,
That made you break this enterprise to me?
When you durst do it, then you were a man:
And to be more than what you were, you would
55   Be so much more the man. Nor time nor place
Did then adhere, and yet you would make both:
They have made themselves, and that their fitness now
Does unmake you. I have given suck, and know
How tender 'tis to love the babe that milks me:
60   I would, while it was smiling in my face,
Have plucked my nipple from his boneless gums,
And dashed the brains out, had I so sworn as you
Have done to this.

MACBETH   If we should fail?

65   LADY MACBETH   We fail?

---

41 **Such** i.e. you are like the drunkard, bold only when inebriated   **account** deem, consider
Art . . . desire? Are you now afraid to be as brave and active as you would like to be (and
claimed to be)?; **act** and **desire** suggest a reference to sexual potency   44 **esteem'st** value as
ornament of life i.e. the crown   **ornament** distinction/adornment   46 **wait upon** follow
47 **cat i'th'adage** "the cat would eat fish but she will not wet her feet"   **adage** proverb
49 **do** the verb can also mean "to have sex"   50 **none** i.e. no man (because killing the king
would be dishonorable and unnatural; in the following line, however, Lady Macbeth
understands "beastlike, irrational")   52 **break** broach, reveal   53 **durst** dared   56 **adhere**
agree, fit   **make both** i.e. make time and place adhere, create an opportunity   57 **that their**
fitness their very suitability   58 **unmake** make incapable/destroy   **given suck** i.e. breast-fed
a baby

But screw your courage to the sticking-place
And we'll not fail. When Duncan is asleep —
Whereto the rather shall his day's hard journey
Soundly invite him — his two chamberlains
70 Will I with wine and wassail so convince,
That memory, the warder of the brain,
Shall be a fume, and the receipt of reason
A limbeck only: when in swinish sleep
Their drenchèd natures lies as in a death,
75 What cannot you and I perform upon
Th'unguarded Duncan? What not put upon
His spongy officers, who shall bear the guilt
Of our great quell?

MACBETH   Bring forth men-children only,
80 For thy undaunted mettle should compose
Nothing but males. Will it not be received,
When we have marked with blood those sleepy two
Of his own chamber and used their very daggers,
That they have done't?

85 LADY MACBETH   Who dares receive it other,
As we shall make our griefs and clamour roar
Upon his death?

MACBETH   I am settled, and bend up
Each corporal agent to this terrible feat.
90 Away, and mock the time with fairest show:
False face must hide what the false heart doth know.

Exeunt

---

66 But only   **screw . . . sticking-place** wind up your courage to the limit   **sticking-place** the
point at which something is made tightly secure (here the metaphor may refer to the groove on
a crossbow into which its cord is fitted, or to the peg on a musical instrument around which
string is tightened)   **68 Whereto the rather** to which all the more readily   **69 chamberlains**
servants who attended the royal bedchamber   **70 wassail** liquor/revelry   **convince**
overcome   **71 warder** keeper, guard   **72 fume** vapor   **receipt** receptacle   **73 limbeck**
apparatus for distilling (i.e. extracting the essence of a liquid)   **swinish** piglike/coarse/
drunken   **76 put upon** blame on/impose on   **77 spongy** i.e. absorbent, saturated with drink
officers servants   **78 quell** murder   **80 undaunted mettle** fearless/intrepid temperament
(**mettle** was undistinguished from "metal," which may lead to a pun on **males**/(chain)mails in
the next line)   **81 received** understood, thought   **85 other** otherwise   **86 As** seeing as,
given that   **88 settled** committed/determined/steady   **bend up** tighten   **89 corporal agent**
bodily faculty/muscle   **90 mock** deceive/imitate   **91 False** deceptive/treacherous/artificial

Act 2 Scene 1   *running scene 8*

Enter Banquo and Fleance, with a Torch [bearer] before him

BANQUO   How goes the night, boy?

FLEANCE   The moon is down: I have not heard the clock.

BANQUO   And she goes down at twelve.

FLEANCE   I take't 'tis later, sir.

5 BANQUO   Hold, take my sword. There's husbandry in

heaven: *Gives his sword*

Their candles are all out. Take thee that too.   *Gives cloak?*

A heavy summons lies like lead upon me,   *Diamond?*

And yet I would not sleep. Merciful powers,

Restrain in me the cursèd thoughts that nature

10 Gives way to in repose.

Enter Macbeth and a Servant with a torch

Give me my sword.— Who's there?   *Takes sword*

MACBETH   A friend.

BANQUO   What, sir, not yet at rest? The king's abed:

He hath been in unusual pleasure,

15 And sent forth great largess to your offices.

This diamond he greets your wife withal,   *Presents a diamond*

By the name of most kind hostess, and shut up

In measureless content.

MACBETH   Being unprepared,

20 Our will became the servant to defect,

Which else should free have wrought.

BANQUO   All's well.

I dreamt last night of the three weyard sisters:

To you they have showed some truth.

25 MACBETH   I think not of them.

Yet, when we can entreat an hour to serve,

2.1   *Location: Macbeth's castle (probably an open-air courtyard within the building)*
1 How . . . night how much of the night has passed, what time is it   **5 husbandry** thrift,
economy   **6 Their . . . out** i.e. the stars are not visible   **7 summons** urge to sleep   **15 largess**
gifts   **offices** servants' quarters   **17 shut up** concluded his speech/went to bed/was wrapped
up   **19 Being . . . wrought** i.e. being unprepared for Duncan's visit, my desire to entertain the
king nobly and generously was hampered by a lack of provisions

We would spend it in some words upon that business,
If you would grant the time.

BANQUO At your kind'st leisure.

30 **MACBETH** If you shall cleave to my consent when 'tis,
It shall make honour for you.

BANQUO So I lose none
In seeking to augment it, but still keep
My bosom franchised and allegiance clear,
35 I shall be counselled.

MACBETH Good repose the while.

BANQUO Thanks, sir: the like to you.

Exeunt Banquo [with Fleance and Torchbearer]

MACBETH Go bid thy mistress, when my drink is ready,
She strike upon the bell. Get thee to bed.— *Exit [Servant]*
40 Is this a dagger which I see before me,
The handle toward my hand? Come, let me clutch thee:
I have thee not, and yet I see thee still.
Art thou not, fatal vision, sensible
To feeling as to sight? Or art thou but
45 A dagger of the mind, a false creation,
Proceeding from the heat-oppressèd brain?
I see thee yet, in form as palpable
As this which now I draw. *Draws his dagger*
Thou marshall'st me the way that I was going,
50 And such an instrument I was to use.
Mine eyes are made the fools o'th'other senses,
Or else worth all the rest. I see thee still,
And on thy blade and dudgeon gouts of blood,
Which was not so before. There's no such thing:
55 It is the bloody business which informs

---

30 **cleave . . . consent** agree with me, support me **when 'tis** when the time comes **32 So** provided that **34 bosom franchised** heart free (of guilt) **35 counselled** guided/open to your opinions **36 the while** in the meantime **43 sensible** perceptible (to the senses) **46 heat-oppressèd** overwhelmed by heat/feverish **47 yet** still **palpable** tangible, capable of being touched **49 marshall'st** guide **the . . . going** i.e. toward my intention/to Duncan's chamber **52 worth . . . rest** more reliable than the other senses **53 dudgeon** hilt **gouts** drops **55 informs** takes on a shape

Thus to mine eyes. Now o'er the one halfworld
Nature seems dead, and wicked dreams abuse
The curtained sleep: witchcraft celebrates
Pale Hecate's off'rings: and withered murder,
60   Alarumed by his sentinel the wolf,
Whose howl's his watch, thus with his stealthy pace,
With Tarquin's ravishing strides, towards his design
Moves like a ghost.— Thou sure and firm-set earth,
Hear not my steps which way they walk, for fear
65   Thy very stones prate of my whereabout
And take the present horror from the time
Which now suits with it.— Whiles I threat, he lives:
Words to the heat of deeds too cold breath gives.   *A bell rings*
I go, and it is done: the bell invites me.
70   Hear it not, Duncan, for it is a knell
That summons thee to heaven or to hell.   *Exit*

Act 2 Scene 2

running scene 8 continues

Enter Lady [Macbeth]

LADY MACBETH   That which hath made them drunk hath made
me bold:
What hath quenched them hath given me fire.—
Hark! Peace!—
It was the owl that shrieked, the fatal bellman
Which gives the stern'st goodnight. He is about it.

---

56 the one halfworld one half of the world   58 curtained screened by the eyelids/veiled by
bed curtains   59 Hecate's off'rings sacrifices to Hecate, Greek goddess of witchcraft and
night, associated with the moon (hence pale)   60 Alarumed moved to action   sentinel
guard, watchman   61 watch signal, watchman's call   62 Tarquin Roman who raped
Lucrece; he was the king's son and this deed led to the overthrow of the Roman monarchy
ravishing intent on rape   design undertaking/scheme   63 sure stable   65 prate . . .
whereabout betray my location   prate speak   66 take . . . it (in breaking the silence) take
on (or "remove") the acute horror of this moment that is so suitable for it   present
immediate/pressing   67 threat threaten (to act)   70 knell toll of a bell rung at funerals or
after a death   2.2   *Location: within Macbeth's castle*   1 them i.e. Duncan's servants
2 quenched extinguished (fire)   3 owl considered a bird of ill omen whose cry heralded death
bellman one who rang a bell to announce a death/night watchman who rang a bell every hour
4 stern'st goodnight harshest and final good night (death)

5   The doors are open, and the surfeited grooms
Do mock their charge with snores: I have drugged their
    possets,
That death and nature do contend about them
Whether they live or die.

Enter Macbeth   *Initially within or*

MACBETH   Who's there? What ho?   *above or unseen*

10 LADY MACBETH   Alack, I am afraid they have awaked,   *by his wife;*
And 'tis not done: th'attempt and not the deed   *with bloody*
Confounds us. Hark! I laid their daggers ready: *daggers*
He could not miss 'em. Had he not resembled
My father as he slept, I had done't.—   *Sees Macbeth*
                                 My husband?

15 MACBETH   I have done the deed. Didst thou not hear a noise?
LADY MACBETH   I heard the owl scream and the crickets cry.
Did not you speak?
MACBETH   When?
LADY MACBETH   Now.
20 MACBETH   As I descended?
LADY MACBETH   Ay.
MACBETH   Hark!
Who lies i'th'second chamber?
LADY MACBETH   Donalbain.
25 MACBETH   This is a sorry sight.   *Looks at his hands*
LADY MACBETH   A foolish thought, to say 'a sorry sight'.
MACBETH   There's one did laugh in's sleep, and one cried
    'Murder!'
That they did wake each other: I stood and heard them.
But they did say their prayers, and addressed them
30 Again to sleep.
LADY MACBETH   There are two lodged together.
MACBETH   One cried 'God bless us' and 'Amen' the other,

---

5 surfeited sated, drunk   **grooms** male servants   **6 mock** make a mockery of/defy/imitate
possets hot spiced drinks often consumed before bed   **7 That** so that   **contend about**
compete for, fight over   **12 Confounds** ruins, defeats   **13 he** i.e. Duncan   **27 one . . . one**
Malcolm and Donalbain (although possibly the grooms)   **29 addressed them** prepared
themselves

As they had seen me with these hangman's hands.
List'ning their fear, I could not say 'Amen',
35   When they did say 'God bless us.'

LADY MACBETH   Consider it not so deeply.

MACBETH   But wherefore could not I pronounce 'Amen'?
I had most need of blessing, and 'Amen'
Stuck in my throat.

40 **LADY MACBETH**   These deeds must not be thought
After these ways: so, it will make us mad.

MACBETH   Methought I heard a voice cry 'Sleep no more,
Macbeth does murder sleep: the innocent sleep,
Sleep that knits up the ravelled sleeve of care,
45   The death of each day's life, sore labour's bath,
Balm of hurt minds, great nature's second course,
Chief nourisher in life's feast'—

LADY MACBETH   What do you mean?

MACBETH   Still it cried 'Sleep no more' to all the house:
50   'Glamis hath murdered sleep, and therefore Cawdor
Shall sleep no more, Macbeth shall sleep no more.'

LADY MACBETH   Who was it that thus cried? Why, worthy thane,
You do unbend your noble strength to think
So brainsickly of things. Go get some water
55   And wash this filthy witness from your hand.
Why did you bring these daggers from the place?
They must lie there: go carry them and smear
The sleepy grooms with blood.

MACBETH   I'll go no more.
60   I am afraid to think what I have done:
Look on't again I dare not.

LADY MACBETH   Infirm of purpose!

---

33 As as if   **hangman's hands** perhaps a general reference to any executioner, though a hangman might have had bloody hands as he sometimes disemboweled the bodies of hanged men   **37 wherefore** why   **40 thought . . . ways** dwelt on in this manner   **41 so** to do so   **44 ravelled** unraveled, frayed   **sleeve** part of the arm of a piece of clothing/silk filament produced by untwisting a thicker thread   **45 bath** soothing bath/healing liquid   **46 Balm** healing ointment   **second course** main, most nourishing dish in a feast   **53 unbend** slacken, weaken   **55 filthy witness** i.e. Duncan's blood   **57 lie** remain (plays on sense of "deceive")

Give me the daggers. The sleeping and the dead   *Takes the daggers*
Are but as pictures: 'tis the eye of childhood
65   That fears a painted devil. If he do bleed,
I'll gild the faces of the grooms withal,
For it must seem their guilt.   *Exit*

Knock within

MACBETH   Whence is that knocking?
How is't with me, when every noise appals me?
70   What hands are here? Ha? They pluck out mine eyes.
Will all great Neptune's ocean wash this blood
Clean from my hand? No, this my hand will rather
The multitudinous seas incarnadine,
Making the green one red.

Enter Lady [Macbeth]

75   LADY MACBETH   My hands are of your colour, but I shame
To wear a heart so white.— I hear a knocking   *Knock*
At the south entry: retire we to our chamber.
A little water clears us of this deed:
How easy is it, then! Your constancy
80   Hath left you unattended.— Hark! More knocking.   *Knock*
Get on your nightgown, lest occasion call us
And show us to be watchers. Be not lost
So poorly in your thoughts.

MACBETH   To know my deed, 'twere best not know
myself.   *Knock*
85   Wake Duncan with thy knocking! I would thou
couldst!   *Exeunt*

---

65 painted pictured/smeared (with blood)   **do bleed** is still bleeding/begins to bleed
afresh (murdered corpses were thought to bleed in the presence of the murderer)
66 gild paint, as with gold leaf (puns on **guilt**)   **68 Whence** from where   **69 appals me**
makes me pale/terrifies me   **71 Neptune** Roman god of the sea   **73 multitudinous**
numerous/containing many waves   **incarnadine** make red, stain with blood   **74 green one**
red green sea entirely red/the green one (i.e. the sea) red   **75 shame** would be ashamed
76 white i.e. cowardly   **77 south entry** southern entrance to the castle   **78 clears**
cleans/frees from accusation   **79 constancy . . . unattended** your firmness has abandoned
you   **81 nightgown** dressing gown   **occasion** events/chance   **82 watchers** those who
remain awake   **83 poorly** miserably/feebly, inadequately   **84 To . . . myself** i.e. being
mentally **lost** is preferable to acknowledging what I have done/if consciousness of what I have
done is to be endured, I must abandon my former self

Act 2 Scene 3

Knocking within. Enter a Porter

PORTER   Here's a knocking indeed! If a man were porter of
hell gate, he should have old turning the key.

Knock

Knock, knock, knock! Who's there, i'th'name of Beelzebub?
Here's a farmer that hanged himself on th'expectation of
5   plenty: come in time, have napkins enough about you: here
you'll sweat for't.

Knock

Knock, knock! Who's there, in th'other devil's name? Faith,
here's an equivocator that could swear in both the scales
against either scale, who committed treason enough for
10   God's sake, yet could not equivocate to heaven: O, come in,
equivocator.

Knock

Knock, knock, knock! Who's there? Faith, here's an English
tailor come hither for stealing out of a French hose: come in,
tailor: here you may roast your goose.

Knock

15   Knock, knock, never at quiet! What are you? But this place is
too cold for hell. I'll devil-porter it no further: I had thought
to have let in some of all professions that go the primrose
way to th'everlasting bonfire.

2.3   2 old plenty of   **3 Beelzebub** common name of a devil   **4 Here's** the Porter begins to
imagine those arriving in hell   **th'expectation of plenty** presumably the farmer anticipated
making a profit by hoarding his grain, only to be confounded by an abundant harvest and
low prices; alternatively, he staked everything on a plentiful harvest that did not materialize
5 come in time you have come at a good time   **napkins** handkerchiefs (to wipe the sweat
resulting from the heat of hell)   **7 other devil** another devil whose name escapes the Porter
(though also suggestive of Macbeth)   **Faith** by my faith (a common oath)   **8 equivocator**
one who uses words ambiguously, so that more than one meaning may apply   **scales** here
specifically the scales of justice   **9 for God's sake** a common oath, but also a reference to
Catholics who used equivocation in court as a way of escaping prosecution   **13 stealing . . .
hose** scrimping on the material used to make a pair of breeches/being too lecherous and dying
of syphilis (tailors were popularly viewed as lustful and this one has let his penis steal out too
often from his breeches; "tail" was slang for "penis")   **14 roast your goose** heat up your
tailor's iron/have sex with your prostitute/contract venereal disease   **17 primrose . . . bonfire**
seemingly attractive but sinful path to eternal damnation

Knock

Anon, anon! I pray you remember the porter.   *Opens the gate*

Enter Macduff and Lennox

20 MACDUFF   Was it so late, friend, ere you went to bed,
That you do lie so late?

PORTER   Faith, sir, we were carousing till the second cock:
and drink, sir, is a great provoker of three things.

MACDUFF   What three things does drink especially provoke?

25 PORTER   Marry, sir, nose-painting, sleep and urine. Lechery,
sir, it provokes and unprovokes: it provokes the desire, but it
takes away the performance. Therefore much drink may be
said to be an equivocator with lechery: it makes him and it
mars him; it sets him on and it takes him off; it persuades
30 him and dishearteus him; makes him stand to and not stand
to: in conclusion, equivocates him in a sleep, and, giving him
the lie, leaves him.

MACDUFF   I believe drink gave thee the lie last night.

PORTER   That it did, sir, i'the very throat on me: but I
35 requited him for his lie, and, I think, being too strong for
him, though he took up my legs sometime, yet I made a shift
to cast him.

Enter Macbeth

MACDUFF   Is thy master stirring?
Our knocking has awaked him: here he comes.   *Porter may exit*

40 LENNOX   Good morrow, noble sir.

MACBETH   Good morrow, both.

MACDUFF   Is the king stirring, worthy thane?

MACBETH   Not yet.

---

19 remember give a tip to   **22 carousing** reveling/drinking toasts   **second cock** second
crowing of the cockerel (3 a.m. or later)   **25 Marry** by the Virgin Mary   **nose-painting**
i.e. reddening of the nose   **29 mars** spoils   **sets . . . off** creates a sexual urge but renders
him impotent   **30 stand . . . to** get an erection and lose it   **31 equivocates . . . sleep** gives
him erotic pleasure in a dream only   **giving . . . lie** deceiving him (as he cannot actually
perform sexually)/laying him flat (as in wrestling)/leaving him without an erection/calling
him a liar/making him urinate   **34 i'the . . . me** literally, in my throat/(deceiving) deliberately,
outrageously   **35 requited** repaid (with violence)   **36 took . . . legs** made me incapable of
walking, pulled my legs out from under me (as a wrestler would)   **made a shift** contrived
37 cast him throw him down/vomit

MACDUFF   He did command me to call timely on him:
45   I have almost slipped the hour.

MACBETH   I'll bring you to him.

MACDUFF   I know this is a joyful trouble to you,
But yet 'tis one.

MACBETH   The labour we delight in physics pain.
50   This is the door.

MACDUFF   I'll make so bold to call,
For 'tis my limited service.   *Exit Macduff*

LENNOX   Goes the king hence today?

MACBETH   He does: he did appoint so.

55   LENNOX   The night has been unruly. Where we lay,
Our chimneys were blown down, and, as they say,
Lamentings heard i'th'air, strange screams of death,
And prophesying with accents terrible
Of dire combustion and confused events
60   New hatched to th'woeful time: the obscure bird
Clamoured the livelong night. Some say the earth
Was feverous and did shake.

MACBETH   'Twas a rough night.

LENNOX   My young remembrance cannot parallel
65   A fellow to it.

Enter Macduff

MACDUFF   O, horror, horror, horror!
Tongue nor heart cannot conceive nor name thee!

MACBETH *and* LENNOX   What's the matter?

MACDUFF   Confusion now hath made his masterpiece.
70   Most sacrilegious murder hath broke ope

---

44 timely early/promptly   45 slipped the hour missed the designated time   48 yet 'tis one
nevertheless it still is a trouble   49 The . . . pain tasks we take pleasure in cure any hardship
they entail   52 limited appointed   54 appoint intend/determine   55 unruly disordered,
turbulent   57 Lamentings cries of grief   58 prophesying foretelling/preaching/uttering
solemnly   accents terrible terrifying utterances   59 dire combustion dreadful confusion/
dangerous tumult   events outcomes   60 New hatched to newly born as offspring to/newly
born into   obscure bird i.e. the owl, bird of darkness   obscure of darkness/hidden
61 livelong long-lasting   64 My . . . to it my youthful memory cannot remember one like it/I
cannot remember one like it even during my youth   67 conceive imagine/comprehend, take
in   69 Confusion disorder/destruction/disaster   70 sacrilegious unholy, profane (literally
"sacrilege" is "stealing what is God's")   ope open

The Lord's anointed temple, and stole thence
The life o'th'building.

MACBETH   What is't you say? The life?

LENNOX   Mean you his majesty?

75 **MACDUFF**   Approach the chamber and destroy your sight
With a new Gorgon. Do not bid me speak:
See, and then speak yourselves.—

Exeunt Macbeth and Lennox

Awake, awake!
Ring the alarum bell. Murder and treason!
80   Banquo and Donalbain! Malcolm, awake!
Shake off this downy sleep, death's counterfeit,
And look on death itself! Up, up, and see
The great doom's image! Malcolm, Banquo,
As from your graves rise up and walk like sprites
85   To countenance this horror! Ring the bell.

Bell rings. Enter Lady [Macbeth]

LADY MACBETH   What's the business,
That such a hideous trumpet calls to parley
The sleepers of the house? Speak, speak!

MACDUFF   O, gentle lady,
90   'Tis not for you to hear what I can speak:
The repetition in a woman's ear
Would murder as it fell.—

Enter Banquo

O, Banquo, Banquo,
Our royal master's murdered!

LADY MACBETH   Woe, alas!
95   What, in our house?

BANQUO   Too cruel anywhere.

---

71 **Lord's anointed temple** God's consecrated house of worship/Duncan's head or body
(**anointed** with holy oil at his coronation)   76 **Gorgon** in Greek mythology, a female monster;
anyone who looked at her was turned to stone   81 **downy** soft, comfortable   **counterfeit**
imitator/likeness   83 **great doom's image** image of Judgment Day, the end of the world
when the dead were supposed to **rise** from their **graves**   84 **sprites** spirits, ghosts
85 **countenance** face/be in keeping with   87 **trumpet** i.e. noise, clamor (a trumpet was also
supposed to sound at Judgment Day)   **parley** conversation/negotiation between enemy forces
(announced with a trumpet call)   91 **repetition** recital, report

Dear Duff, I prithee contradict thyself
And say it is not so.

Enter Macbeth, Lennox and Ross   *Perhaps with*

MACBETH   Had I but died an hour before this chance,   *Attendants*

100   I had lived a blessèd time, for from this instant
There's nothing serious in mortality:
All is but toys: renown and grace is dead.
The wine of life is drawn, and the mere lees
Is left this vault to brag of.

Enter Malcolm and Donalbain

105   DONALBAIN   What is amiss?

MACBETH   You are, and do not know't:
The spring, the head, the fountain of your blood
Is stopped, the very source of it is stopped.

MACDUFF   Your royal father's murdered.

110   MALCOLM   O, by whom?

LENNOX   Those of his chamber, as it seemed, had done't:
Their hands and faces were all badged with blood,
So were their daggers, which unwiped we found
Upon their pillows. They stared and were distracted:

115   No man's life was to be trusted with them.

MACBETH   O, yet I do repent me of my fury,
That I did kill them.

MACDUFF   Wherefore did you so?

MACBETH   Who can be wise, amazed, temp'rate and furious,

120   Loyal and neutral in a moment? No man.
Th'expedition of my violent love
Outrun the pauser, reason. Here lay Duncan,
His silver skin laced with his golden blood,

---

99 chance moment/event/misfortune   **101 mortality** life   **102 toys** trifles, insignificant
things   **renown and grace** honor   **103 drawn** drained (from a barrel)   **lees** dregs
104 left left in   **vault** wine cellar/world beneath the arched sky   **brag** boast, be proud
108 stopped ended/stopped-up   **112 badged** marked as if with a badge worn by liveried
servants   **114 stared** looked stunned, horror-struck/gazed fixedly   **distracted** agitated/
confused   **119 amazed** stunned/confused/dismayed   **temp'rate** calm, composed, restrained
121 Th'expedition the haste   **violent** passionate/impetuous (plays on the sense of
"destructive, bloody")   **122 pauser** provoker of hesitation and self-restraint (the faculty of
reason)

And his gashed stabs looked like a breach in nature

125　For ruin's wasteful entrance: there the murderers,
　　　Steeped in the colours of their trade, their daggers
　　　Unmannerly breeched with gore. Who could refrain
　　　That had a heart to love, and in that heart
　　　Courage to make's love known?

130　LADY MACBETH　　Help me hence, ho!　　　　　*Faints or feigns*
　　　MACDUFF　　Look to the lady.　　　　　　　　　*to do so*
　　　MALCOLM　　Why do we hold our tongues,　　*Aside to Donalbain*
　　　That most may claim this argument for ours?
　　　DONALBAIN　　What should be spoken here, where
　　　　　our fate,　　　　　　　　　　　　　　*Aside to Malcolm*
135　Hid in an auger hole, may rush and seize us?
　　　Let's away: our tears are not yet brewed.
　　　MALCOLM　　Nor our strong sorrow　　　　*Aside to Donalbain*
　　　Upon the foot of motion.
　　　BANQUO　　Look to the lady.—　　　　　　*Lady Macbeth may*
140　And when we have our naked frailties hid,　　*be helped off*
　　　That suffer in exposure, let us meet
　　　And question this most bloody piece of work
　　　To know it further. Fears and scruples shake us:
　　　In the great hand of God I stand, and thence
145　Against the undivulged pretence I fight
　　　Of treasonous malice.
　　　MACDUFF　　And so do I.
　　　ALL　　So all.
　　　MACBETH　　Let's briefly put on manly readiness

---

124 breach flaw/gap in fortifications made by an onslaught of heavy blows　125 wasteful destructive　126 Steeped dyed/soaked　127 Unmannerly improperly　breeched covered, as if wearing breeches (puns on breach)　129 make's make his　132 Why . . . ours? Why do we remain silent when this subject has most to do with us?　135 auger hole small hole drilled with a carpenter's tool (auger), i.e. undetectable hiding place　rush . . . us Donalbain fears that his father's murderer may now seek to harm him and his brother　seize ambush　136 brewed i.e. ready to be shown　138 Upon . . . motion ready to move　140 our . . . hid i.e. temporarily put aside our horror and distress/got dressed　142 question discuss/inquire into　143 scruples doubts　144 thence i.e. with God's help　145 Against . . . malice I shall fight against the unknown purpose that lies behind this treasonous and hostile act　149 briefly quickly　manly readiness i.e. clothes/manly resolve

150   And meet i'th'hall together.

ALL   Well contented.

Exeunt [all but Malcolm and Donalbain]

MALCOLM   What will you do? Let's not consort with them:
To show an unfelt sorrow is an office
Which the false man does easy. I'll to England.

155 DONALBAIN   To Ireland, I. Our separated fortune
Shall keep us both the safer: where we are,
There's daggers in men's smiles; the nea'er in blood,
The nearer bloody.

MALCOLM   This murderous shaft that's shot
160   Hath not yet lighted, and our safest way
Is to avoid the aim. Therefore to horse,
And let us not be dainty of leave-taking,
But shift away: there's warrant in that theft
Which steals itself when there's no mercy left.   *Exeunt*

Act 2 Scene 4   *running scene 9*

Enter Ross with an Old Man

OLD MAN   Threescore and ten I can remember well,
Within the volume of which time I have seen
Hours dreadful and things strange: but this sore night
Hath trifled former knowings.

5   ROSS   Ha, good father,
Thou see'st the heavens, as troubled with man's act,
Threatens his bloody stage: by th'clock 'tis day,
And yet dark night strangles the travelling lamp.

---

152 consort associate, accompany   **153 office** task/role   **157 the . . . bloody** i.e. the more closely one is related to Duncan, the more likely one is to be murdered   **159 shaft** i.e. of an arrow   **160 lighted** alighted, landed   **162 dainty of leave-taking** scrupulous about formal goodbyes   **163 shift away** leave secretly   **warrant** justification·   **164 steals** purloins/slips away   **2.4**   *Location: somewhere near Macbeth's castle, Inverness*   **1 Threescore and ten** seventy (years); a score is twenty   **3 dreadful** frightening   **sore** harsh, grievous   **4 trifled former knowings** made previous experiences insignificant   **5 father** respectful term of address for an old man   **6 heavens** sky/heavenly powers/roof over a **stage**   **act** deed/theatrical performance/division of a play   **8 travelling lamp** i.e. the sun

Is't night's predominance or the day's shame
10   That darkness does the face of earth entomb
When living light should kiss it?

OLD MAN   'Tis unnatural,
Even like the deed that's done. On Tuesday last,
A falcon, tow'ring in her pride of place,
15   Was by a mousing owl hawked at and killed.

ROSS   And Duncan's horses — a thing most strange and
certain —
Beauteous and swift, the minions of their race,
Turned wild in nature, broke their stalls, flung out,
Contending gainst obedience, as they would
20   Make war with mankind.

OLD MAN   'Tis said they ate each other.

ROSS   They did so, to th'amazement of mine eyes
That looked upon't.

Enter Macduff

Here comes the good Macduff.—
How goes the world, sir, now?

25   MACDUFF   Why, see you not?

ROSS   Is't known who did this more than bloody deed?

MACDUFF   Those that Macbeth hath slain.

ROSS   Alas, the day,
What good could they pretend?

30   MACDUFF   They were suborned:
Malcolm and Donalbain, the king's two sons,
Are stol'n away and fled, which puts upon them
Suspicion of the deed.

ROSS   Gainst nature still:
35   Thriftless ambition, that will ravin up

---

9 **predominance** greater power/ascendancy (as of a planet or star)   **shame** i.e. at the murder
of Duncan   13 **Even** exactly   14 **tow'ring** mounting in order to swoop down on her prey
(falconry term)   **pride of place** the highest point in her flight   15 **mousing owl** i.e. inferior
bird that usually feeds on mice   **hawked at** attacked in flight   17 **minions** darlings, favorites
19 **as** as if   29 **pretend** intend   30 **suborned** bribed   35 **Thriftless** wasteful, unprofitable
ravin up devour greedily

Thine own life's means! Then 'tis most like
The sovereignty will fall upon Macbeth.

MACDUFF   He is already named and gone to Scone
To be invested.

40   ROSS   Where is Duncan's body?

MACDUFF   Carried to Colmekill,
The sacred storehouse of his predecessors
And guardian of their bones.

ROSS   Will you to Scone?

45   MACDUFF   No, cousin, I'll to Fife.

ROSS   Well, I will thither.

MACDUFF   Well, may you see things well done there. Adieu,
Lest our old robes sit easier than our new!

ROSS   Farewell, father.

50   OLD MAN   God's benison go with you, and with those
That would make good of bad, and friends of foes!   *Exeunt*

Act 3 Scene 1

running scene 10

Enter Banquo

BANQUO   Thou hast it now: king, Cawdor, Glamis, all
As the weyard women promised, and I fear
Thou played'st most foully for't. Yet it was said
It should not stand in thy posterity,

5   But that myself should be the root and father
Of many kings. If there come truth from them —
As upon thee, Macbeth, their speeches shine —
Why, by the verities on thee made good,

---

36 life's means resources necessary for survival/source of life (i.e. father)   **like** likely
38 named selected   **Scone** ancient city north of Perth, traditional location for Scottish coronations   **39 invested** formally given authority/dressed in the royal garments
41 Colmekill the Western Hebridean island of Iona, the ancient burial place for Scottish kings
46 thither go there (to Scone)   **48 Lest . . . new** i.e. in case our former situation proves preferable to what is to come   **50 benison** blessing   **3.1** *Location: the Scottish royal palace; exact location unspecified*   **3 foully** wickedly, sinfully   **4 It . . . posterity** the kingship would not remain in your line of descendants   **7 shine** illuminate/look upon favorably   **8 verities** truths   **made good** fulfilled

May they not be my oracles as well,

10   And set me up in hope? But hush, no more.

Sennet sounded. Enter Macbeth as King, Lady [Macbeth as Queen],
Lennox, Ross, Lords and Attendants

MACBETH   Here's our chief guest.

LADY MACBETH   If he had been forgotten,
It had been as a gap in our great feast
And all-thing unbecoming.

15   MACBETH   Tonight we hold a solemn supper, sir,   *To Banquo*
And I'll request your presence.

BANQUO   Let your highness
Command upon me, to the which my duties
Are with a most indissoluble tie

20   Forever knit.

MACBETH   Ride you this afternoon?

BANQUO   Ay, my good lord.

MACBETH   We should have else desired your good advice —
Which still hath been both grave and prosperous —

25   In this day's council: but we'll take tomorrow.
Is't far you ride?

BANQUO   As far, my lord, as will fill up the time
'Twixt this and supper: go not my horse the better,
I must become a borrower of the night

30   For a dark hour or twain.

MACBETH   Fail not our feast.

BANQUO   My lord, I will not.

MACBETH   We hear our bloody cousins are bestowed
In England and in Ireland, not confessing

35   Their cruel parricide, filling their hearers
With strange invention: but of that tomorrow,

Sennet trumpet fanfare signaling a procession   **14 all-thing unbecoming** inappropriate in
every way   **15 solemn** formal, ceremonious   **18 Command upon** lay your commands on
20 knit united, bound   **23 else** otherwise   **24 still** always   **grave and prosperous** wise and
profitable   **25 council** i.e. of state officials who advised the king   **28 this** now   **go . . . better**
if my horse does not go sufficiently quickly   **30 twain** two   **33 cousins** i.e. Malcolm and
Donalbain   **bestowed** lodged   **35 parricide** murder of one's father   **36 invention**
fabrications, lies

When therewithal we shall have cause of state
Craving us jointly. Hie you to horse. Adieu,
Till you return at night. Goes Fleance with you?

40 BANQUO   Ay, my good lord. Our time does call upon's.
    MACBETH   I wish your horses swift and sure of foot,
    And so I do commend you to their backs. Farewell.

Exit Banquo

Let every man be master of his time
Till seven at night. To make society

45 The sweeter welcome, we will keep ourself
    Till supper-time alone: while then, God be with you!

Exeunt Lords. [*Macbeth and a Servant remain*]

Sirrah, a word with you. Attend those men
Our pleasure?

    SERVANT   They are, my lord, without the palace gate.

50 MACBETH   Bring them before us.   *Exit Servant*
    To be thus is nothing, but to be safely thus:
    Our fears in Banquo stick deep,
    And in his royalty of nature reigns that
    Which would be feared. 'Tis much he dares,

55 And to that dauntless temper of his mind,
    He hath a wisdom that doth guide his valour
    To act in safety. There is none but he
    Whose being I do fear: and under him
    My genius is rebuked, as it is said

60 Mark Antony's was by Caesar. He chid the sisters
    When first they put the name of king upon me,
    And bade them speak to him: then prophet-like
    They hailed him father to a line of kings:
    Upon my head they placed a fruitless crown,

---

37 therewithal with it, in addition   **cause . . . jointly** affairs of state claiming equal attention
42 commend entrust   **44 To . . . welcome** in order to make socializing more delightful
46 while until   **47 Sirrah** sir (term of address to a social inferior)   **Attend . . . pleasure?** Are
those men waiting for me?   **49 without** outside   **51 thus** in this position, i.e. king   **52 stick**
are fixed/pierce, stab   **55 to** in addition to   **dauntless temper** fearless temperament
58 being personage/existence   **59 genius** personal governing spirit   **rebuked** forcibly
retrained/reproached   **60 Mark . . . Caesar** the Roman general Mark Antony was defeated
by Octavius Caesar   **chid** upbraided, rebuked   **64 fruitless** useless/childless

65   And put a barren sceptre in my grip,
        Thence to be wrenched with an unlineal hand,
        No son of mine succeeding. If't be so,
        For Banquo's issue have I filed my mind:
        For them the gracious Duncan have I murdered:
70   Put rancours in the vessel of my peace
        Only for them, and mine eternal jewel
        Given to the common enemy of man
        To make them kings: the seeds of Banquo kings.
        Rather than so, come fate into the list,
75   And champion me to th'utterance!— Who's there?

Enter Servant and two Murderers

        Now go to the door, and stay there till we call.—   *To Servant*

                                         Exit Servant

        Was it not yesterday we spoke together?

MURDERERS It was, so please your highness.

MACBETH   Well then, now have you considered of my
80   speeches? Know that it was he in the times past which held
you so under fortune, which you thought had been our
innocent self: this I made good to you in our last conference,
passed in probation with you how you were borne in hand,
how crossed, the instruments, who wrought with them, and
85   all things else that might to half a soul and to a notion crazed
say 'Thus did Banquo.'

FIRST MURDERER You made it known to us.

MACBETH   I did so, and went further, which is now our point of
second meeting. Do you find your patience so predominant

65 barren infertile   **sceptre** ornamental rod held by a monarch (possible phallic connotations
here)   **66 unlineal** not descended directly (from Macbeth)   **68 issue** offspring   **filed** defiled,
corrupted   **69 gracious** generous/virtuous/possessed of divine grace   **70 rancours** bitter
hatred/poison   **vessel** cup (perhaps recalling the Holy Communion cup)   **71 eternal jewel**
i.e. soul   **72 common . . . man** i.e. the devil   **74 list** designated combat area at a tournament
75 champion me support/challenge, i.e. in combat   **th'utterance** the limit (death)
79 Well . . . ever? these two speeches are lineated as verse in Folio, but so irregularly that they
are likely to be mistakenly set as prose   **80 he** i.e. Banquo   **held . . . fortune** i.e. prevented
you from improving your fortunes   **82 made good** demonstrated   **conference** conversation
83 passed in probation proved   **borne in hand** deceived   **84 crossed** thwarted
instruments means/agents   **wrought** worked   **85 notion** mind

90   in your nature that you can let this go? Are you so gospelled
to pray for this good man and for his issue, whose heavy
hand hath bowed you to the grave and beggared yours for
ever?

FIRST MURDERER   We are men, my liege.

95   MACBETH   Ay, in the catalogue ye go for men,
As hounds and greyhounds, mongrels, spaniels, curs,
Shoughs, water-rugs and demi-wolves are clept
All by the name of dogs: the valued file
Distinguishes the swift, the slow, the subtle,
100   The housekeeper, the hunter, every one
According to the gift which bounteous nature
Hath in him closed, whereby he does receive
Particular addition from the bill
That writes them all alike: and so of men.
105   Now, if you have a station in the file,
Not i'th'worst rank of manhood, say't,
And I will put that business in your bosoms
Whose execution takes your enemy off,
Grapples you to the heart and love of us,
110   Who wear our health but sickly in his life,
Which in his death were perfect.

SECOND MURDERER   I am one, my liege,
Whom the vile blows and buffets of the world
Hath so incensed that I am reckless what
115   I do to spite the world.

FIRST MURDERER   And I another,
So weary with disasters, tugged with fortune,

---

90 gospelled filled with the teachings of the Gospel (the New Testament)   **92 yours** i.e. your issue, children   **95 catalogue** official list   **go for** pass for   **96 curs** dogs, especially watchdogs or sheepdogs   **97 Shoughs** lapdogs   **water-rugs** long-haired waterdogs (trained to retrieve waterfowl)   **demi-wolves** dogs that are half wolf   **clept** called   **98 valued file** list classified according to value   **99 subtle** wily   **100 housekeeper** watchdog   **101 bounteous** generous **102 closed** enclosed   **103 Particular . . . alike** special distinction unlike the general list in which they all sound the same   **105 station** position/place to stand   **file** list/row (of soldiers) **106 rank** quality/row (of soldiers)   **108 execution** enactment (plays on the sense of "murder") **109 Grapples** attaches tightly   **110 in his life** while he (Banquo) lives   **111 perfect** complete/ entirely healthy   **113 buffets** blows/beatings   **117 tugged with** knocked about by

That I would set my life on any chance
To mend it or be rid on't.

120 MACBETH   Both of you know Banquo was your enemy.

MURDERERS   True, my lord.

MACBETH   So is he mine, and in such bloody distance
That every minute of his being thrusts
Against my near'st of life: and though I could
125 With barefaced power sweep him from my sight
And bid my will avouch it, yet I must not,
For certain friends that are both his and mine,
Whose loves I may not drop, but wail his fall
Who I myself struck down. And thence it is
130 That I to your assistance do make love,
Masking the business from the common eye
For sundry weighty reasons.

SECOND MURDERER   We shall, my lord,
Perform what you command us.

135 FIRST MURDERER   Though our lives—

MACBETH   Your spirits shine through you. Within this hour at
    most
I will advise you where to plant yourselves,
Acquaint you with the perfect spy o'th'time,
The moment on't, for't must be done tonight,
140 And something from the palace, always thought
That I require a clearness. And with him —
To leave no rubs nor botches in the work —
Fleance his son, that keeps him company,
Whose absence is no less material to me
145 Than is his father's, must embrace the fate

---

118 set stake, gamble   **119 mend** improve   **on't** of it   **122 distance** hostility, discord
123 thrusts stabs   **124 near'st of life** vital parts   **126 bid . . . it** justify it on the grounds that
it is my wish   **127 For** on account of   **128 wail** I must lament   **130 to . . . love** do wooingly
entreat your help   **132 sundry** various   **135 Though our lives—** the First Murderer is
interrupted as he declares that he and his companion will carry out the deed even if their lives
depend upon it   **137 advise** inform   **138 perfect spy o'th'time** perhaps "exact awareness of
the time (to do the deed)," though some editors suppose the line may be a reference to the
Third Murderer   **140 something** some distance   **always . . . clearness** it being always
remembered that I must be considered guiltless   **142 rubs nor botches** impediments or flaws
144 material of consequence

Of that dark hour. Resolve yourselves apart:
I'll come to you anon.

MURDERERS   We are resolved, my lord.

MACBETH   I'll call upon you straight: abide within.—

[*Murderers may exit*]

150   It is concluded. Banquo, thy soul's flight,
If it find heaven, must find it out tonight.   *Exeunt*

Act 3 Scene 2   *running scene 10 continues*

Enter Macbeth's Lady and a Servant

LADY MACBETH   Is Banquo gone from court?

SERVANT   Ay, madam, but returns again tonight.

LADY MACBETH   Say to the king, I would attend his leisure
For a few words.

5   SERVANT   Madam, I will.   *Exit*

LADY MACBETH   Naught's had, all's spent,
Where our desire is got without content:
'Tis safer to be that which we destroy
Than by destruction dwell in doubtful joy.

Enter Macbeth

10   How now, my lord? Why do you keep alone,
Of sorriest fancies your companions making,
Using those thoughts which should indeed have died
With them they think on? Things without all remedy
Should be without regard: what's done is done.

15   MACBETH   We have scorched the snake, not killed it:
She'll close and be herself, whilst our poor malice
Remains in danger of her former tooth.
But let the frame of things disjoint, both the worlds suffer,

146 **Resolve yourselves apart** determine matters (or work up your resolution) in private
149 **straight** straight away   **abide** remain   **3.2**   6 **spent** wasted   7 **content** contentedness,
peace of mind   9 **doubtful** uncertain, fearful   11 **sorriest fancies** wretched imaginings
12 **Using** entertaining   13 **them . . . on** i.e. past events/Duncan   14 **regard** thought,
consideration   15 **scorched** slashed   16 **close** heal up   **poor malice** feeble animosity
17 **her former tooth** the snake's original fang   18 **let . . . suffer** let the ordered universe
collapse, heaven and earth perish

Ere we will eat our meal in fear and sleep
20   In the affliction of these terrible dreams
That shake us nightly. Better be with the dead,
Whom we, to gain our peace, have sent to peace,
Than on the torture of the mind to lie
In restless ecstasy. Duncan is in his grave:
25   After life's fitful fever he sleeps well.
Treason has done his worst: nor steel, nor poison,
Malice domestic, foreign levy, nothing
Can touch him further.

LADY MACBETH   Come on,
30   Gentle my lord, sleek o'er your rugged looks:
Be bright and jovial among your guests tonight.

MACBETH   So shall I, love, and so I pray be you.
Let your remembrance apply to Banquo:
Present him eminence, both with eye and tongue:
35   Unsafe the while, that we
Must lave our honours in these flattering streams
And make our faces vizards to our hearts,
Disguising what they are.

LADY MACBETH   You must leave this.
40   **MACBETH**   O, full of scorpions is my mind, dear wife!
Thou know'st that Banquo and his Fleance lives.

LADY MACBETH   But in them nature's copy's not eterne.

MACBETH   There's comfort yet: they are assailable:
Then be thou jocund. Ere the bat hath flown
45   His cloistered flight, ere to black Hecate's summons

---

21 **shake** afflict/make tremble   22 **to . . . peace** have sent to death as a means of fulfilling our desires   23 **on . . . lie** Macbeth is thinking of the rack, a bedlike torture instrument that stretched the limbs   24 **ecstasy** frenzy   25 **fitful** restless/full of fits brought on by a high temperature   26 **nor** neither   27 **Malice domestic** civil war   **foreign levy** the raising of enemy armies by foreign countries   30 **Gentle my lord** my gentle (i.e. noble) lord   **sleek** smooth   **rugged** rough, troubled   33 **remembrance** attention, regard   34 **Present him eminence** show him respect, honor him   35 **Unsafe . . . streams** (our position) being unsafe at the moment, we must cleanse our reputation in streams of flattery/as long as we have to flatter in this way, we remain unsafe   36 **lave** wash   37 **vizards** masks   42 **copy** abundance/pattern from which copies (i.e. descendants) are made/lease (of life), i.e. legal "copyhold" is   **eterne** everlasting   44 **jocund** cheerful   45 **cloistered** in or around cloisters (covered walkways adjoining buildings)

The shard-born beetle with his drowsy hums
Hath rung night's yawning peal, there shall be done
A deed of dreadful note.

LADY MACBETH   What's to be done?

50   MACBETH   Be innocent of the knowledge, dearest chuck,
Till thou applaud the deed.— Come, seeling night,
Scarf up the tender eye of pitiful day,
And with thy bloody and invisible hand
Cancel and tear to pieces that great bond

55   Which keeps me pale. Light thickens,
And the crow makes wing to the rooky wood:
Good things of day begin to droop and drowse,
Whiles night's black agents to their preys do rouse.—
Thou marvell'st at my words: but hold thee still.

60   Things bad begun make strong themselves by ill.
So prithee go with me.   *Exeunt*

Act 3 Scene 3   *running scene 11*

Enter three Murderers

FIRST MURDERER   But who did bid thee join with us? *To Third Murderer*
THIRD MURDERER   Macbeth.
SECOND MURDERER   He needs not our mistrust, since he delivers
Our offices and what we have to do

5   To the direction just.

---

46 shard-born born in dung   **47 yawning** sleepy (with connotations of "yawning open," like
the mouth of a bell that **peals** to announce the arrival of night)   **48 note** noteworthiness/
notoriety (puns on the sense of "musical note, chime")   **50 chuck** chick (term of endearment)
51 seeling blinding (falconry term referring to the sewing together of a young bird's eyelids for
training purposes)   **52 Scarf up** blindfold   **tender** gentle/young   **pitiful** compassionate,
merciful   **54 bond** bond of (Banquo's) life/moral law that prohibits murder (the image is of a
legal contract)   **55 pale** white with fear or cowardice (puns on "paled" meaning "fenced in")
56 makes wing flies   **rooky** filled with rooks (often undistinguished from the **crow**; both
regarded as birds of ill omen)   **58 rouse** rouse themselves   **59 hold thee still** remain calm
3.3   *Location: about a mile from the Scottish royal palace*   3 He . . . mistrust we need
not suspect him   **delivers Our offices** brings details of our duties   **5 To . . . just** exactly in
keeping with the instructions we received

FIRST MURDERER   Then stand with us.
The west yet glimmers with some streaks of day.
Now spurs the lated traveller apace
To gain the timely inn, and near approaches
10   The subject of our watch.
THIRD MURDERER   Hark, I hear horses.
BANQUO   Give us a light there, ho!   *Within*
SECOND MURDERER   Then 'tis he: the rest
That are within the note of expectation
15   Already are i'th'court.
FIRST MURDERER   His horses go about.
THIRD MURDERER   Almost a mile: but he does usually,
So all men do, from hence to th'palace gate
Make it their walk.
Enter Banquo and Fleance, with a torch
20   SECOND MURDERER   A light, a light!
THIRD MURDERER   'Tis he.
FIRST MURDERER   Stand to't.
BANQUO   It will be rain tonight.
FIRST MURDERER   Let it come down.   *He puts out the torch*
25   BANQUO   O, treachery! Fly, good Fleance,
fly, fly, fly!   *They attack Banquo*
Thou mayst revenge.— O slave!   *He dies. Fleance flees*
THIRD MURDERER   Who did strike out the light?
FIRST MURDERER   Was't not the way?
THIRD MURDERER   There's but one down: the son is fled.
30   SECOND MURDERER   We have lost best half of our affair.
FIRST MURDERER   Well, let's away, and say how much is done.
                                                      Exeunt

---

8 **lated** belated   **apace** speedily   9 **gain . . . inn** reach the inn in good time   14 **within . . .
expectation** on the guest list   16 **go about** are walked to the stables/are walked to cool them
down   22 **Stand to't** get ready/stand firm   24 **come down** i.e. the rain/the attack   28 **way**
plan, thing to do

Act 3 Scene 4

Banquet prepared. Enter Macbeth, Lady [Macbeth], Ross, Lennox,
Lords and Attendants

MACBETH   You know your own degrees, sit down: at first
And last the hearty welcome.   *They sit*

LORDS   Thanks to your majesty.

MACBETH   Ourself will mingle with society

5   And play the humble host:
Our hostess keeps her state, but in best time
We will require her welcome.

LADY MACBETH   Pronounce it for me, sir, to all our friends,
For my heart speaks they are welcome.

Enter First Murderer [at the door]

10   MACBETH   See, they encounter thee with their hearts' thanks.
Both sides are even: here I'll sit i'th'midst.
Be large in mirth, anon we'll drink a measure
The table round.—   *Moves to the door*
    There's blood upon thy face.   *To First Murderer*

FIRST MURDERER   'Tis Banquo's then.

15   MACBETH   'Tis better thee without than he within.
Is he dispatched?

FIRST MURDERER   My lord, his throat is cut: that I did for him.

MACBETH   Thou art the best o'th'cut-throats.
Yet he's good that did the like for Fleance:

20   If thou didst it, thou art the nonpareil.

FIRST MURDERER   Most royal sir, Fleance is scaped.

MACBETH   Then comes my fit again. I had else been perfect,
Whole as the marble, founded as the rock,

3.4 *Location: a banqueting hall in the Scottish royal palace*   **1 degrees** ranks
(according to which the guests would be seated)   **at . . . last** to everyone   **4 with society**
among the guests   **6 keeps her state** remains in her throne   **in best time** at the appropriate
moment   **7 require her welcome** ask her to welcome you   **10 encounter** respond to
11 Both . . . even there is an equal number of people sitting on each side of the table   **12 large**
in mirth unrestrained in merrymaking   **drink . . . round** drink a toast with every guest/all join
in a collective toast   **15 thee . . . within** on your outside rather than within his body
16 dispatched killed   **20 the nonpareil** without equal   **21 is scaped** has escaped   **22 fit**
paroxysm of fear   **perfect** complete/flawless/entirely sane   **23 founded** grounded, secure

As broad and general as the casing air:
25 But now I am cabined, cribbed, confined, bound in
To saucy doubts and fears. But Banquo's safe?
FIRST MURDERER   Ay, my good lord: safe in a ditch he bides,
With twenty trenchèd gashes on his head,
The least a death to nature.
30 MACBETH   Thanks for that.—
There the grown serpent lies: the worm that's fled
Hath nature that in time will venom breed,
No teeth for th'present.— Get thee gone: tomorrow
We'll hear ourselves again.   *Exit Murderer*
35 LADY MACBETH   My royal lord,
You do not give the cheer: the feast is sold
That is not often vouched, while 'tis a-making,
'Tis given with welcome. To feed were best at home:
From thence, the sauce to meat is ceremony:
40 Meeting were bare without it.
Enter the Ghost of Banquo, and sits in Macbeth's place
MACBETH   Sweet remembrancer.
Now, good digestion wait on appetite,
And health on both!
LENNOX   May't please your highness sit.
45 MACBETH   Here had we now our country's honour roofed,
Were the graced person of our Banquo present,
Who may I rather challenge for unkindness
Than pity for mischance.

---

24 **broad and general** widely ranging and universal   **casing** surrounding (but also,
paradoxically, "enclosing")   25 **cabined** confined (as in a cabin or hut)   **cribbed** shut up (as
in a crib or cattle stall)   26 **saucy** insolent   **safe** taken care of, i.e. dead   27 **bides** remains
28 **trenchèd** trenchlike, deeply cut   29 **least . . . nature** very least of which would be fatal
31 **worm** baby snake   34 **hear ourselves** converse   36 **give the cheer** welcome your guests/
participate in the merriment   **the . . . welcome** the feast that is not affirmed throughout to
be one that is given warmly and freely seems like an event the guests are having to pay for
37 **vouched** avouched, guaranteed   38 **To . . . home** if it is only mere eating that is involved,
one is better off at home   39 **From thence** away from home   **ceremony** courtesy
40 **Meeting** socializing (puns on **meat**)   **bare** basic/worthless   42 **remembrancer** one who
reminds   45 **had we** we would have   **country's honour** i.e. the nobility, the glory of Scotland
roofed under one roof   46 **graced** honored   47 **challenge** take to task, rebuke
48 **mischance** some mishap (preventing him from attending the feast)

ROSS His absence, sir,

50 Lays blame upon his promise. Please't your highness
To grace us with your royal company?

MACBETH The table's full.

LENNOX Here is a place reserved, sir.

MACBETH Where?

55 LENNOX Here, my good lord. What is't that moves your
highness?

MACBETH Which of you have done this?

LORDS What, my good lord?

MACBETH Thou canst not say I did it: never shake
Thy gory locks at me.

60 ROSS Gentlemen, rise: his highness is not well.   *The Lords*

LADY MACBETH Sit, worthy friends: my lord is often thus,   *begin to*
And hath been from his youth. Pray you keep seat,   *rise*
The fit is momentary: upon a thought
He will again be well. If much you note him,

65 You shall offend him and extend his passion:
Feed, and regard him not.—
Are you a man?   *Lady Macbeth*

MACBETH   Ay, and a bold one, that dare look on that   *and*
Which might appal the devil.   *Macbeth speak aside*

70 LADY MACBETH O, proper stuff!
This is the very painting of your fear:
This is the air-drawn dagger which you said
Led you to Duncan. O, these flaws and starts —
Impostors to true fear — would well become

75 A woman's story at a winter's fire,
Authorized by her grandam. Shame itself!

---

50 Lays . . . promise brings his promise (to attend) into disrepute   **55 moves** stirs,
affects/angers   **59 gory locks** hair matted with blood   **63 upon a thought** in a moment
(the time it takes to have a thought)   **64 note him** pay attention to him   **65 passion**
overwhelming emotion/fit of rage/seizure/outburst of madness   **66 regard** heed/look at
70 proper stuff absolute rubbish   **71 painting . . . fear** image of your fear itself/image created
by your fear   **72 air-drawn** drawn like a picture in the air/drawn, as from a sheath, out of the
air   **73 flaws** bursts of emotion (plays on the sense of "defects")   **starts** nervous movements,
fits, outbursts   **74 Impostors to** false versions, imitators of   **become** suit   **76 Authorized**
originally told and affirmed as true by   **grandam** grandmother

Why do you make such faces? When all's done,
You look but on a stool.

MACBETH   Prithee see there! Behold, look, lo!— How say you?
80   Why, what care I? If thou canst nod, speak too.
If charnel houses and our graves must send
Those that we bury back, our monuments
Shall be the maws of kites.   [*Exit Ghost*]

LADY MACBETH   What, quite unmanned in folly?

85   MACBETH   If I stand here, I saw him.

LADY MACBETH   Fie, for shame!

MACBETH   Blood hath been shed ere now, i'th'olden time,
Ere human statute purged the gentle weal:
Ay, and since too, murders have been performed
90   Too terrible for the ear. The time has been
That, when the brains were out, the man would die,
And there an end: but now they rise again
With twenty mortal murders on their crowns,
And push us from our stools: this is more strange
95   Than such a murder is.

LADY MACBETH   My worthy lord,
Your noble friends do lack you.

MACBETH   I do forget.—
Do not muse at me, my most worthy friends,   *Aloud*
100   I have a strange infirmity which is nothing
To those that know me. Come, love and health to all,
Then I'll sit down.— Give me some wine: fill full.—   *A servant*
Enter Ghost   *fills his goblet*
I drink to th'general joy o'th'whole table,
And to our dear friend Banquo, whom we miss:

---

79 lo look   How what   81 charnel houses buildings containing bones of the dead
82 monuments . . . kites only tombs shall be the stomachs of birds of prey   84 unmanned
made feeble, unmanly   folly foolishness, mental weakness/sin   86 Fie an expression of
disgust or indignation   88 Ere . . . weal before civil law cleansed and made peaceful the
commonwealth   human of people/humane   93 mortal murders fatal injuries   crowns
heads   94 stools seats (at the feast)/thrones   97 lack miss/need   99 muse wonder
100 infirmity illness, weakness (physical or mental)   101 love . . . all Macbeth proposes a toast

105 Would he were here! To all, and him, we thirst,
And all to all.

LORDS   Our duties and the pledge.   *They drink*

MACBETH   Avaunt, and quit my sight! Let the earth   *Sees the*
hide thee!   *Ghost*

Thy bones are marrowless, thy blood is cold:
110 Thou hast no speculation in those eyes
Which thou dost glare with.

LADY MACBETH   Think of this, good peers,
But as a thing of custom: 'tis no other,
Only it spoils the pleasure of the time.

115 MACBETH   What man dare, I dare.
Approach thou like the rugged Russian bear,
The armed rhinoceros, or th'Hyrcan tiger:
Take any shape but that, and my firm nerves
Shall never tremble: or be alive again
120 And dare me to the desert with thy sword.
If trembling I inhabit then, protest me
The baby of a girl. Hence, horrible shadow!
Unreal mock'ry, hence!— Why, so: being gone,   [*Exit Ghost*]
I am a man again.— Pray you sit still.   *To the Lords*

125 LADY MACBETH   You have displaced the mirth, broke the good
meeting
With most admired disorder.

MACBETH   Can such things be,
And overcome us like a summer's cloud,
Without our special wonder? You make me strange

---

105 **thirst** wish to drink/long to see   106 **all to all** may everyone drink to everyone else
107 **duties** loyalty and respect   **pledge** toast   108 **Avaunt** begone   110 **speculation** power
of sight   116 **rugged** rough, shaggy, wild   117 **armed** armored (i.e. with a tough skin)
th'Hyrcan from Hyrcania, in classical times the region south of the Caspian Sea   118 **that**
i.e. that of Banquo   120 **dare . . . desert** challenge me to a fight in a desolate place
121 **trembling I inhabit** trembling possesses me/if I remain indoors out of fear   **protest**
declare   122 **The . . . girl** a baby girl/a girl's doll   **shadow** ghost, illusion, dark thing
123 **mock'ry** imitation/impudent counterfeit   125 **displaced the mirth** put an end to the
merriment   126 **admired** wondered at   128 **overcome** cover, overwhelm   129 **special**
particular   **make . . . owe** cause me to feel (or view me as being) a stranger to my own nature

130 Even to the disposition that I owe,
When now I think you can behold such sights
And keep the natural ruby of your cheeks
When mine is blanched with fear.

ROSS   What sights, my lord?

135 LADY MACBETH   I pray you speak not: he grows worse and worse:
Question enrages him. At once, goodnight.
Stand not upon the order of your going,
But go at once.

LENNOX   Goodnight, and better health
140 Attend his majesty.

LADY MACBETH   A kind goodnight to all.

Exeunt Lords. [Macbeth and Lady Macbeth remain]

MACBETH   It will have blood, they say: blood will have blood.
Stones have been known to move and trees to speak,
Augurs and understood relations have
145 By magot-pies and choughs and rooks brought forth
The secret'st man of blood. What is the night?

LADY MACBETH   Almost at odds with morning, which is which.

MACBETH   How say'st thou, that Macduff denies his person
At our great bidding?

150 LADY MACBETH   Did you send to him, sir?

MACBETH   I hear it by the way, but I will send.
There's not a one of them but in his house
I keep a servant fee'd. I will tomorrow —
And betimes I will — to the weyard sisters:
155 More shall they speak, for now I am bent to know
By the worst means, the worst. For mine own good,

---

133 blanched whitened   **136 At once** all of you/immediately   **137 Stand . . . once** do not
observe the protocol of leaving in order of rank   **144 Augurs** prophecies made by interpreting
the behavior of birds   **understood relations** interpreted accounts/connections between
things   **145 magot-pies** magpies (thought to be birds of ill omen, like **choughs** and **rooks**)
choughs crows   **146 secret'st . . . blood** most hidden murderer   **What . . . night?** What is
the time of night?   **147 at odds** contending, striving   **148 How say'st thou** what do you
say (to the fact)   **denies his person** refuses to come   **150 send** i.e. send a messenger
151 by the way indirectly   **152 them** i.e. the nobles   **153 fee'd** paid (to spy)   **will** will go
154 betimes speedily/early   **155 bent** determined   **156 means** methods

All causes shall give way. I am in blood
Stepped in so far, that, should I wade no more,
Returning were as tedious as go o'er.
160 Strange things I have in head, that will to hand,
Which must be acted ere they may be scanned.

LADY MACBETH   You lack the season of all natures, sleep.

MACBETH   Come, we'll to sleep. My strange and self-abuse
Is the initiate fear that wants hard use:
165 We are yet but young in deed.   *Exeunt*

Act 3 Scene 5

Thunder. Enter the three Witches meeting Hecate

FIRST WITCH   Why, how now, Hecate? You look angerly.

HECATE   Have I not reason, beldams as you are,
Saucy and overbold? How did you dare
To trade and traffic with Macbeth
5 In riddles and affairs of death;
And I, the mistress of your charms,
The close contriver of all harms,
Was never called to bear my part
Or show the glory of our art?
10 And, which is worse, all you have done
Hath been but for a wayward son,
Spiteful and wrathful, who, as others do,
Loves for his own ends, not for you.
But make amends now: get you gone,

---

157 **All . . . way** all other affairs shall be put aside   158 **should I** even if I were to   159 **were** would be   **tedious** wearisome/time-consuming   **go o'er** going on   160 **head** (my) mind **to hand** be carried out   161 **scanned** examined, scrutinized   162 **season** food preservative such as salt/period of time assigned to an event/time during which a plant ripens 163 **strange and self-abuse** strange self-abuse   **strange** extraordinary/alienating   **self-abuse** violation of myself/self-deception   164 **initiate** new, inexperienced   **wants** lacks/needs **hard use** toughening, persistent experience   165 **young in deed** inexperienced in action (**in deed** puns on indeed)   **3.5   *Location: unspecified. This scene is probably by Thomas Middleton, apparently added for performances after Shakespeare's retirement*** 1 **angerly** angry   2 **beldams** hags   3 **saucy** impudent   4 **trade and traffic** have dealings with 7 **close** secret   8 **bear** carry out   9 **art** magic   11 **wayward** perverse, willful

15   And at the pit of Acheron
      Meet me i'th'morning: thither he
      Will come to know his destiny:
      Your vessels and your spells provide,
      Your charms and everything beside.
20   I am for th'air. This night I'll spend
      Unto a dismal and a fatal end:
      Great business must be wrought ere noon.
      Upon the corner of the moon
      There hangs a vap'rous drop profound:
25   I'll catch it ere it come to ground,
      And that distilled by magic sleights,
      Shall raise such artificial sprites
      As by the strength of their illusion
      Shall draw him on to his confusion.
30   He shall spurn fate, scorn death, and bear
      His hopes 'bove wisdom, grace and fear.
      And you all know, security
      Is mortals' chiefest enemy.
      Music and a song
      Hark, I am called: my little spirit, see,
35   Sits in a foggy cloud and stays for me.   [*Exit*]
      Sing within: 'Come away, come away' *etc.*
      FIRST WITCH   Come, let's make haste: she'll soon be back
            again.   *Exeunt*

---

15 pit of Acheron hell   **Acheron** a river in Hades, the classical underworld   **18 vessels** receptacles (presumably cauldrons)   **provide** prepare/be equipped with   **20 spend** use
21 dismal devastating/ominous   **fatal** deadly/destined   **22 wrought** brought about/ performed   **24 vap'rous drop** in response to powerful enchantments, the moon was supposed to release a foam that transformed the things it fell upon   **profound** deep, complex/hanging heavily   **26 sleights** tricks, cunning   **27 artificial** false/produced by artifice or magic
28 illusion illusory nature/power to deceive   **29 confusion** destruction/mental disorder, irrationality   **30 spurn** reject   **31 'bove** above, beyond reach of   **grace** virtue/fortune/ divine salvation   **32 security** confidence in one's safety   **35 stays** waits   **36 Come . . .** *etc.* for text of song, see pp. 95–96

Act 3 Scene 6

Enter Lennox and another Lord

LENNOX   My former speeches have but hit your thoughts,
Which can interpret further: only I say
Things have been strangely borne. The gracious Duncan
Was pitied of Macbeth, marry, he was dead:
5   And the right-valiant Banquo walked too late,
Whom you may say — if't please you — Fleance killed,
For Fleance fled: men must not walk too late.
Who cannot want the thought how monstrous
It was for Malcolm and for Donalbain
10   To kill their gracious father? Damnèd fact!
How it did grieve Macbeth! Did he not straight
In pious rage the two delinquents tear
That were the slaves of drink and thralls of sleep?
Was not that nobly done? Ay, and wisely too,
15   For 'twould have angered any heart alive
To hear the men deny't. So that I say
He has borne all things well, and I do think
That had he Duncan's sons under his key —
As, an't please heaven, he shall not — they should find
20   What 'twere to kill a father: so should Fleance.
But, peace! For from broad words and cause he failed
His presence at the tyrant's feast, I hear
Macduff lives in disgrace. Sir, can you tell
Where he bestows himself?

3.6   *Location: Scotland, exact location unspecified*   **1 hit** coincided with
2 Which . . . further i.e. there is no need for Lennox to elaborate   **only I** I only   **3 borne**
tolerated/managed   **4 pitied of** lamented by   **he was dead** i.e. Macbeth only pitied Duncan
after he was dead   **5 walked too late** was alive only too recently/was out too late at night
(there are reverberations of death in the words: **walked** often referred to the appearances
of a ghost and **late** could mean dead)   **8 cannot . . . thought** does not think   **want** lack
monstrous unnatural   **10 fact** crime/truth   **11 straight** straight away   **12 pious** loyal,
dutiful   **13 thralls** captives, slaves   **17 well** i.e. for himself   **18 under his key** locked up
19 an't if it   **20 so should Fleance** i.e. were Fleance to be imprisoned he too would be
punished for killing his father   **21 from** as a result of   **broad** frank, unrestrained
cause . . . presence because he failed to attend   **24 bestows himself** is lodging

25   LORD   The son of Duncan —
                   From whom this tyrant holds the due of birth —
                   Lives in the English court, and is received
                   Of the most pious Edward with such grace
                   That the malevolence of fortune nothing
30   Takes from his high respect. Thither Macduff
                   Is gone to pray the holy king, upon his aid
                   To wake Northumberland and warlike Siward,
                   That by the help of these — with him above
                   To ratify the work — we may again
35   Give to our tables meat, sleep to our nights,
                   Free from our feasts and banquets bloody knives,
                   Do faithful homage, and receive free honours,
                   All which we pine for now: and this report
                   Hath so exasperate their king that he
40   Prepares for some attempt of war.
     LENNOX   Sent he to Macduff?
     LORD   He did: and with an absolute 'Sir, not I',
                   The cloudy messenger turns me his back
                   And hums, as who should say, 'You'll rue the time
45   That clogs me with this answer.'
     LENNOX   And that well might
                   Advise him to a caution, t'hold what distance
                   His wisdom can provide. Some holy angel

---

25 son of Duncan i.e. Malcolm   **26 holds . . . birth** withholds his birthright (the crown)
28 Of by   **pious** devout, holy   **Edward** Edward the Confessor, who ruled England from 1042
to 1066   **grace** honor/favor/divine virtue   **29 malevolence of fortune** i.e. Malcolm's
misfortunes   **30 Takes** detracts   **respect** courtesy/regard (for Malcolm)   **31 pray** ask,
entreat (but surrounding references to Edward's holiness add a religious sense)   **upon his
aid** in aid of Malcolm   **32 wake** rouse, stir   **Northumberland** Earl (or possibly, people)
of Northumberland, a county in the north of England   **Siward** son of the Earl of
Northumberland   **34 ratify** sanction, approve   **35 meat** food   **36 Free . . . banquets** free
our feasts and banquets from   **37 homage** acts of allegiance   **free** freely given/noble/
unpolluted   **38 report** account (of the situation in Scotland)   **39 exasperate** exasperated
(i.e. incensed)   **their king** i.e. Edward   **41 he** i.e. Macbeth   **42 absolute** resolved/blunt
'Sir, not I' Macduff's words to the messenger   **43 cloudy** frowning/gloomy   **turns me**
i.e. turns (**me** is emphatic; the lord was not present)   **44 hums** i.e. makes a noise of displeasure
who should if to   **rue** regret   **45 clogs** burdens, hampers   **47 Advise . . . caution** serve to
warn him   **distance** i.e. from Macbeth

Fly to the court of England and unfold
50   His message ere he come, that a swift blessing
May soon return to this our suffering country
Under a hand accursed.

LORD   I'll send my prayers with him.   *Exeunt*

Act 4 Scene 1   *running scene 15*

Thunder. Enter the three Witches

FIRST WITCH Thrice the brinded cat hath mewed.

SECOND WITCH   Thrice and once the hedge-pig whined.

THIRD WITCH Harpier cries: 'tis time, 'tis time!

FIRST WITCH Round about the cauldron go:
5   In the poisoned entrails throw.
Toad, that under cold stone
Days and nights has thirty-one
Sweltered venom sleeping got,
Boil thou first i'th'charmèd pot.   *They dance around*

10   ALL   Double, double, toil and trouble: *the cauldron*
Fire burn, and cauldron bubble.

SECOND WITCH   Fillet of a fenny snake,
In the cauldron boil and bake:
Eye of newt and toe of frog,
15   Wool of bat and tongue of dog,
Adder's fork and blindworm's sting,
Lizard's leg and howlet's wing,
For a charm of powerful trouble,
Like a hell-broth boil and bubble.

---

50 that so that   51 suffering . . . accursed country suffering under an accursed hand
4.1 *Location: unspecified; an interior space, perhaps a cavern*   1 brinded having fur
marked with darker streaks (probably tabby)   2 hedge-pig hedgehog   3 Harpier the Third
Witch's familiar   5 entrails intestines or bodily insides generally/contents of the cauldron
7 Days . . . got for thirty-one days and nights has exuded poison produced while sleeping
8 Sweltered sweated, exuded   10 toil labor/dissent, turmoil   trouble effort/disorder/distress
12 fillet slice (of meat)   fenny muddy/from the fens (swamps)   15 Wool downy hair
16 fork forked tongue   blindworm adder/slow-worm (legless lizard)   17 howlet owlet,
young owl

20   ALL   Double, double, toil and trouble:
                  Fire burn, and cauldron bubble.
     THIRD WITCH Scale of dragon, tooth of wolf,
                  Witches' mummy, maw and gulf
                  Of the ravined salt-sea shark,
25   Root of hemlock digged i'th'dark,
                  Liver of blaspheming Jew,
                  Gall of goat, and slips of yew
                  Slivered in the moon's eclipse,
                  Nose of Turk and Tartar's lips,
30   Finger of birth-strangled babe
                  Ditch-delivered by a drab,
                  Make the gruel thick and slab:
                  Add thereto a tiger's chaudron,
                  For th'ingredients of our cauldron.
35   ALL   Double, double, toil and trouble:
                  Fire burn, and cauldron bubble.
     SECOND WITCH   Cool it with a baboon's blood,
                  Then the charm is firm and good.
     Enter Hecate and the other three Witches
     HECATE   O, well done: I commend your pains,
40   And everyone shall share i'th'gains.
                  And now about the cauldron sing
                  Like elves and fairies in a ring,
                  Enchanting all that you put in.
     Music and a song: 'Black spirits', etc.
                        [*Exit Hecate and the other three Witches?*]

23 mummy substance used for embalming/dead flesh itself/substance made from dead bodies
and used in magic (properly called "mummia")   maw throat/stomach   gulf throat/stomach
24 ravined ravaged by hunger/glutted with its prey   25 hemlock poisonous plant
26 blaspheming i.e. denying Christian beliefs   27 slips sprigs/cuttings   yew yew tree (often
planted in graveyards and associated with death)   28 Slivered cut off   29 Tartar person from
Central Asia (like the Turk, a Muslim)   30 birth-strangled strangled at birth, probably by the
mother (and thus unbaptized)   31 Ditch-delivered born in a ditch   drab prostitute
32 slab viscous, glutinous   33 chaudron intestines/insides in general   *Enter . . . Witches*
the following sequence (Hecate's speech and the song) is probably by Thomas Middleton,
apparently added for performances after Shakespeare's retirement; there are six witches in the
song (see p. 96)   *'Black spirits', etc.* for text of song, see p. 96

SECOND WITCH   By the pricking of my thumbs,

45   Something wicked this way comes.   *Knock*

Open, locks, whoever knocks.

Enter Macbeth

MACBETH   How now, you secret, black and midnight hags?

What is't you do?

ALL   A deed without a name.

50   MACBETH   I conjure you, by that which you profess —

Howe'er you come to know it — answer me:

Though you untie the winds and let them fight

Against the churches, though the yeasty waves

Confound and swallow navigation up,

55   Though bladed corn be lodged and trees blown down,

Though castles topple on their warders' heads,

Though palaces and pyramids do slope

Their heads to their foundations, though the treasure

Of nature's germens tumble all together,

60   Even till destruction sicken, answer me

To what I ask you.

FIRST WITCH   Speak.

SECOND WITCH   Demand.

THIRD WITCH   We'll answer.

65   FIRST WITCH   Say, if thou'dst rather hear it from our mouths

Or from our masters?

MACBETH   Call 'em: let me see 'em.

FIRST WITCH   Pour in sow's blood, that hath eaten

Her nine farrow: grease that's sweaten

70   From the murderer's gibbet throw

Into the flame.

---

44 pricking tingling   **47 black** deadly/evil/associated with the black arts   **50 conjure** call upon solemnly (plays on sense of "magically invoke")   **profess** claim to know about/practice as a trade   **52 Though** even if   **53 yeasty** frothy   **54 Confound** destroy, overthrow **navigation** shipping   **55 bladed corn** i.e. where the blade (leaf) is still folded around the seed-containing ear   **lodged** beaten flat   **56 warders** guards   **57 slope** bend down **59 germens** seeds/essential parts   **tumble all together** collapse into whirling chaos/all fall at once   **60 sicken** grows nauseously sated/begins to be destroyed itself   **69 farrow** piglets **sweaten** sweated   **70 gibbet** gallows

ALL   Come high or low,
    Thyself and office deftly show!

Thunder. First Apparition, an armed head

MACBETH   Tell me, thou unknown power—

75   FIRST WITCH He knows thy thought:
    Hear his speech, but say thou nought.

FIRST APPARITION   Macbeth, Macbeth, Macbeth: beware Macduff,
    Beware the Thane of Fife. Dismiss me. Enough.   *He descends*

MACBETH   Whate'er thou art, for thy good caution, thanks:

80   Thou hast harped my fear aright. But one word more—

FIRST WITCH He will not be commanded. Here's another,
    More potent than the first.

Thunder. Second Apparition, a bloody child

SECOND APPARITION   Macbeth, Macbeth, Macbeth!

MACBETH   Had I three ears, I'd hear thee.

85   SECOND APPARITION   Be bloody, bold and resolute: laugh to scorn
    The power of man, for none of woman born
    Shall harm Macbeth.   *Descends*

MACBETH   Then live, Macduff: what need I fear of thee?
    But yet I'll make assurance double sure,

90   And take a bond of fate: thou shalt not live,
    That I may tell pale-hearted fear it lies,
    And sleep in spite of thunder.

Thunder. Third Apparition, a child crowned, with a tree in his hand

                              What is this
    That rises like the issue of a king
    And wears upon his baby-brow the round

95   And top of sovereignty?

ALL   Listen, but speak not to't.

THIRD APPARITION   Be lion-mettled, proud, and take no care
    Who chafes, who frets, or where conspirers are:

---

73 office function   *armed* armored, i.e. wearing a helmet   *descends* i.e. through
the trapdoor   **80 harped** hit upon, guessed   **aright** rightly   **89 assurance** the Second
Apparition's promise/sense of personal security   **90 bond** contract, legal guarantee   **thou**
i.e. Macduff   **94 round And top** crown   **97 lion-mettled** of a lion's temperament (fierce,
regal, courageous)   **98 chafes, who frets** is roused and angry/enrages and vexes you

Macbeth shall never vanquished be until
100   Great Birnam Wood to high Dunsinane Hill
Shall come against him.   *Descend*
MACBETH   That will never be:
Who can impress the forest, bid the tree
Unfix his earth-bound root? Sweet bodements, good!
105   Rebellious dead, rise never till the wood
Of Birnam rise, and our high-placed Macbeth
Shall live the lease of nature, pay his breath
To time and mortal custom. Yet my heart
Throbs to know one thing: tell me, if your art
110   Can tell so much: shall Banquo's issue ever
Reign in this kingdom?
ALL   Seek to know no more.
MACBETH   I will be satisfied: deny me this,
And an eternal curse fall on you! Let me know.
115   Why sinks that cauldron? And what noise
is this?   *Hautboys*   *Cauldron sinks*
FIRST WITCH   Show.
SECOND WITCH   Show.
THIRD WITCH   Show.
ALL   Show his eyes, and grieve his heart:
120   Come like shadows, so depart!
*A show of eight kings and Banquo last: [the eighth king] with a glass
in his hand*
MACBETH   Thou art too like the spirit of Banquo: down!
Thy crown does sear mine eyeballs: and thy hair,
Thou other gold-bound brow, is like the first:

---

100 **Birnam . . . him** Birnam Wood moves itself to attack Macbeth at Dunsinane Hill (about ten miles north of Perth; Birnam Wood is about fifteen miles farther northwest)   **103 impress** conscript, enlist into an army   **104 bodements** predictions   **105 Rebellious dead** i.e. Banquo, who will not stay in his grave   **107 lease of nature** natural lifespan   **108 mortal custom** death, the customary way of humanity/the usual length of human life/life's rent (**custom**)   **120** so in the same manner   *eight kings* supposedly descended from Banquo; James VI of Scotland and I of England, king when Shakespeare wrote the play, claimed descent from Banquo   *glass* magic mirror or crystal that could show the future   **122 sear** burn/ dazzle   **123 Thou other** Macbeth now addresses the second king   **gold-bound brow** i.e. crowned head

A third is like the former.— Filthy hags,
125   Why do you show me this?— A fourth? Start, eyes!
What, will the line stretch out to th'crack of doom?
Another yet? A seventh? I'll see no more:
And yet the eighth appears, who bears a glass
Which shows me many more: and some I see
130   That two-fold balls and treble sceptres carry.
Horrible sight! Now I see 'tis true,
For the blood-boltered Banquo smiles upon me,
And points at them for his.   [*Exeunt kings and Banquo*]
                                        What, is this so?

FIRST WITCH   Ay, sir, all this is so: but why
135   Stands Macbeth thus amazedly?—
Come, sisters, cheer we up his sprites
And show the best of our delights.
I'll charm the air to give a sound,
While you perform your antic round,
140   That this great king may kindly say,
Our duties did his welcome pay.   *Music*

The Witches dance and vanish

MACBETH   Where are they? Gone? Let this pernicious hour
Stand aye accursèd in the calendar!—
Come in, without there!

Enter Lennox

145   LENNOX   What's your grace's will?
MACBETH   Saw you the weyard sisters?
LENNOX   No, my lord.
MACBETH   Came they not by you?
LENNOX   No, indeed, my lord.
150   MACBETH   Infected be the air whereon they ride,

---

125 Start gape/burst from your sockets   126 th'crack of doom peal of thunder at Judgment
Day   130 two-fold . . . sceptres two orbs and three scepters; probably refers to King James,
the actual monarch of England and Scotland (two orbs), and titular king of Britain, France,
and Ireland (three scepters)   132 blood-boltered clogged with blood/with hair matted with
blood   133 his i.e. his descendants   135 amazedly stunned, bewildered   136 sprites spirits,
mood   139 antic round bizarre, grotesque dance   140 kindly graciously, courteously
141 Our . . . pay our respectful behavior was an appropriate display of hospitality and
reverence   142 pernicious ruinous   143 aye forever   144 without you who are outside

And damned all those that trust them! I did hear
The galloping of horse: who was't came by?

LENNOX   'Tis two or three, my lord, that bring you word
Macduff is fled to England.

155   MACBETH   Fled to England?

LENNOX   Ay, my good lord.

MACBETH   Time, thou anticipat'st my dread exploits: *Aside*
The flighty purpose never is o'ertook
Unless the deed go with it. From this moment
160   The very firstlings of my heart shall be
The firstlings of my hand. And even now,
To crown my thoughts with acts, be it thought and done:
The castle of Macduff I will surprise,
Seize upon Fife, give to th'edge o'th'sword
165   His wife, his babes, and all unfortunate souls
That trace him in his line. No boasting like a fool,
This deed I'll do before this purpose cool.
But no more sights!— Where are these gentlemen?   *To Lennox*
Come, bring me where they are.   *Exeunt*

Act 4 Scene 2
running scene 16

Enter Macduff's Wife, her Son and Ross

LADY MACDUFF   What had he done to make him fly the land?

ROSS   You must have patience, madam.

LADY MACDUFF   He had none:
His flight was madness: when our actions do not,
5   Our fears do make us traitors.

---

152 horse horses   **157 anticipat'st** forestall, hinder   **dread exploits** fearsome enterprises
(i.e. the intended murder of Macduff)   **158 flighty** fleeting, swift   **o'ertook** overtaken
159 the . . . it the action accompanies the intention promptly   **160 The . . . hand** i.e. the
moment I decide to do something, I will act upon that thought   **firstlings** first-born things
163 surprise ambush, attack and seize   **164 Fife** the region of which Macduff is thane
give . . . o'th'sword i.e. slaughter   **166 trace . . . line** follow him in his lineage, are descended
from him   **168 sights** visions   **4.2   *Location: Macduff's castle, Fife*   4 when . . .
traitors** even when we have committed no treasonous act, fearful behavior makes us appear
guilty

ROSS   You know not
Whether it was his wisdom or his fear.

LADY MACDUFF   Wisdom? To leave his wife, to leave his babes,
His mansion and his titles in a place
10 From whence himself does fly? He loves us not:
He wants the natural touch, for the poor wren —
The most diminutive of birds — will fight,
Her young ones in her nest, against the owl.
All is the fear and nothing is the love;
15 As little is the wisdom, where the flight
So runs against all reason.

ROSS   My dearest coz,
I pray you school yourself: but, for your husband,
He is noble, wise, judicious, and best knows
20 The fits o'th'season. I dare not speak much further,
But cruel are the times when we are traitors
And do not know ourselves, when we hold rumour
From what we fear, yet know not what we fear,
But float upon a wild and violent sea
25 Each way and none. I take my leave of you:
Shall not be long but I'll be here again.
Things at the worst will cease, or else climb upward
To what they were before. My pretty cousin,
Blessing upon you!

30 LADY MACDUFF   Fathered he is, and yet he's fatherless.

ROSS   I am so much a fool, should I stay longer
It would be my disgrace and your discomfort.
I take my leave at once.

Exit Ross

---

9 titles all to which he is entitled (lands, his thaneship)   **11 wants . . . touch** lacks natural instincts/family feeling   **13 in** being in   **17 coz** cousin (used for any relative, or as an affectionate term of address to a friend)   **18 school** control   **for** as for   **19 judicious** prudent, of good judgment   **20 fits o'th'season** violent and unpredictable disturbances of the current time   **21 we . . . ourselves** we are declared traitors though we do not recognize ourselves as such/when loyalties become confused and we do not know whom to trust **22 hold . . . fear** make rumors out of the things we are afraid of   **25 Each . . . none** (being tossed) in every direction and thus never making progress   **27 climb upward** improve **28 pretty cousin** i.e. Lady Macduff's son   **32 It . . . discomfort** i.e. because I would weep/because I might be discovered by Macbeth's spies

LADY MACDUFF   Sirrah, your father's dead, and what will you do
35   now? How will you live?

SON   As birds do, mother.

LADY MACDUFF   What, with worms and flies?

SON   With what I get, I mean, and so do they.

LADY MACDUFF   Poor bird, thou'dst never fear the net nor lime,
40   the pitfall nor the gin.

SON   Why should I, mother? Poor birds they are not set
for. My father is not dead, for all your saying.

LADY MACDUFF   Yes, he is dead. How wilt thou do for a father?

SON   Nay, how will you do for a husband?

45   **LADY MACDUFF**   Why, I can buy me twenty at any market.

SON   Then you'll buy 'em to sell again.

LADY MACDUFF   Thou speak'st with all thy wit, and yet, i'faith,
with wit enough for thee.

SON   Was my father a traitor, Mother?

50   **LADY MACDUFF**   Ay, that he was.

SON   What is a traitor?

LADY MACDUFF   Why, one that swears and lies.

SON   And be all traitors that do so?

LADY MACDUFF   Everyone that does so is a traitor, and must be
55   hanged.

SON   And must they all be hanged that swear and lie?

LADY MACDUFF   Every one.

SON   Who must hang them?

LADY MACDUFF   Why, the honest men.

60   **SON**   Then the liars and swearers are fools, for there are
liars and swearers enough to beat the honest men and hang
up them.

LADY MACDUFF   Now, God help thee, poor monkey! But how wilt
thou do for a father?

---

39 Poor pitiful/impoverished   **lime** sticky substance spread on branches as a means of
catching birds   **40 pitfall** trap in which a cover falls over a hole   **gin** snare   **41 Poor . . . for**
i.e. they are only set for superior birds   **52 swears and lies** vows and then breaks his word
61 hang up hang

65 SON   If he were dead, you'd weep for him: if you would
     not, it were a good sign that I should quickly have a new
     father.

LADY MACDUFF   Poor prattler, how thou talk'st!

Enter a Messenger

MESSENGER   Bless you, fair dame. I am not to you known,
70   Though in your state of honour I am perfect.
     I doubt some danger does approach you nearly:
     If you will take a homely man's advice,
     Be not found here: hence with your little ones.
     To fright you thus, methinks, I am too savage:
75   To do worse to you were fell cruelty,
     Which is too nigh your person. Heaven preserve you!
     I dare abide no longer.   *Exit Messenger*

LADY MACDUFF   Whither should I fly?
     I have done no harm. But I remember now
80   I am in this earthly world, where to do harm
     Is often laudable, to do good sometime
     Accounted dangerous folly. Why then, alas,
     Do I put up that womanly defence
     To say I have done no harm?—
85   What are these faces?

Enter Murderers

FIRST MURDERER   Where is your husband?

LADY MACDUFF   I hope in no place so unsanctified
     Where such as thou mayst find him.

FIRST MURDERER   He's a traitor.

90 SON   Thou liest, thou shag-eared villain!

FIRST MURDERER   What, you egg? Young fry of
     treachery!   *Stabs him*

---

68 prattler chatterer   **70 in . . . perfect** I am fully acquainted with your honorable status
and reputation   **71 doubt** fear   **nearly** imminently/closely   **72 homely** plain, simple
75 do . . . you i.e. to harm you physically/not to warn you at all   **fell** fierce   **76 nigh your
person** close to you   **87 unsanctified** unconsecrated, unholy   **90 shag-eared** with cropped
ears (a punishment for criminals; the mutilated ear might have an uneven appearance); some
editors prefer "shag-haired," shaggy hair being a traditional attribute of **stage** villains
91 egg i.e. very young thing   **fry** spawn, offspring

SON   He has killed me, mother. Run away, I pray
you!

Dies

Exit [Lady Macduff,] crying 'Murder!'
[pursued by the Murderers]

Act 4 Scene 3

Enter Malcolm and Macduff

MALCOLM   Let us seek out some desolate shade, and there
Weep our sad bosoms empty.

MACDUFF   Let us rather
Hold fast the mortal sword, and like good men
5   Bestride our downfall birthdom. Each new morn
New widows howl, new orphans cry, new sorrows
Strike heaven on the face, that it resounds
As if it felt with Scotland and yelled out
Like syllable of dolour.

10   MALCOLM   What I believe I'll wail;
What know, believe; and what I can redress,
As I shall find the time to friend, I will.
What you have spoke, it may be so, perchance.
This tyrant, whose sole name blisters our tongues,
15   Was once thought honest. You have loved him well:
He hath not touched you yet. I am young, but something
You may discern of him through me, and wisdom
To offer up a weak, poor, innocent lamb
T'appease an angry god.
20   MACDUFF   I am not treacherous.

4.3   *Location: the English royal court*   1 desolate barren/lonely/miserable   **shade**
shadowy or reclusive place   **4 fast** firmly   **mortal** deadly   **5 Bestride . . . birthdom** protect
our fallen birthright (as one would stand astride and defend a fallen soldier on the battlefield)
7 that so that   **9 Like . . . dolour** the same cry of sorrow   **10 wail** lament   **12 to friend**
favorable, on my side   **13 perchance** perhaps   **14 sole name** name alone   **15 honest**
honorable   **16 touched** harmed   **something . . . me** you may detect something of him in me
17 wisdom you may deem it wisdom   **19 angry god** i.e. Macbeth

MALCOLM   But Macbeth is.
    A good and virtuous nature may recoil
    In an imperial charge. But I shall crave your pardon:
    That which you are my thoughts cannot transpose;
25   Angels are bright still, though the brightest fell:
    Though all things foul would wear the brows of grace,
    Yet grace must still look so.

MACDUFF   I have lost my hopes.

MALCOLM   Perchance even there where I did find my doubts.
30   Why in that rawness left you wife and child,
    Those precious motives, those strong knots of love,
    Without leave-taking? I pray you,
    Let not my jealousies be your dishonours,
    But mine own safeties. You may be rightly just,
35   Whatever I shall think.

MACDUFF   Bleed, bleed, poor country!
    Great tyranny, lay thou thy basis sure,
    For goodness dare not check thee: wear thou thy wrongs,
    The title is affeered!— Fare thee well, lord.
40   I would not be the villain that thou think'st
    For the whole space that's in the tyrant's grasp,
    And the rich east to boot.

MALCOLM   Be not offended:
    I speak not as in absolute fear of you.
45   I think our country sinks beneath the yoke:

---

22 recoil degenerate, give way (plays on sense of "rebound like a firearm that has been shot")
23 imperial charge royal command (**charge** plays on sense of "quantity of gunpowder in a firearm")   **24 That . . . transpose** my (suspicious) thoughts cannot change you from what you really are   **25 the brightest** i.e. Lucifer, or Satan, the brightest angel who was cast out of heaven for defying God   **26 foul** sinful/dirty, tarnished   **wear . . . grace** assume the appearance of goodness (thus casting suspicion on true goodness)   **27 look so** look like itself **29 there** i.e. Scotland   **doubts** suspicions   **30 rawness** vulnerability/incompleteness (without **leave-taking**)   **31 motives** incentives (to loving, protective behavior)   **32 leave-taking** formal farewell/permission to depart   **33 Let . . . safeties** do not think that my suspicions are intended to shame and insult you, but that they arise from concern for my own security   **37 basis sure** foundation firmly   **38 check** restrain/rebuke   **39 title is affeered** (Macbeth's) title is confirmed; plays on sense of "affeared," i.e. Malcolm is frightened to claim his title   **42 to boot** in addition   **45 yoke** wooden apparatus worn on the neck of a captive or conquered enemy used to subdue and prevent escape

It weeps, it bleeds, and each new day a gash
Is added to her wounds. I think withal
There would be hands uplifted in my right,
And here from gracious England have I offer
50 Of goodly thousands: but, for all this,
When I shall tread upon the tyrant's head,
Or wear it on my sword, yet my poor country
Shall have more vices than it had before,
More suffer, and more sundry ways than ever,
55 By him that shall succeed.

MACDUFF   What should he be?

MALCOLM   It is myself I mean, in whom I know
All the particulars of vice so grafted
That, when they shall be opened, black Macbeth
60 Will seem as pure as snow, and the poor state
Esteem him as a lamb, being compared
With my confineless harms.

MACDUFF   Not in the legions
Of horrid hell can come a devil more damned
65 In evils to top Macbeth.

MALCOLM   I grant him bloody,
Luxurious, avaricious, false, deceitful,
Sudden, malicious, smacking of every sin
That has a name, but there's no bottom, none,
70 In my voluptuousness: your wives, your daughters,
Your matrons and your maids, could not fill up
The cistern of my lust, and my desire
All continent impediments would o'erbear

---

47 withal moreover   48 right rightful cause   49 England the King of England
50 thousands i.e. of soldiers   54 more sundry in more diverse   55 succeed follow (Macbeth;
with a play on sense of "inherit the throne")   56 What who   58 particulars individual
features/detailed aspects   so grafted are so merged (as in horticulture: a shoot from one plant
is grafted onto the stem of another)   59 opened revealed/unfurled (like a bud)   61 Esteem
regard, value   62 confineless boundless   63 legions multitudes/armies   65 top surpass
67 Luxurious lustful   avaricious greedy for wealth   68 Sudden impetuous, violently hasty,
unpredictable   70 voluptuousness lust for pleasure   71 matrons married women   maids
virgins   72 cistern large water tank   73 continent restrictive/chaste/containing (perhaps
with vaginal connotations)   o'erbear overflow/crush (with my body weight during rape)

That did oppose my will. Better Macbeth
75   Than such an one to reign.

MACDUFF   Boundless intemperance
In nature is a tyranny: it hath been
Th'untimely emptying of the happy throne
And fall of many kings. But fear not yet
80   To take upon you what is yours: you may
Convey your pleasures in a spacious plenty,
And yet seem cold. The time you may so hoodwink.
We have willing dames enough: there cannot be
That vulture in you to devour so many
85   As will to greatness dedicate themselves,
Finding it so inclined.

MALCOLM   With this there grows
In my most ill-composed affection such
A stanchless avarice that, were I king,
90   I should cut off the nobles for their lands,
Desire his jewels and this other's house:
And my more-having would be as a sauce
To make me hunger more, that I should forge
Quarrels unjust against the good and loyal,
95   Destroying them for wealth.

MACDUFF   This avarice
Sticks deeper, grows with more pernicious root
Than summer-seeming lust, and it hath been
The sword of our slain kings. Yet do not fear:
100   Scotland hath foisons to fill up your will

---

74 will sexual desire/penis   **76 Boundless . . . tyranny** in human nature, excessive lack
of control is a form of tyranny over the self   **80 what is yours** i.e. the Scottish throne
81 Convey manage, carry out (secretly)   **82 cold** chaste/lacking in sexual passion
hoodwink blindfold, i.e. deceive   **84 so . . . inclined** the number of women who will offer
themselves to a man in your royal position once they realize you desire them   **88 ill-
composed affection** character constituted of evil/poorly constituted disposition
89 stanchless unstoppable   **90 cut off** kill   **91 his** i.e. one man's   **92 more-having** greater
wealth/greed for more   **93 forge** fabricate, invent   **98 summer-seeming** befitting summer,
i.e. youth (lust may wane with age)   **99 sword . . . kings** i.e. means by which they died (e.g. in
wars motivated by greed)   **100 foisons** plentiful resources

Of your mere own. All these are portable,
With other graces weighed.

MALCOLM   But I have none. The king-becoming graces,
As justice, verity, temp'rance, stableness,
105   Bounty, perseverance, mercy, lowliness,
Devotion, patience, courage, fortitude,
I have no relish of them, but abound
In the division of each several crime,
Acting it many ways. Nay, had I power, I should
110   Pour the sweet milk of concord into hell,
Uproar the universal peace, confound
All unity on earth.

MACDUFF   O Scotland, Scotland!

MALCOLM   If such a one be fit to govern, speak:
115   I am as I have spoken.

MACDUFF   Fit to govern?
No, not to live. O nation miserable,
With an untitled tyrant bloody-sceptred,
When shalt thou see thy wholesome days again,
120   Since that the truest issue of thy throne
By his own interdiction stands accused
And does blaspheme his breed?— Thy royal father
Was a most sainted king: the queen that bore thee,
Oft'ner upon her knees than on her feet,
125   Died every day she lived. Fare thee well.
These evils thou repeat'st upon thyself

---

101 Of . . . own of your very own, belonging entirely to you (as king)   these i.e. these vices
you mention   portable bearable, endurable   102 weighed counterbalanced   103 king-
becoming befitting a king (plays on the idea of one who is about to gain kingship)   104 verity
truthfulness   temp'rance moderation, self-restraint   105 Bounty kindness, generosity
lowliness humility   107 relish trace/taste for   abound . . . crime i.e. I am full of all possible
aspects of vice   108 division category/variation   several individual   110 concord
harmony, peace   111 Uproar bring into a state of uproar   118 untitled without rightful title
119 wholesome healthy   121 interdiction prohibition   122 blaspheme slanders/commits
sacrilege (to the sainted Duncan)   breed his family line   123 sainted saintly, holy
124 upon her knees i.e. in prayer   125 Died . . . lived spent every day of her life in a state
of holy readiness for death   126 repeat'st upon utter against/recount about

Hath banished me from Scotland.— O my breast,
Thy hope ends here!

MALCOLM   Macduff, this noble passion,
130   Child of integrity, hath from my soul
Wiped the black scruples, reconciled my thoughts
To thy good truth and honour. Devilish Macbeth
By many of these trains hath sought to win me
Into his power, and modest wisdom plucks me
135   From over-credulous haste: but God above
Deal between thee and me! For even now
I put myself to thy direction and
Unspeak mine own detraction: here abjure
The taints and blames I laid upon myself
140   For strangers to my nature. I am yet
Unknown to woman, never was forsworn,
Scarcely have coveted what was mine own,
At no time broke my faith, would not betray
The devil to his fellow, and delight
145   No less in truth than life. My first false speaking
Was this upon myself. What I am truly
Is thine and my poor country's to command:
Whither indeed, before thy here-approach,
Old Siward with ten thousand warlike men,
150   Already at a point, was setting forth.
Now we'll together, and the chance of goodness
Be like our warranted quarrel. Why are you silent?

MACDUFF   Such welcome and unwelcome things at once
'Tis hard to reconcile.

---

127 **Hath . . . Scotland** have destroyed any hope I had of returning to Scotland/are exactly
those, which, in Macbeth, caused me to flee Scotland   131 **scruples** doubts   133 **trains**
tricks, stratagems (i.e. sending an apparently sympathetic nobleman to try and lure Malcolm
back to Scotland)   134 **plucks** withholds   135 **over-credulous** too readily believing
137 **direction** guidance   138 **Unspeak . . . detraction** take back the harmful things I said
about myself   **abjure** renounce   139 **taints** (moral) stains   140 **For** as being   141 **Unknown
to woman** i.e. a virgin   **forsworn** perjured, a breaker of oaths   142 **Scarcely . . . own** have
hardly ever desired even what I myself owned   145 **false speaking** lie   146 **this upon myself**
i.e. the false statements he made about his character   148 **here-approach** arrival here
150 **at a point** prepared, ready   151 **we'll** we'll set forth   **the . . . quarrel** may our success
match the degree to which our cause is justified

Enter a Doctor

155 MALCOLM   Well, more anon.— Comes the king forth, I pray
          you?

    DOCTOR   Ay, sir, there are a crew of wretched souls
    That stay his cure: their malady convinces
    The great assay of art, but at his touch —
    Such sanctity hath heaven given his hand —
160 They presently amend.   *Exit*

    MALCOLM   I thank you, doctor.

    MACDUFF   What's the disease he means?

    MALCOLM   'Tis called the evil:
    A most miraculous work in this good king,
165 Which often, since my here-remain in England,
    I have seen him do. How he solicits heaven
    Himself best knows: but strangely-visited people,
    All swoll'n and ulcerous, pitiful to the eye,
    The mere despair of surgery, he cures,
170 Hanging a golden stamp about their necks
    Put on with holy prayers: and 'tis spoken,
    To the succeeding royalty he leaves
    The healing benediction. With this strange virtue
    He hath a heavenly gift of prophecy,
175 And sundry blessings hang about his throne
    That speak him full of grace.

Enter Ross

    MACDUFF   See who comes here.

    MALCOLM   My countryman, but yet I know him not.

---

157 stay await   **cure** kings were believed to possess a healing touch   **convinces** defeats
158 assay of art efforts of medical practitioners   **159 sanctity** holiness   **160 presently**
amend immediately recover   **163 the evil** "the king's evil," i.e. scrofula, an inflammation of
the lymph nodes, which the monarch's touch was believed to cure   **165 here-remain** stay
166 solicits entreats (through prayer)   **167 strangely-visited** severely afflicted   **169 mere**
absolute   **170 stamp** coin   **171 'tis spoken** it is said   **172 succeeding royalty** king's
successors   **173 benediction** grace, blessing   **strange** inexplicable   **176 speak him** declare
him to be   **178 countryman** i.e. fellow Scot   **know** recognize (presumably Ross's clothing
identifies him as Malcolm's countryman, or perhaps Malcolm means that sorrow has so
altered Ross that he seems like a different man)

MACDUFF		My ever-gentle cousin, welcome hither.
180	MALCOLM	I know him now. Good God betimes remove

MALCOLM The means that makes us strangers!

ROSS Sir, amen.

MACDUFF Stands Scotland where it did?

ROSS Alas, poor country,
185 Almost afraid to know itself. It cannot
Be called our mother, but our grave; where nothing
But who knows nothing is once seen to smile:
Where sighs and groans and shrieks that rend the air
Are made, not marked: where violent sorrow seems
190 A modern ecstasy. The dead man's knell
Is there scarce asked for who, and good men's lives
Expire before the flowers in their caps,
Dying or ere they sicken.

MACDUFF O, relation too nice, and yet too true!

195 MALCOLM What's the newest grief?

ROSS That of an hour's age doth hiss the speaker:
Each minute teems a new one.

MACDUFF How does my wife?

ROSS Why, well.

200 MACDUFF And all my children?

ROSS Well, too.

MACDUFF The tyrant has not battered at their peace?

ROSS No, they were well at peace when I did leave 'em.

MACDUFF Be not a niggard of your speech: how goes't?

205 ROSS When I came hither to transport the tidings
Which I have heavily borne, there ran a rumour
Of many worthy fellows that were out,

---

179 **ever-gentle** ever noble   180 **betimes** hastily   181 **means** circumstances (more
specifically, Macbeth)   186 **nothing . . . nothing** no one other than a fool   189 **marked** paid
attention to   190 **modern ecstasy** commonplace frenzy   **The . . . who** i.e. no one bothers to
inquire about who has died when they hear the funeral bell toll as death has become so
common   193 **or . . . sicken** before becoming ill   194 **relation** report, account   **nice**
detailed/accurate/extraordinary, strange   196 **hiss the speaker** mock the speaker (as the
news is already out of date)   197 **teems** gives rise to, breeds   203 **at peace** i.e. dead (though
Macbeth continues to understand the sense of "untroubled")   204 **niggard of** miser in
206 **heavily** sorrowfully/as a burden   207 **out** i.e. preparing for war/committed to rebellion

Which was to my belief witnessed the rather,
For that I saw the tyrant's power afoot.
210 Now is the time of help.— Your eye in Scotland   *To Malcolm*
Would create soldiers, make our women fight,
To doff their dire distresses.

MALCOLM   Be't their comfort
We are coming thither. Gracious England hath
215 Lent us good Siward and ten thousand men:
An older and a better soldier none
That Christendom gives out.

ROSS   Would I could answer
This comfort with the like. But I have words
220 That would be howled out in the desert air,
Where hearing should not latch them.

MACDUFF   What concern they?
The general cause? Or is it a fee-grief
Due to some single breast?

225 ROSS   No mind that's honest
But in it shares some woe, though the main part
Pertains to you alone.

MACDUFF   If it be mine,
Keep it not from me, quickly let me have it.

230 ROSS   Let not your ears despise my tongue for ever,
Which shall possess them with the heaviest sound
That ever yet they heard.

MACDUFF   Hum! I guess at it.

ROSS   Your castle is surprised, your wife and babes
235 Savagely slaughtered: to relate the manner

---

208 **witnessed the rather** further confirmed   209 **power** army   **afoot** on the march
210 **eye** i.e. you, your presence   212 **doff** cast off (as one would a garment)   213 **Be't** let it be
216 **An . . . out** i.e. there is not an older or better soldier in all Christendom   217 **gives out**
reports, proclaims   219 **the like** i.e. similarly encouraging news   220 **would** should   **desert**
lonely, desolate   221 **latch** take hold of, receive   223 **general cause** i.e. the woes of Scotland
fee-grief grief owned by one person only (a term derived from legal language relating to
property)   231 **possess them with** put them in possession of/cause them to become
(demonically) possessed by   **heaviest** most sorrowful, grievous   234 **surprised** ambushed
235 **manner** way in which they were killed, details

Were, on the quarry of these murdered deer,
To add the death of you.

MALCOLM   Merciful heaven!
What, man, ne'er pull your hat upon your brows:
240   Give sorrow words. The grief that does not speak
Whispers the o'er-fraught heart and bids it break.

MACDUFF   My children too?

ROSS   Wife, children, servants, all that could be found.

MACDUFF   And I must be from thence! My wife killed too?

245   ROSS   I have said.

MALCOLM   Be comforted:
Let's make us med'cines of our great revenge,
To cure this deadly grief.

MACDUFF   He has no children.— All my pretty ones?
250   Did you say all? O hell-kite! All?
What, all my pretty chickens and their dam
At one fell swoop?

MALCOLM   Dispute it like a man.

MACDUFF   I shall do so,
255   But I must also feel it as a man:
I cannot but remember such things were
That were most precious to me. Did heaven look on
And would not take their part? Sinful Macduff,
They were all struck for thee! Naught that I am,
260   Not for their own demerits, but for mine,
Fell slaughter on their souls. Heaven rest them now!

MALCOLM   Be this the whetstone of your sword. Let grief
Convert to anger: blunt not the heart, enrage it.

MACDUFF   O, I could play the woman with mine eyes

---

236 **quarry** heap of deer killed at a hunt   **deer** puns on "dear"   239 **pull . . . brows** a conventional gesture of grief   241 **Whispers** whispers to   **o'er-fraught** overburdened 244 **must . . . thence** had to be away from home   249 **He** refers either to Macbeth or to Malcolm   250 **hell-kite** bird of prey from hell   251 **dam** mother   252 **fell swoop** cruel swooping down of the **hell-kite**   253 **Dispute** fight against   259 **struck** killed violently and suddenly   **Naught** wicked, sinful person   260 **demerits** faults   261 **Fell** quibbles on the adjectival sense of "cruel"   262 **whetstone** stone on which swords are sharpened 264 **play . . . eyes** i.e. weep

265   And braggart with my tongue! But, gentle heavens,
          Cut short all intermission. Front to front
          Bring thou this fiend of Scotland and myself:
          Within my sword's length set him. If he scape,
          Heaven forgive him too!
270 **MALCOLM**   This tune goes manly.
          Come, go we to the king. Our power is ready:
          Our lack is nothing but our leave. Macbeth
          Is ripe for shaking, and the powers above
          Put on their instruments. Receive what cheer you may:
275   The night is long that never finds the day.   *Exeunt*

Act 5 Scene 1

running scene 18

Enter a Doctor of Physic and a Waiting-Gentlewoman

DOCTOR   I have two nights watched with you, but can perceive no truth in your report. When was it she last walked?

GENTLEWOMAN   Since his majesty went into the field, I have seen
5   her rise from her bed, throw her nightgown upon her, unlock her closet, take forth paper, fold it, write upon't, read it, afterwards seal it, and again return to bed; yet all this while in a most fast sleep.

DOCTOR   A great perturbation in nature, to receive at once
10   the benefit of sleep and do the effects of watching. In this slumbery agitation, besides her walking and other actual performances, what — at any time — have you heard her say?

---

265 **braggart** play one who brags, i.e. gives out a braying cry/talks emptily and ceaselessly
266 **intermission** pause in action   **Front to front** face to face   268 **scape** escape   270 **tune** style (of speech)/tone/frame of mind   271 **power** army   272 **Our . . . leave** it remains only to obtain formal permission to depart (from the English king)   273 **ripe for shaking** i.e. ready to fall (like ripe fruit from a tree)   **powers above** heavenly powers   274 **Put . . . instruments** urge on their agents (us)/put on their weapons   **5.1**   *Location: Macbeth's castle at Dunsinane*   **Physic** medicine   1 **watched** remained awake   3 **walked** sleepwalked
4 **field** battlefield (i.e. prepared for war)   6 **closet** cabinet   9 **perturbation** disturbance
10 **effects of watching** appearance and actions of waking   11 **agitation** disturbed state of mind/nervous activity

GENTLEWOMAN   That, sir, which I will not report after her.

15 DOCTOR   You may to me, and 'tis most meet you should.

GENTLEWOMAN   Neither to you nor anyone, having no witness to confirm my speech.

Enter Lady [Macbeth], with a taper

Lo you, here she comes. This is her very guise, and, upon my life, fast asleep. Observe her: stand close.   *They stand aside*

20 DOCTOR   How came she by that light?

GENTLEWOMAN   Why, it stood by her. She has light by her continually: 'tis her command.

DOCTOR   You see her eyes are open.

GENTLEWOMAN   Ay, but their sense are shut.

25 DOCTOR   What is it she does now? Look how she rubs her hands.

GENTLEWOMAN   It is an accustomed action with her to seem thus washing her hands: I have known her continue in this a quarter of an hour.

30 LADY MACBETH   Yet here's a spot.

DOCTOR   Hark, she speaks. I will set down what comes from her, to satisfy my remembrance the more strongly.

LADY MACBETH   Out, damned spot! Out, I say!— One: two: why then, 'tis time to do't.— Hell is murky.— Fie, my lord, fie, a
35 soldier, and afeard? What need we fear who knows it, when none can call our power to account?— Yet who would have thought the old man to have had so much blood in him?

DOCTOR   Do you mark that?

LADY MACBETH   The Thane of Fife had a wife: where is she
40 now?— What, will these hands ne'er be clean?— No more o'that, my lord, no more o'that: you mar all with this starting.

---

15 meet suitable   *taper* candle   **18 guise** custom/manner   **19 close** concealed   **31 set down** write down   **32 satisfy** meets the needs of, confirm   **remembrance** memory
33 One: two Lady Macbeth imagines she hears the striking of a clock or perhaps the bell she was to strike as a signal to Macbeth   **36 none . . . account** no one can hold us responsible as we are now so powerful   **39 Thane of Fife** Macduff   **41 mar** spoil   **42 starting** nervousness/fits, outbursts

DOCTOR   Go to, go to: you have known what you should not.

GENTLEWOMAN   She has spoke what she should not, I am sure of
45   that: heaven knows what she has known.

LADY MACBETH   Here's the smell of the blood still. All the
perfumes of Arabia will not sweeten this little hand. O, O, O!

DOCTOR   What a sigh is there! The heart is sorely charged.

GENTLEWOMAN   I would not have such a heart in my bosom for
50   the dignity of the whole body.

DOCTOR   Well, well, well.

GENTLEWOMAN   Pray God it be, sir.

DOCTOR   This disease is beyond my practice. Yet I have
known those which have walked in their sleep who have died
55   holily in their beds.

LADY MACBETH   Wash your hands, put on your nightgown, look
not so pale. I tell you yet again, Banquo's buried; he cannot
come out on's grave.

DOCTOR   Even so?

60 LADY MACBETH   To bed, to bed. There's knocking at the gate.
Come, come, come, come, give me your hand. What's done
cannot be undone. To bed, to bed, to bed.   *Exit Lady [Macbeth]*

DOCTOR   Will she go now to bed?

GENTLEWOMAN   Directly.

65 DOCTOR   Foul whisp'rings are abroad. Unnatural deeds
Do breed unnatural troubles: infected minds
To their deaf pillows will discharge their secrets.
More needs she the divine than the physician.
God, God forgive us all! Look after her:
70   Remove from her the means of all annoyance,
And still keep eyes upon her. So, goodnight.
My mind she has mated, and amazed my sight.
I think, but dare not speak.

GENTLEWOMAN   Goodnight, good doctor.   *Exeunt*

---

43 Go to expression of reproof similar to "come come" (probably directed at Lady Macbeth)
48 sorely charged grievously burdened   **50 dignity** worth, high status   **52 be** i.e. be well
53 practice medical skill   **58 on's** of his   **59 Even so?** i.e. is that how it is   **68 divine** priest
70 annoyance injury (here self-harm)   **71 still** continually   **72 mated** bewildered

Act 5 Scene 2

Drum and Colours. Enter Menteith, Caithness, Angus, Lennox [and]
Soldiers

MENTEITH   The English power is near, led on by Malcolm,
His uncle Siward and the good Macduff.
Revenges burn in them, for their dear causes
Would to the bleeding and the grim alarm
5   Excite the mortified man.

ANGUS   Near Birnam Wood
Shall we well meet them: that way are they coming.

CAITHNESS   Who knows if Donalbain be with his brother?

LENNOX   For certain, sir, he is not: I have a file
10   Of all the gentry: there is Siward's son,
And many unrough youths that even now
Protest their first of manhood.

MENTEITH   What does the tyrant?

CAITHNESS   Great Dunsinane he strongly fortifies.
15   Some say he's mad, others that lesser hate him
Do call it valiant fury: but for certain
He cannot buckle his distempered cause
Within the belt of rule.

ANGUS   Now does he feel
20   His secret murders sticking on his hands,
Now minutely revolts upbraid his faith-breach.
Those he commands move only in command,
Nothing in love: now does he feel his title

5.2   *Location: near Dunsinane   Drum and Colours* drummer and bearer of military
flags   **3 dear** heartfelt/noble/grievous   **causes** motives for revenge, grounds for action
4 bleeding shedding of blood/bloody (**alarm**)   **alarm** call to arms   **5 Excite . . . man** rouse
even a dead or insensible man   **9 file** list   **11 unrough** beardless, i.e. young   **12 Protest**
declare, assert   **14 Dunsinane** i.e. the castle   **17 buckle . . . rule** i.e. legally (or morally)
justify his grounds for fighting; the image is of a diseased and bloated belly one cannot buckle
a belt around   **distempered** disordered/diseased   **cause** grounds for action/illness
20 sticking i.e. with blood   **21 minutely** every minute   **upbraid** reproach, censure   **faith-
breach** breaking of (secular and spiritual) loyalty   **22 move . . . love** only obey because they
are following orders, not out of love for their king

SEYTON   'Tis not needed yet.

MACBETH   I'll put it on.

　　　　Send out more horses: skirr the country round:

　　　　Hang those that talk of fear. Give me mine armour.—

Seyton gets the armor

40　　　　How does your patient, doctor?

DOCTOR   Not so sick, my lord,

　　　　As she is troubled with thick-coming fancies

　　　　That keep her from her rest.

MACBETH   Cure her of that.

45　　　　Canst thou not minister to a mind diseased,

　　　　Pluck from the memory a rooted sorrow,

　　　　Raze out the written troubles of the brain,

　　　　And with some sweet oblivious antidote

　　　　Cleanse the stuffed bosom of that perilous stuff

50　　　　Which weighs upon the heart?

DOCTOR   Therein the patient

　　　　Must minister to himself.

MACBETH   Throw physic to the dogs, I'll none of it.—

　　　　Come, put mine armour on: give me my staff.— *To Attendants,*

55　　　　Seyton, send out. Doctor, the thanes fly from me.— *who arm him*

　　　　Come, sir, dispatch.— If thou couldst, doctor, cast

　　　　The water of my land, find her disease,

　　　　And purge it to a sound and pristine health,

　　　　I would applaud thee to the very echo,

60　　　　That should applaud again.— Pull't off, I say.— *To Attendants*

　　　　What rhubarb, cyme, or what purgative drug *To Doctor*

　　　　Would scour these English hence? Hear'st thou of them?

---

38 skirr scour, pass speedily through　　**41 Not so sick** not so much physically ill
42 thick-coming thronging　　**fancies** imaginings, delusions　　**47 Raze out** erase, wipe out
48 oblivious inducing oblivion, forgetfulness　　**49 stuffed** over-full/oppressed　　**54 staff** rod of
office/spear or clublike weapon　　**55 send out** i.e. send out **more horses**　　**56 dispatch** hurry
up　　**cast The water** make a diagnosis by examining the urine　　**58 pristine** original, former
60 Pull't off either an instruction to remove a piece of armor that is proving difficult to put
on or has been put on incorrectly, or Macbeth has changed his mind about wearing his armor
at all　　**61 rhubarb** plant used to make purgative drugs　　**cyme** senna, a plant used to make
purgative drugs and sometimes mixed with rhubarb for this purpose　　**62 scour** cleanse, purge

DOCTOR   Ay, my good lord: your royal preparation
Makes us hear something.

65   MACBETH   Bring it after me.—   *To Seyton or Attendants*
I will not be afraid of death and bane,
Till Birnam Forest come to Dunsinane.

DOCTOR   Were I from Dunsinane away and clear,   *Aside*
Profit again should hardly draw me here.   *Exeunt*

Act 5 Scene 4   *running scene 21*

*Drum and Colours. Enter Malcolm, Siward, Macduff, Siward's Son,
Menteith, Caithness, Angus and Soldiers, marching*

MALCOLM   Cousins, I hope the days are near at hand
That chambers will be safe.

MENTEITH   We doubt it nothing.

SIWARD   What wood is this before us?

5   MENTEITH   The wood of Birnam.

MALCOLM   Let every soldier hew him down a bough
And bear't before him: thereby shall we shadow
The numbers of our host and make discovery
Err in report of us.

10   A SOLDIER   It shall be done.

SIWARD   We learn no other but the confident tyrant
Keeps still in Dunsinane and will endure
Our setting down before't.

MALCOLM   'Tis his main hope:

15   For where there is advantage to be given,

---

63 **preparation** mobilized army/military proceedings   65 **it** probably the armor removed a few
lines earlier   66 **bane** murder/destruction   68 **clear** safe/free/untroubled   69 **hardly** with
great difficulty   **5.4   *Location: near Birnam Wood*   2 chambers** private rooms (like the
bedchamber in which Duncan was murdered)   3 **nothing** not at all   7 **shadow** conceal
8 **host** army   **discovery** military reconnaissance   9 **Err** be mistaken   12 **Keeps** remains
(with connotations of defensive preservation)   13 **setting down** encampment for a siege
15 **where . . . given** while they could have advantaged Macbeth (through loyalty)/wherever it
is possible to advantage the English forces/where military advantage must be conceded to the
English (who are about to besiege the castle)/when they had the opportunity (i.e. were not
confined to the castle during a siege)

Both more and less have given him the revolt,
And none serve with him but constrainèd things
Whose hearts are absent too.

MACDUFF   Let our just censures
20   Attend the true event, and put we on
Industrious soldiership.

SIWARD   The time approaches
That will with due decision make us know
What we shall say we have and what we owe.
25   Thoughts speculative their unsure hopes relate,
But certain issue strokes must arbitrate:
Towards which advance the war.   *Exeunt, marching*

Act 5 Scene 5   *running scene 22*

Enter Macbeth, Seyton, and Soldiers with Drum and Colours

MACBETH   Hang out our banners on the outward walls:
The cry is still 'They come.' Our castle's strength
Will laugh a siege to scorn: here let them lie
Till famine and the ague eat them up.
5   Were they not forced with those that should be ours,
We might have met them dareful, beard to beard,
And beat them backward home.

A cry within of women

What is that noise?

SEYTON   It is the cry of women, my good lord.

Exit or goes to the door

MACBETH   I have almost forgot the taste of fears:
10   The time has been my senses would have cooled

---

16 **more . . . revolt** people of both high and low social status have deserted Macbeth
19 **Let . . . event** let an exact assessment be made only after the outcome of the actual battle
23 **due** appropriate, necessary (plays on the sense of "owing")   24 **owe** own/are required to
repay   25 **Thoughts . . . arbitrate** speculation deals with uncertain hopes; for a definitive
outcome, combat must be the deciding factor   **5.5** *Location: Macbeth's castle at
Dunsinane*   4 **ague** fever   5 **forced** reinforced   6 **dareful** defiantly/boldly

To hear a night-shriek, and my fell of hair
Would at a dismal treatise rouse and stir
As life were in't. I have supped full with horrors:
Direness, familiar to my slaughterous thoughts,

15   Cannot once start me.—   *Seyton re-enters or comes forward*

Wherefore was that cry?   *To Seyton*

SEYTON   The queen, my lord, is dead.

MACBETH   She should have died hereafter:
There would have been a time for such a word.
Tomorrow, and tomorrow, and tomorrow,

20   Creeps in this petty pace from day to day
To the last syllable of recorded time:
And all our yesterdays have lighted fools
The way to dusty death. Out, out, brief candle.
Life's but a walking shadow, a poor player

25   That struts and frets his hour upon the stage
And then is heard no more. It is a tale
Told by an idiot, full of sound and fury,
Signifying nothing.

Enter a Messenger

Thou com'st to use thy tongue: thy story quickly.

30   MESSENGER   Gracious my lord,
I should report that which I say I saw,
But know not how to do't.

MACBETH   Well, say, sir.

MESSENGER   As I did stand my watch upon the hill,

---

11 fell of hair entire head of hair   **12 treatise** tale   **13 As** as if   **supped full** had my fill of horror/dined in the company of horrors (i.e. Banquo's ghost)   **14 Direness** dreadfulness, horror   **15 start me** make me start   **17 She . . . hereafter** she should have died at a future time/she would have died at some point anyway   **18 such a word** i.e. news of her death   **20 petty** slow/insignificant   **21 syllable** most minute portion/basic element of a word   **recorded** written/narrated/remembered   **22 lighted** lit the way for (with a **candle**)   **23 dusty** i.e. characterized by the dust to which all mortals return   **24 shadow** insubstantial thing/illusion/ghost/actor (the theatrical sense is picked up in **fools** and **player**)   **poor** wretched/unskilled   **25 frets** wears out/worries his way through/rants and rages (in the manner of a bad actor)   **27 fury** fierce passion/frenzy, madness/wild anger/violence   **29 thy story quickly** relate your news at once   **34 did . . . watch** was on guard

35   I looked toward Birnam, and anon methought
       The wood began to move.

MACBETH   Liar and slave!

MESSENGER Let me endure your wrath if't be not so.
       Within this three mile may you see it coming:
40   I say, a moving grove.

MACBETH   If thou speak'st false,
       Upon the next tree shall thou hang alive
       Till famine cling thee: if thy speech be sooth,
       I care not if thou dost for me as much.—
45   I pull in resolution, and begin
       To doubt th'equivocation of the fiend
       That lies like truth. 'Fear not, till Birnam Wood
       Do come to Dunsinane', and now a wood
       Comes toward Dunsinane.— Arm, arm, and out!
50   If this which he avouches does appear,
       There is nor flying hence nor tarrying here.—
       I 'gin to be aweary of the sun,
       And wish th'estate o'th'world were now undone.—
       Ring the alarum bell! Blow wind, come wrack,
55   At least we'll die with harness on our back.   *Exeunt*

Act 5 Scene 6

running scene 23

Drum and Colours. Enter Malcolm, Siward, Macduff and their army,
with boughs

MALCOLM   Now near enough. Your leafy screens throw down,
       And show like those you are. You, worthy uncle,
       Shall with my cousin, your right noble son,
       Lead our first battle. Worthy Macduff and we

43 cling shrivel   **sooth** truth   **44 dost . . . much** do the same for me   **45 pull in resolution**
(am forced to) rein in my firmness of purpose; some editors emend to "pall"   **46 fiend** i.e. the
Third Apparition   **50 avouches** affirms   **51 nor . . . . here** no point either fleeing from here
or remaining   **52 'gin** begin   **53 th'estate** the kingdom/condition/settled order   **54 wrack**
ruin, destruction   **55 harness** armor   **5.6** *Location: outside Macbeth's castle at*
Dunsinane   **2 show** appear   **uncle** i.e. Siward   **4 battle** battalion

5   Shall take upon's what else remains to do,
       According to our order.

SIWARD   Fare you well.
       Do we but find the tyrant's power tonight,
       Let us be beaten if we cannot fight.

10   MACDUFF   Make all our trumpets speak: give them all breath,
       Those clamorous harbingers of blood and death.

Exeunt. Alarums continued

Act 5 Scene 7
running scene 23 continues

Enter Macbeth

MACBETH   They have tied me to a stake: I cannot fly,
       But bear-like I must fight the course. What's he
       That was not born of woman? Such a one
       Am I to fear, or none.

Enter Young Siward

5   YOUNG SIWARD   What is thy name?

MACBETH   Thou'lt be afraid to hear it.

YOUNG SIWARD   No, though thou call'st thyself a hotter name
       Than any is in hell.

MACBETH   My name's Macbeth.

10   YOUNG SIWARD   The devil himself could not pronounce a title
       More hateful to mine ear.

MACBETH   No, nor more fearful.

YOUNG SIWARD   Thou liest, abhorrèd tyrant: with my sword
       I'll prove the lie thou speak'st.

Fight and Young Siward slain

15   MACBETH   Thou wast born of woman.
       But swords I smile at, weapons laugh to scorn,
       Brandished by man that's of a woman born.   *Exit*

---

6 **order** arrangement, battle plan   8 **Do** i.e. if   **power** army   11 **harbingers** forerunners, messengers   **5.7**   2 **bear-like** like a bear tied to a **stake** and baited with dogs, a popular form of entertainment   **course** designated bout, during which the bear was attacked by dogs   8 **is** that is

Alarums. Enter Macduff

MACDUFF   That way the noise is. Tyrant, show thy face.
If thou be'st slain, and with no stroke of mine,
20   My wife and children's ghosts will haunt me still.
I cannot strike at wretched kerns, whose arms
Are hired to bear their staves: either thou, Macbeth,
Or else my sword with an unbattered edge
I sheathe again undeeded. There thou shouldst be:
25   By this great clatter, one of greatest note
Seems bruited. Let me find him, Fortune,
And more I beg not.   *Exit. Alarums*

Enter Malcolm and Siward

SIWARD   This way, my lord. The castle's gently rendered:
The tyrant's people on both sides do fight,
30   The noble thanes do bravely in the war,
The day almost itself professes yours,
And little is to do.

MALCOLM   We have met with foes that strike beside us.

SIWARD   Enter, sir, the castle.   *Exeunt. Alarum*

Enter Macbeth

35   MACBETH   Why should I play the Roman fool and die
On mine own sword? Whiles I see lives, the gashes
Do better upon them.

Enter Macduff

MACDUFF   Turn, hell-hound, turn.

MACBETH   Of all men else I have avoided thee.
40   But get thee back: my soul is too much charged
With blood of thine already.

---

21 kerns lightly armed foot soldiers   **22 staves** staffs used as weapons   **24 undeeded**
without its having carried out any action   **25 note** reputation/notoriety (plays on the sense
of "musical note")   **26 bruited** loudly announced   **28 gently rendered** calmly (or easily)
surrendered   **31 The . . . yours** i.e. you have almost won   **33 strike beside us** fight alongside
us/deliberately miss when they strike at us   **35 play . . . sword** i.e. do as the Romans did
and commit suicide when defeated   **36 lives** anyone living   **39 men else** other men
40 charged burdened; plays on the senses of "blamed/accused (of a crime)"

MACDUFF   I have no words:
My voice is in my sword, thou bloodier villain
Than terms can give thee out.   *Fight. Alarum*

45   MACBETH   Thou losest labour.
As easy mayst thou the intrenchant air
With thy keen sword impress as make me bleed.
Let fall thy blade on vulnerable crests:
I bear a charmèd life, which must not yield
50   To one of woman born.

MACDUFF   Despair thy charm,
And let the angel whom thou still hast served
Tell thee: Macduff was from his mother's womb
Untimely ripped.

55   MACBETH   Accursèd be that tongue that tells me so,
For it hath cowed my better part of man.
And be these juggling fiends no more believed
That palter with us in a double sense,
That keep the word of promise to our ear
60   And break it to our hope. I'll not fight with thee.

MACDUFF   Then yield thee, coward,
And live to be the show and gaze o'th'time:
We'll have thee, as our rarer monsters are,
Painted upon a pole, and underwrit,
65   'Here may you see the tyrant.'

MACBETH   I will not yield
To kiss the ground before young Malcolm's feet
And to be baited with the rabble's curse.
Though Birnam Wood be come to Dunsinane,

---

44 **terms . . . out** words can proclaim you to be   45 **losest labour** waste time   46 **intrenchant** unable to be cut   47 **keen** sharp (plays on the sense of "eager, fervent")   **impress** make a physical impression, mark   48 **crests** helmets, heads   52 **angel** personal governing spirit/ Lucifer   54 **Untimely** prematurely (Macduff was born by Caesarian section)   56 **cowed** overawed, intimidated   **better . . . man** i.e. courage, manly spirit   57 **juggling** deceiving/ equivocating   58 **palter** equivocate   59 **keep . . . hope** only fulfill their promises verbally rather than in the manner we expected   62 **show . . . o'th'time** sideshow or public spectacle of the age   64 **Painted . . . pole** (your picture) painted on a sign, as an advertisement for the attraction   **underwrit** written underneath   68 **rabble** mob of commoners

70   And thou opposed, being of no woman born,
        Yet I will try the last. Before my body
        I throw my warlike shield. Lay on, Macduff,
        And damned be him that first cries, 'Hold, enough!'

                                          Exeunt fighting. Alarums
        Enter fighting, and Macbeth slain

                            [*Exit Macduff with Macbeth's body*]
        *Retreat and flourish. Enter, with Drum and Colours, Malcolm, Siward,
        Ross, Thanes and Soldiers*

        MALCOLM   I would the friends we miss were safe arrived.
75   SIWARD   Some must go off: and yet, by these I see
        So great a day as this is cheaply bought.
        MALCOLM   Macduff is missing, and your noble son.
        ROSS   Your son, my lord, has paid a soldier's debt: *To Siward*
        He only lived but till he was a man,
80   The which no sooner had his prowess confirmed
        In the unshrinking station where he fought,
        But like a man he died.
        SIWARD   Then he is dead?
        ROSS   Ay, and brought off the field. Your cause of sorrow
85   Must not be measured by his worth, for then
        It hath no end.
        SIWARD   Had he his hurts before?
        ROSS   Ay, on the front.
        SIWARD   Why then, God's soldier be he!
90   Had I as many sons as I have hairs
        I would not wish them to a fairer death:
        And so his knell is knolled.
        MALCOLM   He's worth more sorrow,
        And that I'll spend for him.

---

70 opposed facing me/hostile to me   **71 try the last** attempt the extreme/undergo the
utmost   **72 Lay on** set to, go about it   **74 would** wish   **75 go off** die   **these** i.e. those
present   **78 soldier's debt** i.e. death   **80 prowess** bravery   **81 unshrinking station** brave
stand   **87 before** on the front of his body (which would show that he had died fighting
honorably, not running away)   **90 hairs** puns on "heirs"   **92 knolled** tolled   **94 spend**
expend (in tears)

95 SIWARD   He's worth no more.
            They say he parted well and paid his score,
            And so God be with him! Here comes newer comfort.
    Enter Macduff with Macbeth's head
    MACDUFF   Hail, king, for so thou art. Behold where stands
            Th'usurper's cursèd head. The time is free:
100   I see thee compassed with thy kingdom's pearl,
            That speak my salutation in their minds,
            Whose voices I desire aloud with mine:
            Hail, King of Scotland!
    ALL   Hail, King of Scotland!   *Flourish*
105 MALCOLM   We shall not spend a large expense of time
            Before we reckon with your several loves
            And make us even with you. My thanes and kinsmen,
            Henceforth be earls, the first that ever Scotland
            In such an honour named. What's more to do
110   Which would be planted newly with the time,
            As calling home our exiled friends abroad
            That fled the snares of watchful tyranny,
            Producing forth the cruel ministers
            Of this dead butcher and his fiend-like queen,
115   Who — as 'tis thought — by self and violent hands
            Took off her life: this, and what needful else
            That calls upon us, by the grace of grace
            We will perform in measure, time and place.
            So thanks to all at once and to each one,
120   Whom we invite to see us crowned at Scone.
                                        Flourish.   Exeunt

---

96 score bill, amount owed   **98 stands** i.e. on a pole or lance   **99 free** liberated from tyranny
100 compassed . . . pearl i.e. surrounded by the finest nobles of Scotland (plays on the idea of
being crowned)   **101 salutation** greeting   **105 spend** waste/pay out   **106 reckon** settle
accounts   **107 make . . . you** i.e. by rewarding the thanes' loyalty   **110 planted . . . time**
performed now as befits the beginning of a new age   **113 ministers** agents   **115 by . . . life**
i.e. committed suicide   **self and violent** her own violent   **116 needful else** other necessary
things   **117 grace of grace** i.e. grace of God (the essence of grace itself)   **118 measure** due
proportion

The Songs (apparently by Thomas Middleton, used in stagings after Shakespeare's retirement)

Song 1: at end of 3.5:

UNSEEN SPIRITS   Come away, come away,   *Above*
    Hecate, Hecate, O come away!
HECATE   I come, I come, I come, I come,
    With all the speed I may,
5   With all the speed I may.
    Where's Stadlin?
UNSEEN SPIRIT   Here.
HECATE   Where's Puckle?
UNSEEN SPIRIT   Here.
10 UNSEEN SPIRITS   And Hoppo too, and Hellway too,
    We lack but you, we lack but you.
    Come away, make up the count.
HECATE   I will but 'noint, and then I mount.
    I will but 'noint, and then I mount.
Malkin, a spirit like a cat, descends
15 UNSEEN SPIRITS   Here comes one down to fetch his dues,
    A kiss, a cull, a sip of blood,
    And why thou stay'st so long I muse, I muse,
    Since the air's so fresh and good.
HECATE   O, art thou come? What news, what news?
20 MALKIN   All goes well to our delight:
    Either come or else
    Refuse, refuse.
HECATE   Now I am furnished for the flight.   *Going up*
    Now I go, O now I fly,
25   Malkin my sweet spirit and I.
    O what a dainty pleasure is this
    To ride in the air
    When the moon shines fair,
    And feast and sing and toy and kiss!

Song 1: **12 the count** the full number **13 'noint** anoint (apply an oil, perhaps in ritual manner) **15 dues** what is owed to him **16 cull** embrace **17 muse** wonder **23 furnished** prepared/equipped

30   Over woods, high rocks and mountains,
      Over seas, our crystal fountains,
      Over steeples, towers, turrets,
      We fly by night 'mongst troops of spirits:
      No ring of bells to our ears sound,
35   No howls of wolves, nor yelps of hounds,
      No, nor the noise of water's breach,
      Nor cannon's throat our height can reach.
UNSEEN SPIRITS   No ring of bells to our ears sound,
      No howls of wolves, nor yelps of hounds,
40   No, nor the noise of water's breach,
      Nor cannon's throat our height can reach.   [*Exeunt*]

Song 2: in 4.1, before Macbeth's entrance:
HECATE   Black spirits and white, red spirits and grey,
      Mingle, mingle, mingle, you that mingle may.
FOURTH WITCH   Titty, Tiffin, keep it stiff in,
      Firedrake, Puckey, make it lucky,
5   Liard, Robin, you must bob in.
ALL   Round, around, around, about, about,
      All ill come running in, all good keep out.
FOURTH WITCH   Here's the blood of a bat.
HECATE   Put in that, O put in that!
10   FIFTH WITCH   Here's leopard's bane.
HECATE   Put in a grain.
FOURTH WITCH   The juice of toad, the oil of adder.
FIFTH WITCH   Those will make the charm grow madder.
HECATE   Put in, there's all, and rid the stench.
15   SIXTH WITCH   Nay, here's three ounces of a red-haired wench.
ALL   Round, around, around, about, about,
      All ill come running in, all good keep out.
                    [*Exit Hecate and the other three Witches*]

---

31 **crystal** an alternative reading in the early musical sources is "mistress"   34 **sound** make
noise/can be heard   36 **breach** breaking (waves)   *Song 2:*   3 **keep . . . in** keep the gruel in
the cauldron viscous   10 **bane** poison   12 **oil** venom   13 **madder** more potent, liable to
provoke frenzy/red-colored (from the plant "madder" used in dyeing)   14 **rid** get rid of
15 **wench** girl/lass (**red-haired** people were sometimes associated with evil)

TEXTUAL NOTES

F = First Folio text of 1623, the only authority for the play
F2 = a correction introduced in the Second Folio text of 1632
F3 = a correction introduced in the Third Folio text of 1663–64
Ed = a correction introduced by a later editor
SD = stage direction
SH = speech heading (i.e. speaker's name)

List of parts = Ed

1.1.1 SH FIRST WITCH = Ed. F = 1. *(throughout)* **3 SH SECOND WITCH** = Ed. F = 2. *(throughout)* **5 SH THIRD WITCH** = Ed. F = 3. *(throughout)* **10 SH SECOND WITCH** = Ed. *Line assigned to All in* F **11 SH THIRD WITCH** = Ed. *Line assigned to All in* F **12 SH ALL** = Ed. *At line 10 in* F

1.2.1 SH DUNCAN = Ed. F = *King. (throughout)* **11 Macdonald** = Ed. F = *Macdonwald* **15 gallowglasses** = Ed. F = Gallowgrosses **16 quarrel** = Ed. F = Quarry **23 ne'er** = Ed. F = neu'r

1.3.33 weyard *always spelled* weyard *or* weyward *in* F, *never* weird **40 Forres** = Ed. F = Soris **59 rapt** = Ed. F = wrapt **117 lose** = Ed. F = loose **145 hair** = Ed. F = Heire

1.4.49 harbinger *spelled* Herbenger *in* F

1.5.1 SH LADY MACBETH = Ed. F = Lady. *(throughout)* **11 lose** = Ed. F = loose **15 human** *spelled* humane *in* F **48 it** = Ed. F = hit

1.6.0 SD *Hautboys spelled* Hoboyes *in* F *(throughout)* **5 martlet** = Ed. F = Barlet **6 mansionry** = Ed. F = Mansonry **10 most** = Ed. F = must **23 hermits** *spelled* Ermites *in* F

1.7.6 shoal = Ed. F = Schoole **11 th'ingredients** *spelled* th'Ingredience *in* F **49 do** = Ed. F = no

2.1.62 strides = Ed. F = sides **63 sure** = Ed. F = sowre **64 way they** = Ed. F = they may

2.3.157 nea'er = Ed. F = neere

2.4.8 travelling *spelled* trauailing *in* F **21 ate** *spelled* eate *in* F **36 life's** = Ed. F = liues **51 SD** *Exeunt* = Ed. F = *Exeunt omnes*

3.1.78 SH MURDERERS = Ed. F = *Murth. (throughout the scene)* **97 clept** *spelled* clipt *in* F

3.3.1 SH FIRST MURDERER = Ed. F = 1. *(throughout the scene)* **2 SH THIRD MURDERER** = Ed. F = 3. *(throughout the scene)* **3 SH SECOND MURDERER** = Ed. F= 2. *(throughout the scene)* **9 and** = F2. F = end

3.4.14 SH FIRST MURDERER = Ed. F = *Mur.* **88 human** *spelled* humane *in* F **90 time** = F2. F = times **165 in deed** = Ed. F = indeed

3.5.26 sleights = Ed. F = slights

3.6.25 son = Ed. F = Sonnes

4.1.59 germens = Ed. F = Germaine **73 SD** *First Apparition* = Ed. F = *1. Apparation* **82 SD** *Second Apparition* = Ed. F = *2. Apparation* **92 SD** *Third Apparition* = Ed. F = *3. Apparation* **100 Birnam** *spelled* Byrnam, Byrnan, Birnan, Byrnane, *and* Birnane *in* F **Dunsinane** = Ed. F = Dunsmane **128 eighth** = F3. F = eight

4.2.1 SH LADY MACDUFF = Ed. F = *Wife.* **25 none** = Ed. F = moue **86 SH FIRST MURDERER** = Ed. F = *Mur.*

4.3.39 Fare = Ed. F= Far **121 accused** *spelled* accust *in* F **148 thy** = F2. F = they **188 rend** = Ed. F = rent **270 tune** = Ed. F = time

5.1.35 fear who = Ed. F = feare?who

5.3.23 disseat *spelled* dis-eate *in* F **38 more** *spelled* moe *in* F **44 Cure her** = Ed. F = Cure **58 pristine** = Ed. F = pristiue

5.4.4 SH SIWARD = Ed. F = *Syew. (throughout the scene; also Syw., at line 11 and Sey. at line 22)*

5.5.41 false = Ed. F = fhlse **45 pull** = F. *Sometimes emended to* pall

5.7.120 SD *Exeunt* = Ed. F = *Exeunt Omnes*

SCENE-BY-SCENE ANALYSIS

ACT 1 SCENE 1

The three weyard sisters arrange to appear to Macbeth later, introducing the supernatural element to the play and establishing a dark, malevolent tone. Their chant of "Fair is foul, and foul is fair" introduces inverted values and the storm invokes nature in disorder.

ACT 1 SCENE 2

An injured captain reports on the battle with the rebel Macdonald. He describes "valiant" Macbeth's brave but violent slaying of Macdonald as he "unseamed him from the nave to th'chops." Ross brings news of Macdonald's Norwegian allies, reporting that they had "terrible numbers" and were assisted by the Thane of Cawdor, traitor against King Duncan, but were defeated by "Bellona's bridegroom"—Macbeth. Duncan pronounces that Cawdor is to be executed and Macbeth is to have his title, ironically asserting that "No more that Thane of Cawdor shall deceive / Our bosom interest."

ACT 1 SCENE 3

Lines 1–38: The three weyard sisters reveal their cruel natures as they wait. They hear Macbeth coming and work a spell until "the charm's wound up," setting in motion events that will gather momentum, a recurrent image throughout the play.

Lines 39–91: Macbeth's comment that the day has been "So foul and fair" echoes the words of the three weyard sisters in Act 1 Scene 1. Banquo's response to the sight of the sisters reinforces their nonhuman qualities: they "look not like th'inhabitants o'th'earth." He says that they "should be women" but their beards suggest otherwise: gender is called into question. Macbeth wants them to speak, which they do, hailing him as "Thane of Glamis," the title he already holds, but then as "Thane of Cawdor" and "king hereafter." Banquo questions Macbeth's response: why does he "start and seem to fear / Things that do sound so fair"? Banquo then asks what the future holds for him. The three weyard sisters tell him that his children shall be kings, and though he will be "lesser" than Macbeth, he will be "greater." Macbeth asks how he is to become the Thane of Cawdor, or king, as this "Stands not within the prospect of belief," but the sisters vanish without further speech. Their ethereal quality is emphasized by Macbeth and Banquo's description of them in terms of "bubbles," "air," and "breath." Banquo questions their existence, but Macbeth focuses on the prophecies.

Lines 92–171: Ross announces that Macbeth is now Thane of Cawdor. Macbeth asks, "Why do you dress me in borrowed robes?" highlighting recurrent images of apparel and of concealment and disguise. Angus explains that Cawdor has been executed for treason. From this point in the scene, Macbeth is divided from the other characters by his increasing number of asides, indicating the separation and tension between the private and public aspects of himself. He asks Banquo if he hopes that his children will become kings, now that part of the prophecy has come true, but Banquo is uncertain, warning that "instruments of darkness tell us truths" only to "betray" us. Macbeth then talks aside about the prophecies, moving toward "the swelling act" of his becoming king. We see that he is already thinking of taking destiny into his own hands as his mind presents him with a "horrid image," and he concludes, "Come what come may," one of his many references to time, destiny, and inevitability.

ACT 1 SCENE 4

Malcolm, King Duncan's elder son, reports Cawdor's execution. Duncan praises Macbeth before announcing that he is settling the succession to the throne onto Malcolm, giving him the title Prince of Cumberland. Macbeth takes his leave to tell Lady Macbeth of Duncan's intended visit and talks in an aside of his "black and deep desires." The contrasts between his asides and his speeches to Duncan emphasize the growing tensions between his ambition and his loyalty.

ACT 1 SCENE 5

Lady Macbeth reads Macbeth's letter reporting the three weyard sisters' prophesies, but fears that he is "too full o'th'milk of human kindness" to "catch the nearest way" of becoming king (i.e. murdering Duncan) and says that without "the valour of [her] tongue," he will not act. Lady Macbeth's spell-like soliloquy invokes spirits to "unsex" her and fill her with "direst cruelty." She rejects her femininity, and with it the associated stereotypes of weakness and compassion. When Macbeth arrives she shows her apparent dominance over him as she urges him to be less open in his emotions and to disguise his true self: "look like th'innocent flower, / But be the serpent under't." She will take care of everything else.

ACT 1 SCENE 6

Lady Macbeth greets Duncan and his court.

ACT 1 SCENE 7

Macbeth's soliloquy reveals his indecision, focusing on the moral consequences of killing Duncan, who is there "in double trust" as his kinsman and his king, but also as his guest. Describing Duncan's goodness, Macbeth acknowledges that there is no impetus to commit murder except his own "Vaulting ambition." When Lady Macbeth interrupts, Macbeth tells her that they cannot go through with the plan. She again shows her dominance and ability to manipulate him by questioning his masculinity: "When you durst do it, then you were a man." Despite this requirement that Macbeth live up to traditional gender roles, she once again rejects them on her own behalf, arguing that having sworn to do something, even pluck a suckling child from her breast and dash its brains out, then she would do it. Her plan is that she will make Duncan's guards drunk, and then, when Duncan is asleep, they will kill him. Macbeth, fired by her daring, says that she should only "Bring forth men-children." He declares himself "settled" on the course of action, concluding that he must hide his "false heart" with a "false face."

ACT 2 SCENE 1

Lines 1–37: As Banquo and his son Fleance discuss the absolute blackness of the night, an image that evokes both evil and secrecy, Macbeth enters. Banquo is surprised that he is "not yet at rest" and tells him that he has dreamed of the three weyard sisters. Macbeth lies, saying "I think not of them," but suggests that he would like to talk to Banquo at some point, ambiguously suggesting that if Banquo remains loyal to Macbeth then it will be beneficial for him. Banquo and Fleance retire.

Lines 38–71: Macbeth sends a servant to tell Lady Macbeth to ring the bell when his drink is ready, a signal that is perhaps also awaited by the audience, thus heightening the tension of his following soliloquy. Once alone, Macbeth sees a dagger floating before him but questions whether it is real or "a false creation" of his "heat-oppressèd brain," as it seems to draw him toward Duncan's room. His speech evokes both the nighttime and an atmosphere of witchcraft and evil, until the bell tolls and he declares, "I go, and it is done," emphasizing irreversible decision in contrast with his questioning tone at the beginning of the speech.

ACT 2 SCENE 2

Lady Macbeth has "drugged" the "possets" (bedtime drinks) of Duncan's grooms so strongly that they are on the brink of death. She is herself feeling "bold" and filled with "fire." When she hears Macbeth, however, her confidence and speech falter as she wonders if the grooms have woken again. She reveals that she could not kill Duncan herself as he "resembled / [Her] father as he slept." Macbeth enters and announces that he has "done the deed." He is distressed and fixates on his inability to repeat "Amen" after Malcolm and Donalbain (or possibly the grooms?) when he overheard them saying their prayers. He also heard a voice cry that "Macbeth does murder sleep." His apparent weakness appears to renew Lady Macbeth's strength, creating another shift in the power dynamic of their relationship. She notices that he has mistakenly brought the grooms' daggers away with him and orders him to take them back. He refuses, and accusing him of being "infirm of purpose," she takes them, intending to smear the grooms in Duncan's blood, so that they will appear guilty. In her absence, Macbeth is disturbed by knocking, and worries that he will never remove the blood from his hands. His wife returns, saying that her hands are the same bloody color as his (a visual symbol of their shared guilt) but that "a little water" will remove the blood and "clear us of this deed." She leads him away to wash and put on his nightgown.

ACT 2 SCENE 3

Lines 1–38: In the play's only episode with a "comic" element, the Porter goes to the door, imagining himself as the gatekeeper of hell, providing ironically grim humor after the events of the previous scene. The repeated knocking emphasizes Macbeth's notion that peace and sleep have been permanently destroyed.

Lines 39–85: Macduff and Lennox ask for Macbeth, who greets them and says that Duncan is not yet awake. He takes them to the king's door and waits with Lennox as Macduff goes in. Lennox describes the "unruly" night that has passed, suggesting that the storm was an omen. Macduff returns in horror, having discovered Duncan's body. He sends the other two in as he shouts to wake the household and calls for the alarm bell to be rung.

Lines 86–164: The confusion that characterizes the rest of this scene, as individuals move on and off stage, shouting or conducting brief, fragmentary dialogue, emphasizes the disorder created by Duncan's murder. Lady Macbeth demands to know why they have been woken, but, ironically, Macduff says that it is not for the ears of a "gentle lady" and announces the murder to Banquo as Macbeth and Lennox re-enter. Macbeth, in his "public" role, gives a formal speech about how "The wine of life is drawn," as Malcolm and Donalbain arrive and hear of their father's death. Lennox explains that it seems Duncan's grooms killed him, as he found them and their daggers covered in blood. Macbeth claims that he killed the grooms in his fury, but as Macduff questions him, Lady Macbeth seems to faint, drawing attention away from her husband. As Macduff and Banquo call for help and Macbeth suggests that they all arm themselves, Malcolm and Donalbain discuss matters. Fearing they may be the next victims, they leave for England and Ireland.

ACT 2 SCENE 4

Ross discusses the strange omens that have surrounded events, such as the darkness that "entombs" the earth even though it is daytime, reflecting Macbeth's reversal of natural order. Macduff arrives to report that Duncan's grooms were responsible for the murder and it is believed that they were hired by Malcolm and Donalbain, who have fled. Ross comments that "sovereignty will fall upon Macbeth," and Macduff says that he has already gone to Scone to be crowned. Ross intends to go to the coronation, but Macduff goes home to Fife.

ACT 3 SCENE 1

Lines 1–46: Banquo contemplates how the three weyard sisters' prophesies have come true for Macbeth, who is now king, but fears that Macbeth has "played" "most foully" in order that they should. He also considers the sisters' predictions for himself, that he will be "the root and father / Of many kings," and wonders if this is true. He stops as he hears the approach of Macbeth and Lady Macbeth, who flatter him as their "chief guest" at a feast that evening. Macbeth asks if Banquo intends to ride with Fleance that afternoon, asking how far he intends to go and urging him not to be back late. He then declares that "every man" will be "master of his time / Till seven," raising the matter of time once again and drawing attention to Macbeth's own attempts to "master" the world around him.

Lines 47–151: When the others have left, Macbeth sends for some men who await him outside the palace. He reflects on Banquo's "royalty of nature," which makes him the one person to fear. He remembers the weyard sisters' prophecy that Banquo will be the father of kings but that he himself wears a "fruitless crown," and therefore he has murdered Duncan and given up his immortal soul on behalf of "Banquo's issue." He is interrupted by the servant bringing in the men: they are hired Murderers. Macbeth reminds them of a previous conversation in which he persuaded them that Banquo had wronged them. He asks if they are ready to kill him. They are, and Macbeth instructs them to kill Fleance as well, that night and away from the palace. The distancing of the deed from the palace, and the placing of the Murderers outside the palace gates at the beginning of this scene suggests Macbeth's continuing attempts to separate his darker personal element from his public face.

ACT 3 SCENE 2

Sending a servant to fetch her husband, Lady Macbeth echoes his words in the previous scene as she contemplates the uncertainty of their achievements when "desire is got without content." When Macbeth arrives, she asks him why he keeps dwelling on the past: "what's done is done." He tells her that they are not yet safe and that he would be better dead and in peace, like Duncan, than living with a tortured mind that is "full of scorpions." She encourages him to be "bright and jovial" with their guests. He replies that she must do the same, particularly with Banquo. He tells her that he has planned "A deed of dreadful note," but refuses to say what it is. His comment "Be innocent of the knowledge, dearest chuck" is strangely tender in contrast to his following invocation to the "seeling night," but also suggests a new division between the two characters as Macbeth begins to work independently of his wife's influence.

ACT 3 SCENE 3

The two Murderers meet up with a third and wait for Banquo and Fleance. The First Murderer strikes out the torch and Banquo is attacked and killed in darkness, but Fleance escapes.

ACT 3 SCENE 4

Lines 1–34: Macbeth addresses his guests with appropriately formal language, emphasizing the ceremonial nature of the banquet. The arrival of the Murderers, however, reinforces the breakdown of order, as this private element of Macbeth's life intrudes upon his public space. There is a marked change in his language as he speaks to them, showing cruel indifference to Banquo's death. When he learns of Fleance's escape, he realizes that he is still not safe.

Lines 35–141: Lady Macbeth reminds her husband of his duties as a host and he returns to take his place at the banquet, observing that Banquo should be there. As he does so, Banquo's ghost sits in Macbeth's place. Macbeth's irrational response causes Ross to suggest that Macbeth is not well, but Lady Macbeth assures everyone that her husband has always had these momentary "fits" and that if they pay too much attention, they "shall offend him." She then turns to Macbeth and, once again questioning his masculinity, asks him, "Are you a man?" She says that he looks "but on a stool." Macbeth is insistent, telling her to look upon the ghost—which no one else can see. The ghost disappears, and again, Lady Macbeth reminds her husband of his guests. He apologizes for his outburst, blaming "a strange infirmity" and calling them all to drink to Banquo, "whom we miss." On cue, the ghost re-enters and Macbeth breaks down again, crying "Hence, horrible shadow!" Lady Macbeth stops Ross from questioning her husband, claiming that to do so will "enrage" him. She tells the guests to leave and "Stand not upon the order of your going," emphasizing the breakdown of social order now that Macbeth is king.

Lines 142–165: Macbeth observes that Macduff is not present at court. He resolves to visit the three weyard sisters again. Lady Macbeth encourages him to sleep. The gathering momentum of events is evident as Macbeth says that as he has come so far he can only go forward, and that they "are yet but young in deed."

ACT 3 SCENE 5

The three weyard sisters meet Hecate, goddess of witchcraft, who is angry about her exclusion from Macbeth's affairs. Before she is called away by spirits, she says that she will be there when Macbeth next consults them, when they will "draw him on to his confusion."

ACT 3 SCENE 6

Lennox meets with another Lord and reports that Fleance is suspected of Banquo's murder, but reveals his suspicions that Macbeth, "the tyrant," is responsible for this and for Duncan's death. The Lord informs Lennox that Macduff has joined Malcolm "in the English court" to ask the English king to make war with Macbeth. Lennox prays for assistance for their "suffering country."

ACT 4 SCENE 1

Lines 1–46: The three weyard sisters are joined by Hecate and three others in singing and dancing, culminating in the announcement that "Something wicked this way comes" as Macbeth enters.

Lines 47–143: Macbeth's sense of his own power is emphasized as he commands the three weyard sisters to give him answers, even if it causes terrible consequences for the world. They agree, but ask if he wants the answers from them or their "masters." Macbeth says to "Call 'em," and the three weyard sisters summon three Apparitions before him. The first, an armed (armored) head, tells him to "beware Macduff." The second, a bloody child, tells him that "none of woman born / Shall harm Macbeth," prompting Macbeth to declare that in this case he need not fear Macduff, but that he will kill him anyway. The Third Apparition, a crowned child holding a tree, declares that Macbeth will be undefeated until Birnam Wood comes against him at Dunsinane Hill. Reassured, Macbeth declares "That will never be" and that he will "live the lease of nature," returning once more to his preoccupation with time. He then asks the sisters if Banquo's "issue" will ever reign, but they refuse to tell him. Confident in his power, Macbeth declares "I will be satisfied" and commands them to answer. In response, the sisters conjure an image of a line of eight kings, all descendants of a "blood-boltered" Banquo, who smiles at Macbeth. Macbeth is left astounded as the three weyard sisters vanish.

Lines 144–169: Macbeth calls Lennox and demands to know if he saw the sisters. Lennox says that he did not and tells Macbeth that messengers have arrived with news of Macduff's flight to England. Macbeth's final aside reveals a sharp contrast to his indecision in Act 1 Scene 7, as he talks of how he will "crown" his "thoughts with acts," "surprise" Macduff's castle, and kill his wife and children.

ACT 4 SCENE 2

Lady Macduff questions Ross about her husband's flight to England, claiming that it was "madness" and that he cannot love her or "his babes" if he has left them in danger. Ross defends Macduff, but cannot stay. Lady Macduff tells her son that his father is dead and cynically responds to his claims that he is not by calling Macduff "a traitor" because he "swears and lies." As they argue, a Messenger brings news of impending danger and urges her to run with her "little ones." Lady Macduff asserts that she has "done no harm," but acknowledges that this is a "womanly defence." The Murderers enter and demand to know Macduff's whereabouts, accusing him of treachery. His son denies this and is killed. Lady Macduff flees, pursued by the Murderers.

ACT 4 SCENE 3

Lines 1–154: In England, Malcolm does not trust Macduff, suspecting that he may have been sent by the tyrant Macbeth, particularly since he has left his family behind. Macduff denies this, but Malcolm tests him by claiming that he is unfit to be king, describing his own vices. At first, Macduff politely denies this, but then breaks down and despairs for his country's future, saying that Malcolm is unfit to live or rule. Malcolm reveals that it was a test and that he now believes in Macduff's "good truth and honour," reassuring him that he has none of the vices he claimed earlier.

Lines 155–275: A doctor says that "a crew of wretched souls" is waiting for the English king to cure them and Malcolm explains to Macduff that the king can cure scrofula. His description of this, using terms such as "holy," "healing," "virtue," and "grace," contrasts with the evil and destruction associated with Macbeth's tyrannical kingship. Ross arrives and reports Scotland's suffering. Macduff asks for news of his family and Ross lies that they are "well." He urges Malcolm to return to Scotland and Malcolm says that he intends to do so, with support from "Gracious England." Ross breaks down and reveals the truth about Macduff's family. Macduff is distraught. When Malcolm urges him to "Dispute it like a man," Macduff says that he will do so, but that he must also "feel it as a man," presenting a more emotional perception of masculinity than that held by the Macbeths.

ACT 5 SCENE 1

A Doctor and a Gentlewoman wait for evidence of Lady Macbeth's recent sleepwalking. The Gentlewoman describes how Lady Macbeth rises while still asleep, writes, and then conceals what she has written, but she refuses to repeat what is said during these episodes. Lady Macbeth enters, rubbing her hands as though she is washing them. Her speeches reveal her guilty conscience about the deaths of Duncan, Lady Macduff, and Banquo as she complains that "the smell of blood" is still on her hands. The repetitive and disjointed nature of her speech reflects her state of mind and contrasts sharply with her previous cool efficiency. The watchers realize the significance of the spectacle but the Doctor says that she is more in need of "divine" help than that of a physician.

ACT 5 SCENE 2

In the first of six short scenes that run into each other—the pace of events is now at its quickest—Lennox and other Scottish noblemen discuss their intention to join with Malcom and Macduff near Birnam Wood. They reveal that "the tyrant" Macbeth is fortifying Dunsinane against the English.

ACT 5 SCENE 3

Macbeth issues orders, confident that the prophecies mean he is invincible. A frightened servant reports that there are "ten thousand" English soldiers and Macbeth sends him away, angry at his cowardice. He calls for Seyton. His speech as he waits reveals a weariness with life: he feels he has "lived long enough" and his actions mean that his life will hold not honor and friendship but "Curses." He instructs Seyton to bring his armor. When he inquires after his wife, the doctor reports that Lady Macbeth is "troubled" and Macbeth tells him to cure her "diseased" mind, but is told that it is a patient alone who can deal with their own conscience.

ACT 5 SCENE 4

The English forces arrive at Birnam Wood and camouflage themselves with tree branches to disguise their numbers.

ACT 5 SCENE 5

As Macbeth defiantly issues orders to Seyton, a cry is heard and Seyton is sent to investigate. Macbeth contemplates how he would once have been disturbed by such a noise, but now that he has "supped full with horrors" he is no longer affected. Seyton returns with news of Lady Macbeth's death, and Macbeth's response is weary and resigned as he describes life as "a walking shadow," a "tale" "Signifying nothing." A messenger brings news that he has seen Birnam Wood moving. Angry, then resigned, Macbeth vows to fight on.

ACT 5 SCENE 6

Malcolm commands the English forces to throw off their camouflage and places the English soldier Siward and his son at the head of the army.

ACT 5 SCENE 7

Macbeth fights, unafraid because he can only be killed by one "not born of woman." He kills young Siward and exits. Macduff passes across the stage, searching for Macbeth, and then Siward leads Malcolm to the defeated castle. Macbeth re-enters, scorning escape in suicide. Macduff finds him and they fight, but Macbeth claims that he bears "a charmed life" because of the prophecy. Macduff replies that he was "from his mother's womb / Untimely ripped." Roused by Macduff's threats that he will be kept captive like "rarer monsters," Macbeth refuses to yield and they exit fighting, then re-enter after "Alarums," and Macbeth is slain. Macduff drags him away. As Malcolm and Siward discuss the battle, Ross informs Siward of his son's death. Macduff enters, bearing Macbeth's severed head, and hails Malcolm as "King of Scotland." Malcolm makes his noblemen into earls and expresses his intention to deal with matters "in measure, time and place," emphasizing a return to order.

MACBETH IN PERFORMANCE: THE RSC AND BEYOND

The best way to understand a Shakespeare play is to see it or ideally to participate in it. By examining a range of productions, we may gain a sense of the extraordinary variety of approaches and inter-pretations that are possible—a variety that gives Shakespeare his unique capacity to be reinvented and made "our contemporary" four centuries after his death.

We begin with a brief overview of the play's theatrical and cine-matic life, offering historical perspectives on how it has been per-formed. We then analyze in more detail a series of productions staged over the last half-century by the Royal Shakespeare Company. The sense of dialogue between productions that can only occur when a company is dedicated to the revival and investigation of the Shakespeare canon over a long period, together with the uniquely comprehensive archival resource of promptbooks, program notes, reviews, and interviews, held on behalf of the RSC at the Shake-speare Birthplace Trust in Stratford-upon-Avon, allows an "RSC stage history" to become a crucible in which the chemistry of the play can be explored.

Finally, we go to the horse's mouth. Modern theater is dominated by the figure of the director, who must hold together the whole play, whereas the actor must concentrate on his or her part. The director's viewpoint is therefore especially valuable. Shakespeare's plasticity is wonderfully revealed when we hear directors of highly successful productions answering the same questions in very different ways.

FOUR CENTURIES OF *MACBETH*: AN OVERVIEW

Macbeth is one of the most frequently performed of all Shakespeare's plays. Its central place in the repertory has resulted in a full stage history. Simon Forman, the Elizabethan quack doctor and astrologer, described a production he saw at the Globe in 1611. Scholars, however, believe that the play with its oblique references to the Gunpowder Plot of 1605 was first written and performed around 1606 as a tribute to King James I, who was also James VI of Scotland. It is impossible to say whether or not Forman gives an accurate account of the production he saw (it has also been suggested that the document is a fabrication, but the balance of evidence very strongly supports its authenticity). His perception may have been filtered through a reading of Holinshed's *Chronicles*, the play's main source. And the version Forman witnessed may have been different from that which survives (see the discussion in the introduction of Middleton's possible revisions). It is striking that he makes no reference to Macbeth's second visit to the weyard sisters. Nevertheless, Forman's report is of inestimable value as the only detailed eyewitness report of the performance of a Shakespearean tragedy in Shakespeare's lifetime:

> There was to be observed first, how Macbeth and Banquo, two noblemen of Scotland, riding through a wood, there stood before them three women, fairies or nymphs, and saluted Macbeth, saying three times unto him, 'Hail, Macbeth, King of Codon, for thou shalt be a king, but shall beget no kings,' etc. Then said Banquo, 'What, all to Macbeth, and nothing to me?' 'Yes,' said the nymphs, 'hail to thee, Banquo, thou shalt beget kings, yet be no king.' And so they departed and came to the court of Scotland, to Duncan, King of Scots, and it was in the days of Edward the Confessor. And Duncan bad them both kindly welcome, and made Macbeth forthwith Prince of Northumberland, and sent him home to his own castle, and appointed Macbeth to provide for him, for he would sup with him the next day at night, and did so. And Macbeth contrived to kill Duncan, and through the persuasion of his wife did that night murder the king in his own castle, being his guest, and there were many prodigies seen that night and the day before. And when Macbeth had murdered the king, the blood on his hands could not be washed off by any means, nor from his

wife's hands, which handled the bloody daggers in hiding them, by which means they became both much amazed and affronted. The murder being known, Duncan's two sons fled, the one to England, the [other to] Wales, to save themselves. They being fled, they were supposed guilty of the murder of their father, which was nothing so. Then was Macbeth crowned king, and then he, for fear of Banquo his old companion, that he should beget kings but be no king himself, he contrived the death of Banquo and caused him to be murdered on the way as he rode. The next night, being at supper with his noblemen whom he had to bid to a feast, to the which also Banquo should have come, he began to speak of noble Banquo and to wish that he were there. And as he thus did, standing up to drink a carouse to him, the ghost of Banquo came and sat down in his chair behind him. and he, turning about to sit down again, saw the ghost of Banquo, which [af]fronted him so, that he fell into a great passion of fear and fury, uttering many words about his murder, by which, when they heard that Banquo was murdered, they suspected Macbeth. Then Macdove fled to England to the king's son, and so they raised an army and came into Scotland, and at Dunston Anys overthrew Macbeth. In the meantime, while Macdove was in England, Macbeth slew Macdove's wife and children, and after, in the battle, Macdove slew Macbeth. Observe also how Macbeth's queen did rise in the night in her sleep and walk, and talked and confessed all, and the doctor noted her words.

Whatever the relationship of Forman's report to the play as it was first performed, there is evidence of the text being cut and adapted from the earliest times. Two early theater promptbooks survive, one based on a copy of the 1623 Folio belonging to the University of Padua, and the other, known as the "Smock Alley" promptbook, on the play as it was performed in Dublin after the 1660s.

Despite being one of the most frequently performed of all Shakespeare's plays, few modern productions include Hecate or the music and songs, although Restoration and many later adaptations featured spectacular visual effects. Samuel Pepys records his view of the play in his diary in 1667 as "one of the best plays for a stage, and variety of dancing and music, that ever I saw." Though alien to modern sensibilities, the idea that *Macbeth* was above all notable for its singing and dancing was commonplace in the late seventeenth- and eighteenth-century theater.

Although we know little of the play's original performance, it is assumed that Richard Burbage, the leading tragedian with the King's Men, played the title role. The main part has been played by the dramatic giants of succeeding ages from Thomas Betterton to David Garrick, John Philip Kemble to Edmund Kean, William Charles Macready to Henry Irving, John Gielgud and Laurence Olivier to Anthony Hopkins, Ian McKellen, and Antony Sher. Approaches to the role vary: Macbeth can be anything from an essentially noble character overcome by ambition to an inherently evil tyrant. The success or failure of productions is generally dependent upon the sheer energy and charisma of the actor taking the central role—it has always been a star vehicle for leading actors. As for Lady Macbeth, though the part would originally have been played by a young male apprentice, it has—together with Cleopatra—become one of the western theater repertoire's leading roles for mature actresses.

Sir William Davenant's adaptation staged at Lincoln's Inn Fields in 1663–64 sought to refine the play to suit the tastes of Restoration audiences by expanding the role of Lady Macduff and making the Macduffs a moral counterbalance to the Macbeths. Davenant eliminated the Porter and added music, singing, and dancing for the three witches, and gave Macbeth a final moral: "Farewell vain World, and what's more vain in it, Ambition." The performance of Thomas Betterton and his wife, Mary Saunderson, as the Macbeths was widely admired and the adaptation remained popular for eighty years until David Garrick announced his intention to present *Macbeth* "as written by Shakespeare" at Drury Lane on 7 January 1744.

Garrick was a new type of actor for a new age. He tried to clear away much of the Restoration baggage—no more flying witches— and to restore the majority of Shakespeare's text, although there was still no Porter, Malcolm was less complex and self-accusatory, and the actor included a dying speech for himself. The key to Garrick's performance was his attempt to create a complex, imaginative unity from the powerful and contradictory elements of the character:

> Through all the soliloquies of anxious reflections in the first act; amidst the pangs of guilty apprehension, and pungent remorse, in the second; through all the distracted terror of the third; all the impetuous curiosity of the fourth, and all the desperation of the fifth, Mr Garrick shews uniform, unabating excellence; scarce a look, motion, or tone, but takes possession of our faculties, and leads them to a just sensibility.[1]

Garrick's Lady Macbeth was Hannah Pritchard, who "in that horrible part had all the merit so well-drawn a character could confer."[2]

Up to that time, Shakespeare was played in contemporary dress—famous paintings of Garrick and Pritchard by Henry Fuseli and Johann Zoffany show the actors dressed in eighteenth-century costume. Charles Macklin was the first producer to attempt historical accuracy, in his 1773 staging of the play. While scenery and costumes were approved, the elderly Macklin's performance was not well received and the rivalry between Macklin's and Garrick's supporters led to riots and the production's closure.

The most famous historical Lady Macbeth was Sarah Siddons playing opposite her brother, John Philip Kemble, at Drury Lane in the last years of the eighteenth century and the first decades of the nineteenth. While the character of Lady Macbeth has been notoriously demonized, from Malcolm's description of her as "fiend-like" onward, successive generations of actors have tried to humanize her. Sarah Siddons writes of an altogether more sympathetic character in her *Memoranda* entitled "Remarks on the Character of Lady Macbeth":

> In this astonishing creature one sees a woman in whose bosom the passion of ambition has almost obliterated all the characteristics of human nature; in whose composition are associated all the subjugating powers of intellect and all the charms and graces of personal beauty. You will probably not agree with me as to the character of that beauty . . . according to my notion, it

is of that character which I believe is generally allowed to be most captivating to the other sex,—fair, feminine, nay, perhaps, even fragile.[3]

Despite the tenor of Siddons's remarks, there seems to be general agreement that this account, written many years later, is hardly an accurate picture of her own performance. As her biographer Roger Manvell suggests, "she always played Lady Macbeth against her own inner conception of how it should be done."[4] Manvell goes on to point out, "from the first the impression she created in the audience was far from this—she inspired sheer awe and terror."[5]

Although Kemble treated Shakespeare's three witches seriously, he nevertheless deployed a chorus of fifty or more singing, dancing, comic witches. The witches were traditionally played by men, usually the company comedians, the argument being that the trage-dians were all busy elsewhere. J. P. Kemble's niece Fanny Kemble complained in her journal that "It has always been customary,—heaven only knows why,—to make low comedians act the witches, and to dress them like old fishwomen . . . with as due a proportion of petticoats as any woman, letting alone witch, might desire, jocose red faces, peaked hats, and broomsticks."[6]

Kemble's Macbeth has been described as essentially "a noble character who degenerates into evil."[7] The leading actor of the next generation was Edmund Kean, a much less orthodox character who presented Macbeth as "a determined, ruthless man who disinte-grates through guilt and fear."[8] The critic William Hazlitt, generally an admirer of Kean, thought his Macbeth "deficient in the poetry of the character."[9]

William Charles Macready played the part for many years with a variety of different leading ladies including Mary Amelia Huddart, Helen Faucit, the American Charlotte Cushman, and Fanny Kemble. His productions strove for historical accuracy in their staging. His performance was contrasted unfavorably, however, with Samuel Phelps's at Sadler's Wells, which drew general praise:

Since Edmund Kean's, we have seen nothing better for vigour and vivid effect. It is essentially distinct from and stands in contrast to Mr Macready's, which, however fine and classical in its conception, is but too obviously open to the Scotch sneer of presenting 'a very respectable gentleman in considerable difficulties;' so studied is it in all its parts, and subdued into commonplace by too much artifice; fretfulness, moreover, substituting high passion in the fifth act. The straightforward and right-earnest energy of Mr Phelps's acting, on the contrary, made all present contemplate the business as one of seriousness and reality; while the occasional pathos of his declamation thrilled the heart within many a rude bosom with unwonted emotion.[10]

The London *Times*'s reviewer was impressed by the originality of the staging and praised the production as a whole: "There is a spirit of freshness diffused over it."[11] Phelps's most distinguished Lady Macbeth was Isabella Glyn, described by one reviewer as "the very heroine of crime—the guardian demon of the crowned assassin—the weird-like accessory and human agent of the mysterious spirits that wait on Nature's mischief."[12]

Charles Kean specialized in spectacular, supposedly historically accurate productions. His *Macbeth*, which opened at Covent Garden in 1840, enjoyed popular success, but while Ellen Kean's Lady Macbeth was favorably reviewed, his Macbeth failed:

In Charles Kean's Macbeth all the tragedy has vanished; sympathy is impossible, because the mind of the criminal is hidden from us. He makes Macbeth ignoble—one whose crime is that of a common murderer, with perhaps a tendency towards Methodism. It is not, however, so much the acting as the 'getting up' of *Macbeth* which will attract the public.[13]

Nineteenth-century actors generally humanized Lady Macbeth, making her feminine and womanly, a good wife, if somewhat misguided. Adelaide Ristori, though, domineered over Tesibaldo Vitaliani's Macbeth in an Italian production at the Lyceum in 1857, which successfully toured Europe and the United States. Edwin Booth played the role successfully in New York in numerous productions with Charlotte Cushman, and also with the Polish-born Helena Modjeska, who, like Helen Faucit, emphasized Lady Macbeth's femininity.

Henry Irving's productions at the Lyceum were spectacular and enormously successful. His dark costumes and subdued lighting for *Macbeth* "blended together to compose a dark, massive, dangerous world."[14] However, his reading of Macbeth as "a bloody-minded hypocritical villain"[15] failed to convince all the critics:

> A Macbeth less luxurious than is now seen cannot be readily conceived. Yet the word is apt, and furnishes a clear indication of the character. Against the over-intellectuality of Macbeth the imaginative power and the marvellous mobility of feature of the actor cannot prevail. The ingenuity, subtlety, picturesqueness, and power of the performance may be granted, but the new Macbeth will not replace the old.[16]

It is clear from the notes that Ellen Terry, Irving's Lady Macbeth, scribbled in the margins of her working script that she shared the prevailing notions about the nature of women. Lady Macbeth's tragedy, as Ellen Terry saw it, lay in an essentially feminine ambition, a misplaced and afterward disillusioned faith in a husband devoid of the stuff of kings: "A woman (all over a woman) who believed in Macbeth with a lurking knowledge of his weakness, but who never found him out to be nothing but a brave soldier and a weakling, until that damned party in the parlor—'The Banquet Scene' as it is called."[17] Ellen Terry judged it right to keep Mrs. Siddons's cold determination while discarding the fiendish aspects of her nature that would have so disturbed Victorian beliefs about the nature of women. Many critics could not accept this "enchanting being" as Shakespeare's Lady Macbeth:

> So exquisite a creature is she as by the flickering firelight she reads her husband's letter, so radiant in robes of indescribable beauty, and with such rhapsody of passionate longing does she lean back to wait for the coming of her lord, we decline to accept her as other than a being out of Arthurian legend.[18]

Despite performing his role in Italian in an otherwise English production, the actor Tommaso Salvini's red-bearded Macbeth combined, according to Robert Louis Stevenson, "pride and the sense of animal well-being" with "moral smallness." His appearance in the final act suggested how "the atmosphere of blood, which pervades the whole tragedy, has entered into the man and subdued him to its own nature; and an indescribable degradation, a slackness and puffiness, has overtaken his features. He has breathed the air of carnage and supped full of horrors."[19] Sarah Bernhardt, meanwhile, played Lady Macbeth in a French prose translation turning the play into "a dull and somewhat vulgar melodrama"[20] in which Bernhardt's histrionic performance was described in the London *Times* as "inadequate and unsatisfactory."[21]

The scholarly Johnston Forbes-Robertson, an acclaimed Hamlet, and sophisticated Mrs. Patrick Campbell were miscast as the Macbeths in the Lyceum's 1898 production. Herbert Beerbohm Tree's spectacular production with Violet Vanbrugh as Lady Macbeth was more successful but included fifteen scene changes and lasted over four hours. *Blackwood's Edinburgh Magazine* complained that Beerbohm Tree "has sought to achieve a pictorial, not a dramatic effect."[22] Meanwhile, the reaction against such overblown productions, which started in Germany, was taken up by William Poel, who founded the Elizabethan Stage Society and staged his plays as far as possible as they had been in Shakespeare's time—on simple thrust stages with minimal scenery and props.

These contrasting production styles continued to compete until Barry Jackson's 1928 Birmingham Repertory Theatre production, directed by H. J. Ayliff, set the play in the period of the First World War:

The battle scenes with which it opened and closed were brought up to date with exploding shells and rattling machine guns. Macbeth was dressed in khaki uniform with riding-breeches, high, polished boots, and a chest covered in medal ribbons. Lady Macbeth appeared in a short, sleeveless cocktail dress, and Lady Macduff and her son were murdered over a

2. Ellen Terry as Lady Macbeth, reading the letter from her husband (Lyceum Theatre, London, 1888).

cup of afternoon tea by killers who entered through a case-ment window.[23]

Critics complained that the poetry of the play was lost in the clipped modern delivery, although Laurence Olivier won praise for his performance as Malcolm. For all its faults, the production led the way "to a new understanding of *Macbeth* as a play about alienation in an amoral modern world, whose hero, Kafka-like, finds himself isolated by his visions from those around him, and who discovers that hell is not a place elsewhere but the nightmare within."[24] As critic Michael Mullin goes on to argue, "Jackson's failed experiment pointed the way and made possible a series of theatrical experiments leading from Komisarjevsky to Guthrie, and finally culminating in Glen Byam Shaw's tour de force at Stratford-upon-Avon in which Sir Laurence Olivier and Vivien Leigh gave what theater historians consider a definitive Macbeth and Lady Macbeth."[25]

John Gielgud was involved in three productions between 1930 and 1952. The first at the Old Vic was directed by Harcourt Williams. Gielgud's romantic Macbeth was admired for its intellectual quality and the quality of the verse-speaking. The critic James Agate judged Martita Hunt's Lady Macbeth, playing opposite Gielgud, to be "too likeable."[26] Gielgud went on to direct the play himself in 1942 at the Piccadilly Theatre, in a performance that, though not to all tastes, the critic Audrey Williamson considered

Poetically . . . the crowning achievement of our time; his 'airborne dagger' seared the eyeballs, and the imaginative impulse was never wholly lost until it dwindled to the yellow flicker of the 'brief candle' and autumn sere. Yet surprisingly our most lyrical actor caught the soldier and murderer too; this was a lithe and virile figure, combining the mud-stained practicability of the warrior with the golden eloquence of the poet: a haunted and haunting performance, with a twilit bitterness at the last.[27]

Gielgud's Stratford-upon-Avon production in 1952 with the amiable Ralph Richardson in the title role was less successful. J. C. Trewin thought that as Lady Macbeth, "Margaret Leighton, at first a tigress burning bright, has the drive, the command that Macbeth lacks."[28]

Expatriate Russian director Theodore Komisarjevsky's 1933 production at Stratford revolutionized the play with an expressionist design against a background of war. Its experimental quality received mixed reviews, but despite initial reservations, many critics recognized its significance: "It was swift and exciting; intelligently directed to suggest presage of impending doom; and when once we had grasped the producer's conventions and intentions all, or nearly all, fell into place naturally and inevitably. The old play was given a new cutting-edge."[29]

Orson Welles's 1936 production at the Lafayette Theatre in Harlem was equally cutting edge, set in Haiti with an all-black cast, including many nonprofessional actors. It became known as the "Voodoo" *Macbeth* and was noted mainly for its theatrical inventiveness and the violence of its imagery, which tended to overshadow individual performances.

Michael Benthall's successful production at the Old Vic with Paul Rogers and Ann Todd was first staged at the Edinburgh Festival in 1954 to great critical acclaim and afterward toured America, but the production that has come to be regarded as one of the two or three most successful of the twentieth century—along with Trevor Nunn's Dench/McKellen version, discussed by the director below—was the 1955 production at Stratford with Laurence Olivier and Vivien Leigh. Glen Byam Shaw's direction was in fact considered rather ordinary; it was Olivier who made the show, as the London *Times*'s critic records:

> The striking thing about the performance is its psychological penetrativeness. It cuts boldly through all sorts of superficial contradictions in the character. The usual difficulty of reconciling the tough warrior with the superstition-ridden neurotic seems scarcely to exist. Attention from first to last is fastened on the mind of Macbeth. Sir Laurence is concerned first to show that his mind is already filled with dangerous thoughts and desires which it dare not formulate till the Weird Sisters give them voice. By various subtleties and ingenuities, each

having the freshness of a new-minted coin, he suggests vividly that the latent nobility of character may yet assert itself against the fatal lure of ambition, but once this hope has gone and dreadful desires have turned to deed the actor treats the deed as a mere incident making possible the psychological drama which follows.[30]

Macbeth's cultural legacy is pervasive due to the relative simplicity of the plot and its archetypal nature, the rise and fall of an ambitious leader, as well as its powerful characterization, especially of Lady Macbeth. It has been frequently adapted into other media—opera, novels, film, television, science fiction, and song—and employed for a variety of purposes from political cartoons and satire to advertising. As Irena Makaryk suggests in her discussion of Ukrainian director Les Kurbas's 1924 modernistic, anti-bourgeois production, "Within the general trend of modernizing Shakespeare in the West from the 1960s on, *Macbeth* has been the 'trademark' avant-garde play, its primitivism and anarchism being particularly attractive characteristics."[31]

Verdi's *Macbeth* was his first adaptation of a Shakespeare play and its brilliance was instantly recognized. First performed at the Teatro della Pergola, Florence, in March 1847, it was revised by Verdi in 1865 for the Paris Opéra, with an added ballet sequence. This is the version generally performed today.

As well as the Ukrainian adaptation discussed by Makaryk, there have been productions across Europe, including a Croatian-language version in 1997 directed by Henryk Baranowski. Welcome Msomi's South African adaptation *uMabatha*, based on the life of the great Zulu warrior Chaka, was staged at the Globe Theatre in 1997. In 1995, the Australian director Simon Woods produced an experimental bilingual English/Japanese version at the Zen Zen Zo theater in Kyoto. The great Japanese director Yukio Ninagawa has created two distinct productions (one in 1980, the other in 2001, both frequently revived), with Samurai allusions fitting to Macbeth's military demeanor, and a design based around a cherry tree, its falling blossoms representative of that transience and mortality to which Macbeth alludes in his speech about the turning leaf. At the climax,

3. Laurence Olivier as Macbeth and Vivien Leigh as Lady Macbeth, directed by Glen Byam Shaw, Stratford-upon-Avon 1955, after the murder on a quasi-realistic stage set characteristic of the period.

cherry blossoms were seen on the branches of Birnam Wood hewn and borne by Malcolm's army.

There have been numerous film versions, including Orson Welles's idiosyncratic 1948 movie which, unlike his stage production, was set in Scotland. Welles cut approximately half the text and gave the play a religious focus, even inventing a new character, the "Holy Father." Welles himself played Macbeth. Ken Hughes's black-and-white film *Joe Macbeth* (1955) sets the play in New York's gangland with simplified dialogue and plot. Cinematography invokes a film noir style, playing with light and shadow, high and low angles.

Roman Polanski's 1971 film with the young Jon Finch and Francesca Annis as the Macbeths was shot in bright technicolor, with much gore, especially in the scene where Macduff's family are slaughtered in their home. It did not go unremarked that Polanski had begun work on the film shortly after his heavily pregnant wife, the actress Sharon Tate, together with three of her friends, was brutally murdered by followers of Charles Manson. The film, financed by Hugh Hefner's Playboy company, was also controversial for Lady Macbeth's nudity in her sleepwalking scene and for its ending, which lacks textual warrant, wherein Donalbain goes to the weyard sisters, as if to initiate a further cycle of ambition and violence.

Akiro Kurosawa's film adaptation *Throne of Blood* (1957), a translation of the plot and setting into Samurai culture, shot in expressionistic black and white, is generally acclaimed as a classic of Japanese cinema. It has been highly influential on western cinema from the *Seven Samurai* remake (*The Magnificent Seven*) onward. A number of stage productions have been filmed, including Trevor Nunn's acclaimed 1971 production for the RSC at The Other Place with Judi Dench and Ian McKellen, and Gregory Doran's at the Swan with Antony Sher and Harriet Walter.

AT THE RSC

Stones Have Been Known to Move and Trees to Speak

Images of blood and darkness dominate the language of Shakespeare's shortest and most exciting tragedy. Fair is foul and foul is fair—from the instant we are plunged into the Scottish play there is a sense of stagnancy, of something rotting and eating away at all the natural and pure things of this world. Witches, vile murder, ghosts, apparitions, and nightmares punctuate the action of the protagonist's story. Is it any surprise that this play has been the inspiration for so much Gothic and horror fiction, and that Roman Polanski's film version is listed in publications and websites that deal with the greatest British horror films of the twentieth century?

Despite the play's historical background and its obvious references to the political world of the time, it is the psychological complexities of the Macbeths, the disintegration of the mind, and the usurpation of good by evil, which have proved the focal point for most modern productions. In a world dominated by the lust for power, Shakespeare gives us a case study of how simply and quickly the evil in man can spread like a virus. How can a person commit or order acts that by their nature deny any human feeling? As critic Stanley Wells points out: "The play's framework of national destiny has proved less attractive to later ages than the personal tragedy of Macbeth played within it; many modern productions adjust the text to throw even more emphasis on Macbeth and his Lady."[32]

Peter Hall's 1967 production focused on the powerful degree to which *Macbeth* is a Christian play. He was led by the religious symbolism in such lines as:

Confusion now hath made his masterpiece.
Most sacrilegious murder hath broke ope
The Lord's anointed temple, and stole thence
The life o'th'building.

The murder of the king is seen as a sacrilegious act, and with it "nature seems dead." In Hall's opening scene, the weyard sisters were shown as huge silhouettes inverting a crucifix on which they poured blood; a cross was carried behind Duncan and, later, behind Malcolm; Duncan wore the white robes of consecrated kingship, and when later Macbeth appeared in the same robes, "the blasphemy was shocking." The religious reading was carried through to the set, which "consisted of a dark, oak interior which looked like a cathedral."[33] Before the dialogue began, there was

a quite sensational statement of purity, virtue, innocence, snatched away to show the evil lying beneath. A great white sheet—an angel's wing?—hung over the stage and, just before the appearance of the witches, fluttered away, flapping into extinction. Its disappearance revealed a blood-red carpet like a heath with clotted heather. One felt that if one pressed one's hand in it blood would ooze out. It was backed by red granite-seeming cliffs and, at times during the action, sections of it were removed to show an arid bone-white expanse—as if it rested on a bleached skeleton. The witches seemed to emerge from beneath this bloody carpet, bearing an inverted cruci-fix . . . *Macbeth* for [Hall] was the 'metaphysics of evil.'[34]

To focus on this religious aspect of the play does help to overcome one of the main stumbling blocks for a production of *Macbeth*: its representation of the supernatural, the need to make a modern secular audience accept a world in which witches, ghosts, and apparitions are powerful forces.

In 1982, by contrast, Howard Davies took religion out of the play and deliberately set out a "policy of demystification."[35] His production

completely jettisoned the atmosphere of blood and darkness in which so many Macbeths have floundered. Instead, he used a direct, clinical style which made no attempt to conceal its theatrical devices. The stage was dominated by two percussionists and their battery of equipment, brilliantly spotlit on an upper level, who punctuated and commented on the action, rather than providing atmosphere.[36]

In his depiction of the supernatural there was an "abandonment of any attempt to impersonate the witches as bearded, skinny-lipped hags, withered and wild in their attire":[37]

The weird sisters were attractive young actresses who performed routines with whirling blankets, and who deliberately fragmented their speeches into 'imperfect' word-games, meaningless until meaning was given to them by Macbeth's response . . . The apparitions were spoken clearly and directly by the watching company, with no attempt at theatrical illusion, and Birnam Wood was merely a forest of drawn swords.[38]

4. Peter Hall production, Stratford 1967: the Macbeths crowned. Sharp contrasts of darkness and light on the set emphasize a reading in terms of primal good and evil.

Although heavily criticized by some, this production's staging choices were praised by many for the way in which the audience were forced to look at the play afresh. The absence of a sense of primordial evil was perhaps a reaction against, or at least an alternative to, the viewpoint presented by the groundbreaking Trevor Nunn production of 1976. By paring the play down to its essentials, Nunn created a palpable intensity and brooding sense of evil, which never let up. A circle painted on the floor of The Other Place studio theater encompassed the action of the play. Used as the main acting space, it symbolized a magic circle in which magicians stood for protection while conjuring and in which the evil of Macbeth would be exorcised. It also represented the "golden round," the religious and ceremonial aspects of kinship.

Trevor Nunn used the opening scene to illustrate the powerful sense apparent throughout the play of the forces of evil ranged against goodness. While Duncan and his court were at prayer, the three witches moved to the centre of the acting circle and began to groan and howl. Their voices became louder, until they drowned out the pious Duncan.[39]

Surrounded by darkness and with the absence of a formal raised stage, the actors performed on a bare floor.

> The audience—less than two hundred of them—sat on three sides of the acting area, two rows deep and elevated above the floor by scaffolding . . . The acting area was defined by a black painted circle round which the actors sat on packing-crates when not engaged in the performance. The audience could thereby see the witches outside the circle as they watched Macbeth fulfilling their prophecies, and see Macduff sitting ignorantly as his family is slaughtered . . . The cast was reduced to fourteen (about the number used when *Macbeth* was first performed) and there was some doubling. The audience . . . were so close to the actors that an extraordinary intimacy was created between them, and the words could be spoken quietly and subtly . . . the play was not so much about damnation as about the minds of the characters . . . In such plain, austere surrounding, the success of the production rested entirely on the actors.[40]

The success of the sparse setting of this production led other directors to reflect the psychological interior of their Macbeths in the set design. Discarding the attempt to recreate any recognizable interior, designers have sought to achieve a similar intimacy and intensity on the main Royal Shakespeare Theatre stage. Jonathan Pryce, who played Macbeth in 1986, said: "I don't see this play set at some particular point where it would have immediate relevance to any particular society. It has resonances throughout time. When a play offers an overview of the human psyche, it seems too narrow to confine it."[41]

In the production played by Pryce, directed by Adrian Noble, Bob Crowley's set "was an illusionist's box where any number of conjuror's tricks might defeat the eye. Doors suddenly appeared, stairs shot out of flush walls. Then the walls themselves began to move.

The Macbeths' world got smaller and smaller until it felt like a coffin."[42] The set was variously described as a "claustrophobic pressure chamber"[43] and an empty box with "a recessed platform surrounded by blank timber walls. It can be anywhere: a heath, the castle, the interior of the hero's skull."[44]

In 1993, Derek Jacobi starred as Macbeth and director Adrian Noble, returning to the play for a second time, made the lead performance the focus of the whole production. Designer Ian MacNeil explained:

> Derek is brilliant at taking you right inside someone's head and exploring their deepest thoughts and emotions. I think that set helps us to do that. Its dark, interior quality allows the production to focus upon what is private and metaphysical in the central character. Basically the set is a black box . . . when colour is introduced it has far greater impact. Lady Macbeth's first entrance in a crimson dress, the sumptuous banquet to greet Duncan's arrival at Dunsinane, the dripping blood on the hands of Macbeth and his wife, the Witches' supernatural pageant, the verdant colours of the scene in England, stand out strikingly amidst the production's brooding darkness.[45]

MacNeil designed a moving bridge that spanned the whole stage and became the site for all the play's magical elements. Piers Ibbotson, the assistant director, described the concept: "the bridge provides a physical manifestation of the play's hierarchy—it shows the witches, and later Banquo's ghost, hovering over the affairs of men."[46]

Considered by many to be a chamber piece, *Macbeth* appears to work better on a more intimate stage. In 1999, Gregory Doran staged the play in the Swan Theatre, a Jacobean-style playhouse built in 1986, which seats around four hundred people. This production was widely considered the best staging by the RSC since Trevor Nunn's 1976 production at The Other Place, a small black-box studio with an even smaller capacity. In contrast to so many other productions, Doran and his designer set the play in a very recognizable modern world: that of Eastern European conflict.

Doran's spare staging is played without interval and hurtles along at tremendous, stomach-lurching speed. It's also performed in modern dress, and in its catalogue of horrors inevitably recalls the murderous strife in former Yugoslavia. Doran never labours specific parallels, however, creating instead an almost hallucinatory impression of the brutality and horror that burns itself into the brain with the intensity of a bad dream . . . the tension is constantly increased by Adrian Lee's deeply unsettling percussive score . . . Almost all the action is set in either half light or murky darkness . . . There are shadows everywhere.[47]

Everything is on the move: uncertain, equivocal. The opening words—the witches' curses—are spoken in darkness. What look like sturdy walls go bendy, as apparitions bulge out of them. When Birnam Wood comes to Dunsinane it does so in such a crepuscular swirl that for a moment it really does appear as an eerie event.[48]

The program notes were written by journalist and broadcaster Fergal Keane, whose experience of reporting from the battlefields gave a unique insight into Macbeth's relevance at the end of the twentieth century:

My life . . . has been a journey through the heartland of the warlords: from Belfast to Pretoria, from Sarajevo to Kosovo, Rwanda to Cambodia, I have met them—the men and women in whom 'vaulting ambition o'erleaps itself' and any greater moral purpose or instinct for humanity. It has been suggested—with grievous lack of insight—that Macbeth is not a play relevant to our times. The truth is that I can hardly imagine a drama more relevant in this age of bloody coups and civil wars. In this year alone a once-trusted general has seized power in Pakistan; in Africa the lords of the gun have been busy turning Congo into a wasteland; in East Timor the warriors of General Wiranto's Special Forces spent months killing their enemies in advance of the referendum for independence. Macbeth irrelevant? Never.[49]

Macbeth: Philosopher, Soldier, and Psychotic

> The huge problem for players of Macbeth is to yoke together those warring opposites of sensitivity and violence, deep depression and coarse brutality. Some Macbeths have shot their bolts by the end of the banquet scene; others save themselves for that fifth act which awaits like the north face of the Eiger.[50]

On explaining the psychological difficulties of soldiers returning from the First World War, the president of the British Psycho-Analytic Association, Ernest Jones, explained that war constituted "an official abrogation of civilized standards" in which men were not only allowed, but encouraged "to indulge in behaviour of a kind that is throughout abhorrent to the civilized mind . . . All sorts of previously forbidden and hidden impulses, cruel, sadistic, murderous and so on, are stirred to greater activity."[51] When we, and the weyard sisters, meet Macbeth, he is halfway between the battlefield and home, physically and psychologically unsettled, between two worlds. The sisters' prophecy has such a startling effect not only because of the regicidal thought that it implants, but also because Macbeth knows what will happen if his psychology of war becomes his domestic psychology, unleashing those "forbidden and hidden impulses" without the constraints normally imposed by the pressures of social conformity. He knows, exceptional warrior that he is, that to cross this barrier will have diabolical consequences.

In 1986, Jonathan Pryce played Macbeth as a psychotic waiting to happen, as a "killing machine with an elegant turn of phrase."[52] The exemplary soldier, used to obeying orders, his Macbeth was initially passive: "To do anything he needs to be given an order. Hitherto he has obeyed his king. Now he receives orders from elsewhere; they happen to express his secret ambition."[53] His descent from dutiful soldier to a "demon of nervous energy"[54] was the centerpiece of the production. The appalling change in Macbeth's character had a powerful and frightening effect. Sinead Cusack, who played Lady Macbeth, pointed out that "she has no knowledge of the hell that she's letting loose in his mind and his life, and what he will become."[55] Whereas most Macbeths in performance try to quickly adopt a mask to conceal their true feeling about the prophecy, Pryce's fainted at the news. His extreme reaction perhaps indicated that he had not just thought about being king, but had already thought about *killing* the king.

> Pryce's performance is a remarkable example of thinking the character through from scratch. He presents us with a boisterous soldier long tormented by 'wicked dreams' but dogged by personal insecurity; and after the murder, he remains recognisably the same person.[56] For a good third of the action he maintains a mask of ingratiation—excessively modest, ready with winning smiles . . . Even when the mask cracks it is only by degrees, and it is not until the climax of the banquet— which he diversifies with burlesque displays of lunacy to put the guests off the scent—that the monster finally hatches out. He takes his wife's hand for the speech on 'night's black agents' and finishes it with a blood-curdling shriek that sends her staggering across the stage; then bursts into laughter at his little joke.[57]

Sinead Cusack described how immediately after this Pryce showed the disintegration of his character's mind and the Macbeths' relationship:

> And then he smeared all my lipstick across my face. He put his hand in my mouth and yanked down my jaw, mocking a kiss. It was a travesty of the embrace, of how it used to be. He was throwing their sexuality back in her face, saying, 'That no longer has power in my life,' scoffing at her with that bark of a laugh. His mania was staggeringly dangerous and she was terrified . . . And deeply hurt. Lost . . . He was completely gone from me and he would never come back. It was a feeling of absolute hopelessness.[58]

In contrast to Pryce, in 1993 Derek Jacobi, an actor known for playing more sensitive characters, brought out the emotional com-

5. Jonathan Pryce as Macbeth with the "apparition" of a child king conjured up in Act 4 Scene 1: "He has no children"—unlike Duncan, Banquo, Macduff, and Siward. Directed by Adrian Noble, 1986.

plexity of Macbeth. He focused on Macbeth's psychological journey, reclaiming him as tragic hero. Of Jacobi's suitability to the role, director Adrian Noble commented:

> I think he's a natural Macbeth but not a natural psychopath. The idea of the man being a psychopath has overlain our perception of the part. If you take the psychopath out of it, the play is a metaphysical debate about what is and what is not. His escalating hallucinations are a metaphor in themselves. It takes in scenes explored in *Lear* and *Hamlet* about madness, the fear of losing control. It's also the best exposition of tyranny and its methods ever written.[59]

Jacobi thoroughly examined Macbeth's decline into evil by tracing the disintegration of his civilian and domestic side, and the usurpation of the better part of himself by the killer instincts that dominate him on the battlefield:

> Macbeth didn't seem to me, at the start, to know more of evil than any other soldier of his time who is used to killing people. What caught my imagination was the effect of evil on him, the changes it brings about. We spent a certain amount of time in rehearsal thinking about what is frightening, what is palpably evil, what is out there; the forces that seem to lurk malevolently around the world of the play. This was an area we tried to work hard on, with as much psychological depth as possible . . . 'So foul and fair a day' does not, it seems to me, refer to the weather: 'foul' is about those heads he's cut off and bowels he's ripped out; 'fair' is because it was all worth it, for this great victory. That is the state of mind he is in, as, just by chance he repeats the phrase that the witches have used . . . Because of the victory he is in a state of high excitement and of emotional exhaustion. He has been killing all day: he is covered with blood. In this state he gets the news: in this state he must react to it. The speed with which things happen in the next phase of the play is to a large extent conditioned by Macbeth's physical and mental state when he receives the

witches' greeting . . . We wanted to present a couple much in love and comfortable with each other. We also wanted to show the contrast between Macbeth the warrior, whose duty is killing and maiming, and Macbeth the husband, the lover, the domestic, cultured man who dances and listens to music. Off the battlefield he isn't in the least gruff or brutal in his behaviour . . . His first words are 'My dearest love,' a very romantic phrase, which he doesn't use again—his language to his wife becomes, indeed, progressively less endearing.[60]

(The last point is questionable: the Macbeths are not seen onstage together after the third act, during which Macbeth is still calling his wife by the tender endearment "dearest chuck.") According to critic Irving Wardle:

Jacobi's open-hearted soldier is also a machiavellian actor (leading the applause for Malcolm's election); his increasing hardness is matched by his increasing vulnerability (as late as the cauldron scene you find him nuzzling for comfort into a passing messenger); and finally this clapped-out warlord regains all his original valor in the fight with Macduff. What Jacobi achieves, thanks largely to his evocation of inner horrors reinforced by a style of delivery that charges iambic lines with sprung rhythm, is to reclaim Macbeth as a hero. Attention always focuses on him; what happens to him matters more than what happens to anyone else; even when organising the massacre of Macduff's family he retains his personal charm. The man who cancels his bond with humanity still commands the sympathy of a morally indefensible reading.[61]

Jacobi also picked up on the fearfulness of Macbeth, his constant awareness that he is slipping into evil:

I went through the play marking the times he speaks of fear, particularly in relation to himself. He does so in every scene: it is paramount for him, the man is constantly fearful . . . The moment before he does the murder he is afraid—the dagger speech is a fearful speech, the utterance of a terrified man. He does the murder for her, and it destroys them both.[62]

"O, full of scorpions is my mind, dear wife!": fear exists because the better part of himself is constantly resisting, fighting and at odds with his actions. When he invokes "pity, like a naked new-born babe," this battle within Macbeth becomes wedded to the language:

> His head is full of the mixture of good and evil. At this moment the evil side of him, which we all possess, is getting the upper hand and in order to balance it he brings up the best, the purest, the most innocent images, of angels, and new-born babies, and the sky. They are all pure, unsullied, wonderful images; goodness pours out of them; they're shining. And on the other side are the dark, blood-driven, evil, dank thoughts.[63]

In order to remain sane, Jacobi's Macbeth cut off the emotional side of his life, something that Lady Macbeth could not do, no matter how she willed it. Having given the order to murder Lady Macduff and her children, this Macbeth went to inspect the aftermath. "That is the true monstrousness; it is that appalling lack of emotion that he has to come to terms with in the end."[64]

Lady Macbeth: From Fiend-like Queen to Grieving Mother

The difficulty for any actress playing Lady Macbeth is the speed with which she is thrown into delivering her most important speeches. There is no buildup, no backstory: from the moment we see her, the actress has to perfect the equivalent of a vertical take-off. From her arresting opening speech to her final madness, Lady Macbeth has a psychological arc which has to be mapped in very few scenes.

Judi Dench played her as a woman obsessed with ambition:

> Slinky costumes were replaced by a drab, black outfit which effectively concealed hair and figure, leaving only hands and mobile features visible . . . As she knelt in hoarse prayer to the

spirits, her demand to be filled with 'direst cruelty' suddenly
appalled her. She broke away with an animal squeal of terror,
hands over her eyes, as if she had come face to face with the
fiend. She had no illusions about the evil she was embracing,
but the thrill of it drew her back. As she reached a final, frantic
ecstasy, arms outstretched to embrace the darkness, they were
ready to receive her husband on his unexpected arrival.[65]

The power of the supernatural was palpable in this intense studio
production, and Lady Macbeth's soliloquy came across as an incan-
tation, a spell. On her words "Hie thee hither," Macbeth, as if magically summoned, appeared onstage.

When discussing their conception of the part, most modern
actresses pick up on the idea that the Macbeths have lost a child, and
build this into their performance. This angle was heavily emphasized
in Adrian Noble's 1986 production, which

> treated the Macbeths—Jonathan Pryce and Sinead Cusack—
> as a childless Strindbergian couple for whom power became a
> substitute for parenthood. When Lady M taunted her husband
> with cowardice, he slapped her on the face . . . the couple went
> on to clasp each other with fierce protectiveness when she
> mentioned the loss of their child: you felt you were watching
> an intimate domestic drama with immense political repercus-
> sions.[66]

Supplanting and subverting the social isolation, feelings of longing,
depression, loneliness, and utter desolation that can afflict parents
who desperately want a child, these Macbeths put their energies into
a twisted form of conception:

> As rehearsals progressed, it was this bleak biological datum—
> 'He hath no children'—that began to focus the tragedy. *Mac-
> beth* became not so much a political tragedy of multiple
> betrayal as a domestic drama, the destruction of a marriage.
> Lacking children, the Macbeths' energies re-directed them-
> selves into obsessions that travestied creativity: they killed

other people's children, turning their kingdom into a waste-land. But when they discovered what it meant to hold a barren sceptre, their childlessness doubly mocked them. There could be no success without succession . . . This Macbeth liked having children around. He liked children's games. The witches' apparitions were children, seductive in white nightgowns, playing blind man's buff with the kneeling king on the floor, giggling their predictions into his ear, then circling him in an endless procession of Banquo's future issue. These same white-gowned children then became Macduff's ambushed family. One of them sat on the floor playing with the assassin's boot-straps before he was picked up and stabbed . . . such images found a contemporary expression for the evil that the play is exploring. The abuse of children is the ultimate taboo, the death of a child is the ultimate grief.[67]

Lady Macbeth sacrifices her womanhood to these "murdering minis-ters." She unsexes herself, suppressing femininity as she seeks to dry up the "milk of human kindness" in both herself and her husband. Her punishment is to be locked in her crime forever, with suicide the only escape. She lives in a constant state of night—neither awake nor asleep, somewhere between life and death (somnambulism was once thought to be the result of demonic possession). In 1986, Sinead Cusack's Lady Macbeth built into the character a physical repulsion, a psychological nausea, prompted by the sight of Dun-can's blood:

And then she sees the blood . . . something happens to her gut. For her, the sight is horrible. It shocks her, the reality of it. She has imagined the killing, but people who have visions are often shocked by the reality when it comes . . . As an actress I tried to show just a little click in my brain that I could store up to use and refer back to later when I had blood on my own hands . . . After that we began talking different languages. We who had needed to touch each other all the time grew distant. When he had killed, neither of us wanted to touch each other.[68]

Often portrayed in modern productions as a mutually dependent couple, sexually and mentally intimate in their first scenes, this physical awkwardness immediately after the murder points forward to the disintegration of their relationship. In Adrian Noble's 1993 production,

> After Duncan's killing, there's a wonderful moment where you can see the seeds of their future estrangement in the awkwardness of the embrace they try to give one another, their intimacy badly hampered by the fact that both of them have bloody hands. Then this Macbeth begins very pointedly to exclude his wife from his deliberations. Watching them seated at either end of the vast dining table after the banquet scene, Lady Macbeth [Cheryl Campbell] stiffening as she hears of the spy-network he has created, you get a desolate sense of the divergent paths they will now take. The hero progresses to brutalising doggedness . . . his wife to madness.[69]

Harriet Walter's startling and powerful performance in 1999 combined the elements of Lady Macbeth's character that make her frightening, very human, and ultimately pitiable: "She has a superb cold authority: her analysis of her husband's scruples is detached rather than scornful. But the self-command isn't overdone: you can always sense the ordinary mortal behind it, the woman who eventually cracks."[70]

Walter cleverly adopted a nervousness to her voice, the kind of throb that only comes when a person tries to be something they are not. There was a real sense of a woman whose potential psychosis had been encouraged by isolation. With no means of support outside of her husband, no network of companions of the kind that develops with the social contact that surrounds children, this Lady Macbeth had had too much time in a world of her own imagining. She came across as Macbeth's equal, aware of the evil she was invoking but drawn to it as a means of revitalizing their marriage. The reference to the fact that she had "given suck" was met with raw pain by man and wife as they reached toward each other at the painful memory. The ending to the banquet scene had an unusual emotional strength

as it signaled the deteriorating minds and marriage of this once intimate partnership:

> At the end of the scene with Banquo's ghost (here conjured up
> purely by Sher's crazed reactions) she subsides into terrible little
> sobbing laughs with her husband that seem to be torn from her
> by the roots. It's like a ghastly parody of their former intimacy.[71]

> Marginalized by power, she also acquires the pathos of internal
> exile as she is excluded from her husband's counsel; and the
> sleepwalking scene, rather than a somnambulistic star turn,
> becomes a fearful exploration of her disordered sub-conscious.[72]

Our understanding today of the psychology of war and post-
traumatic stress has informed modern productions of *Macbeth*. Many
soldiers sensitive to the injustices of war, who have witnessed terrible
sights and perpetrated terrible acts, suffer a mental shock that can
lead to insomnia, compulsive behavior, visions of violence and the
dead coming back to life. The irony for Macbeth is that these disturbances occur not as a consequence of armed combat in the battlefield but as a result of regicide in his own home. Having been
"paltered with in a double sense," he has changed from war hero to
dishonorable villain. His acute awareness of this is what makes him
continue to be human. By the same account, Lady Macbeth's mental
anguish is intensified to unbearable levels because the feelings of
compassion and humanity that she has tried to repress cannot be
extinguished. No one who heard it will ever forget the noise, somewhere between an animal whimper and an existential howl, that
Judi Dench conjured out of herself in the sleepwalking scene.

THE DIRECTOR'S CUT: INTERVIEWS WITH TREVOR NUNN, GREGORY DORAN, AND RUPERT GOOLD

Sir Trevor Nunn is the most successful and one of the most highly
regarded of modern British theater directors. Born in 1940, he was
a brilliant student at Cambridge, strongly influenced by the literary
close reading of Dr. F. R. Leavis. At the age of just twenty-eight he

succeeded Peter Hall as Artistic Director of the RSC, where he remained until 1978. He greatly expanded the range of the company's work and its ambition in terms of venues and touring. He also achieved huge success in musical theater and subsequently became artistic director of the National Theatre in London. His productions are always full of textual insights, while being clean and elegant in design. Among his most admired Shakespearean work has been a series of tragedies with Ian McKellen in leading roles: *Macbeth* (1976, with Judi Dench, in the dark, intimate space of The Other Place), *Othello* (1989, with McKellen as Iago and Imogen Stubbs as Desdemona), and *King Lear* (2007, in the Stratford Complete Works Festival, on world tour, and then in London). The *Macbeth* discussed here is widely regarded as one of the greatest and most influential productions of the twentieth century and a version of it was filmed.

Gregory Doran, born in 1958, studied at Bristol University and the Bristol Old Vic theater school. He began his career as an actor, before becoming associate director at the Nottingham Playhouse. He played some minor roles in the RSC ensemble before directing for the company, first as a freelance, then as associate and subsequently chief associate director. His productions, several of which have starred his partner Antony Sher, are characterized by extreme intelligence and lucidity. He has made a particular mark with several of Shakespeare's lesser-known plays and the revival of works by his Elizabethan and Jacobean contemporaries. His 1999 *Macbeth*, with Sher and Harriet Walter in the leading roles, was highly acclaimed and a version of it was filmed.

Rupert Goold was born in 1977. He studied at Cambridge and was an assistant director at the Donmar Warehouse under Sam Mendes. After undertaking a range of experimental work, in 2006–07 he directed two highly acclaimed Shakespearean productions with the veteran stage and television actor Patrick Stewart: *The Tempest*, part of the RSC's year-long Complete Works Festival, and the intimate modern-dress *Macbeth* at the Minerva Theatre, Chichester, which transferred to London's West End, the Brooklyn Academy of Music, and finally Broadway. It garnered multiple awards in London and was nominated for six Tony awards in New York. In 2009 Goold became an associate director of the RSC.

At the end of the play Malcolm describes the Macbeths as a "dead butcher" and his "fiend-like queen": but there's got to be more to them than that, hasn't there? In the case of Lady Macbeth in particular, there's a long tradition of actresses wrestling with her human side ("Had he not resembled / My father," and all that).

Nunn: In many ways, *Macbeth* concentrates thematically on the nature of evil, and therefore, the play is also, through the strands of the Banquo story and the Malcolm/Macduff story climaxing in the England scene, about the nature of goodness. But something else explains the *structure* of the play, and binds its many elements together; it is an examination of belief, or as we more commonly say, faith. The successful, highly regarded, trustworthy general Macbeth is inclined to believe the weyard sisters encountered on the heath, and equally clearly his comrade and friend Banquo is not. When the first element of the sisters' strange prophecy comes true, Macbeth is persuaded entirely to believe in their prophetic utterances, to the point of writing to his wife about this "road to Damascus" revelation. She is obviously more than willing to be recruited to this belief, and thereafter she clings to it as extremely as a fundamentalist terrorist to religious validation.

Macbeth's waverings endanger both him and his wife, to the point where his belief in the prophecies has to be revitalized if he is to go on. His return visit to the witches, indicating that, despite the bad news about Fleance, Macbeth is invulnerable, fuels the final section of the play, as the invading warriors imbued with the opposite (and very Christian) faith are carried along by their own certainties. The end comes in the form of a "bad joke" as the revitalized Macbeth realizes that the phrase "born of woman," which will protect him against all-comers, doesn't include a child entering the world by means of a primitive Caesarean. Macbeth's next words, after taking in that his faith has been founded on a semantic quibble, are "I'll not fight with thee." His belief has dissolved, and with it his resolution, his invulnerability, and his sense of destiny.

Doran: Lady Macbeth is certainly not a "fiend-like queen." I think she is driven to do something that she doesn't allow herself to think through; she has a kind of myopia. Whereas Macbeth thinks rather a lot—too much, in a way—she suppresses her imagination. Lady Macbeth has only one very short soliloquy in the entire play, when she realizes that she has become queen at the cost of having blood on her hands:

> Naught's had, all's spent,
> Where our desire is got without content:
> 'Tis safer to be that which we destroy
> Than by destruction dwell in doubtful joy.

I think she realizes that her husband no longer has any real use for her. At the end of the banquet scene she realizes that Macbeth has left her, he has moved on, and is going to continue to secure himself as king and eliminate his enemies. She seems to have no knowledge of his plans anymore. We discovered a moment whereby she picked up a candle to light her way to her bedchamber as she left the banqueting table and all the other candles went out; it was the influence of the three weyard sisters, who had been under the table all the time. In other words, Lady Macbeth is haunted by her conscience, and what Harriet [Walter] made clear in the sleepwalking scene is that here is a woman who has insisted that her husband do this terrible deed in order to get the crown, and then immediately finds both the emptiness of the role and also that her relationship with her husband has somehow diminished. And I think that is very poignant.

As for Macbeth as a "butcher," the experience of watching the play is that you don't feel Macbeth is just a ruthless tyrant. That's partly due to how he is haunted and how the play's imagery supports that. He says, "O, full of scorpions is my mind, dear wife!" and "They have tied me to a stake: I cannot fly," as if he is some terrible bear chained to a stake and attacked by dogs. The imagery supports his status as almost a victim. You get a sense in performance that once he has realized the sin he has committed, his struggle to carry on living makes him worthy of our pity. And Lady Macbeth's sleepwalking scene, where you see how much she is being punished by her own conscience, is a devastating portrayal of a human soul in disintegration.

Goold: History is written by the victors, and so in one sense that is all they are. One of the things the play seems to be exploring is the tension between social and political identity versus the individual psyche. However, in Lady Macbeth's case I also always thought that it was important that she was, to a certain degree, a two-dimensional character—a "fiend-like queen." It is her single-minded remorseless ambition that is set against Macbeth's huge complexity. Too often I think great actresses try and give backstory or humanity to a woman who, while we can pity her hugely, never shows us she is more than a psychopath. It is that chilling viciousness that makes the part so iconic and so potent.

How did you invoke the sense of the supernatural for a modern audience who might be more skeptical about those aspects of the play than theatergoers would have been in Shakespeare's day?

Nunn: My production dressed Duncan more as a priest than a military king, so that he had an iconic, rather papal aura which not only suggested a prevailing religious conformity in the social structure, but accentuated the heinous and unthinkable quality of the murder. Apart from that emphasis, there was very little of a hieratic nature in the presentation because extreme naturalistic credibility was the aim and intention of all that we did with a text rich in imagery, but equally daring in the use of slang, conversational rhythm, interrupted thought, and the vocabulary of domestic squabble. In The Other Place, it was possible to speak without projection, indeed to whisper and be heard by everyone, and this gave a sense for the audience not so much of being at a play as of overhearing conversations which put everybody present in equal danger. When Macbeth and Lady Macbeth were at the point of committing the murder of Duncan, I had placed all the other actors at vantage points invisibly around the theater, and asked them to breathe heavily, as if sleeping. The effect, of a silence so profound that people peacefully and innocently asleep in the house could be clearly heard, was genuinely gripping and terrifying, as well as prefiguring Macbeth's nightmare that he will sleep no more, that he has murdered sleep. Ian McKellen and

Judi Dench were quite extraordinary in their ability to observe the rules of the text but make exchanges like this seem totally naturalistic, almost improvised. This "experience" of sleep also connected to Lady Macbeth sleepwalking in her fitful confessional, which again we tried to make as real as if caught on a hospital CCTV camera.

Doran: I noticed that the word "fear" (and linked to it "afraid," "fearsome," "fearful") is a very important theme in the play. At the beginning of rehearsals I got everybody in the company to describe a time when they had been really afraid: afraid for their safety, the safety of their children; afraid of spiders, heights, whatever. People described in detail their experiences of fear and we tried to tap into the reality of what that experience is: what it does to the human body; what it does to your breath; and how we could communicate that sense of fear.

In terms of how to get the audience to feel that fear, we decided very early to play the first scene—the very short scene with the three witches—in total darkness. When we suddenly turned all the lights out, including the exit signs, so there was total blackout, we discovered that people have a very primal attitude to darkness. I once did Peter Shaffer's *Black Comedy* at the Donmar. The play opens with the very interesting convention that the lights don't go on and you hear the characters talking as if they're in full light, and then suddenly all the lights go on and the characters continue the rest of the play as if they are in total darkness. At the first preview I made sure there was a total blackout and stood at the back of the auditorium to make sure that nobody came in and broke it. Within a minute or two a lady scuttled up the aisle and banged into me, trying to get out because she couldn't tolerate the darkness. I thought if that can happen in a sixties' light comedy, perhaps I ought to use it for *Macbeth*!

So for the first scene we suddenly went to blackout and, after people had got over their initial shock, it was a very eerie experience. We then heard the witches talking in the darkness. When you see the witches for the first time people often think, "Oh, so that's how they're doing the witches." The fact that you couldn't see them gave the scene a real intensity. It made you really listen to it. In the early previews we dropped in three little amplifiers at exactly the height where the witches would have been standing. The actors were backstage and their voices came through via microphone. Then when they said "Hover through the fog and filthy air," we flew out the amplifiers over the audience's heads, so that what you thought was the voice of a woman in front of you suddenly flew over your head. But it was so freaky, and people became so disturbed by it, only a minute or two into the play, that we decided it was too much.

I think as always with Shakespeare part of what we were trying to do was surprise people: make them think that something was what they thought it was and then suddenly it was not. The whole back wall of the Swan was in fact a fake back wall. Everybody knew the Swan, it looked like the wall of the Swan, but when we came to the apparition scene suddenly the apparitions pushed through the wall. The wall had sections which were painted and textured like brick, but were actually made of wetsuit material, so that when the actors pushed their faces into it they came through the wall. Something solid suddenly became fluid. Then at the end of the banquet, just as Lady Macbeth left the stage with her candle, all of the other candles left on the table suddenly, magically, went out. In fact it was the witches, who had been hidden under the table through the entire scene, pulling the wicks down through the table. Then they threw the table up and appeared to the audience. It shocked them silly because the chairs went flying and the banquet table suddenly flew into the air. We then went straight on into the next scene where Macbeth visits the witches.

We took all those moments and tried genuinely to work out how you frighten an audience, and how to create the equivalent effect that Shakespeare suggests for a skeptical modern audience.

Goold: I always felt the key to the supernatural was less in finding a modern correlative than in playing up the political world in which the play operates. Ghosts, witches, and visions are fearsome in their own right, but what makes them terrifying is when they prey on the minds of political figures in positions of power. They are manifestations of political crisis as much as a paranormal worldview, so we just always tried to ground and make detailed the paranoid police state that Scotland becomes in the play and that seemed to make the supernatural all the more shocking.

**More specifically, the weird or "weyard" sisters have been vari-
ously played as old hags, classical Fates, alluring nymphs, and
many interpretations in-between: how did you and your cast set
about realizing them?**

Nunn: It was very important in our production that "the witches"
were entirely believable, not just to Macbeth but to everybody in the
audience. I think this production was the very first small-scale intimate staging of the play, to an audience of about two hundred,
ranged on three sides of the action. It was also played without interval (whether that had been done before, I don't know) so the black
mass ritual meticulously observed by the three witches at the very
beginning set up a disturbing atmosphere from which there was no
escape until the glimmer of Christianity arrived like a fragile dawn at
the end. The sisters were varied in age, a senior white-haired witch
very much in control of the proceedings. A second witch, of an age
to be her daughter, took instruction from the elder, but both of these
were dependent on the third, who was young enough to be the third
generation. She it was who became tranced, and provided each time
the visionary or prophetic information. We redistributed the lines
designated First, Second, and Third in the Folio so that each sister's
contribution was specific and in character, and so that we avoided
generalized ghoulishness or choric posturing. They were individuals
and they were believable.

Doran: We decided that it's the wrong way round with *Macbeth* to try
and begin with the witches. It's not a society terrorized by the
witches. It's a society which has produced the witches and made
them scapegoats. It is interesting that the greatest witch persecu-
tions have happened at times of civil crisis: during the Civil War, for
example. There is the sense that at such times we require these tar-
gets to give vent to our national fears. The weyard sisters became for
us a product of the fear already existing in society, rather than something that was making that society afraid. The way we tried to do
that was to look at the weyard sisters from their point of view. I
rehearsed them separately from the rest of the play, so that whenever
we rehearsed their scenes I would work with the weyard sisters
beforehand and we would decide how they would play the scene, but

we wouldn't tell the other actors. We tried one idea that the witches couldn't speak until they were asked a question, and they needed Macbeth to ask them that question. Then when he addressed them they could reveal their understanding of the future to him. The problem was that Banquo then asked the question as well, and they also had to tell him the future, which messed up their plan. Other days we tried other aspects of the witches: their vindictiveness; or perhaps their heightened sexuality; or we would try exploring the idea that they were high on drugs. But the other actors never know the route the witches had taken; the weirdness of the way they performed was all that was apparent to them. That meant that they remained this outside group. In rehearsal we never called them witches. Other people did, but they referred to themselves as the weyard sisters. We took their own personal agendas very seriously, so that they were real people, with real appetites.

The strangeness of the witches of course keeps the play ticking with this terrible undertow of fear. We had them make one or two extra appearances. At the moment when Banquo and Fleance are attacked by robbers while out riding, we had the witches silently watching. Right at the end of the play we see Malcolm become king. But of course the witches tell Banquo that his offspring will become king, so we finished the play with Fleance arriving with one of the trinkets that he had found from the witches, and clearly thinking "My time will come." So there was this sense of an endless cycle of violence and retribution.

Goold: The sisters are by far the hardest thing to get right in the play, not least because they dominate the opening act, and yet their second scene, with the tale of the pilot and his wife, is impenetrable, extraneous, and poorly written (probably by Middleton). I longed to cut it, but the witches have to establish themselves if they are to resonate, so a solution has to be found. I took inspiration from Wes Craven, who said he came up with Freddy Krueger by thinking about when people felt safest and then threatening that (sleep, in the case of *A Nightmare on Elm Street*). For most sensibilities a neutral watchful chorus of blank Norns [in Norse myth, the three goddesses of fate] is attractive, but the problem with the witches is that they just have to be evil, petty, and vicious—the text only supports that read-ing. For a variety of reasons I hit on the idea of them being nurses—again, people we trust and look to in times of need and custodians of life and death in most people's lives, so more problematic if they are evil. Nurses would also be needed in the warfare of the first act and so would fit in unnoticed around a battlefield. That was something very important to me; I had always felt the first act of the play can be very bitty in performance—the leaping locations, the complexity of the civil war backstory, and the sheer challenge of the language in the opening scenes can all make the play hard to get into. I had a hunch that creating two long opening scenes, one in a field hospital and the next in the kitchen of Glamis castle, would give the piece a slower, more monumental growth and then allow the play's action to accelerate from Act 3 on. I also think it is a mistake to have the witches ever-present, which is what blights so many fringe and regional productions where the witches have to double as every-thing from Fleance to the various doctors. While this can have moments of seeming insight, most of the time it is both distracting and robs the witches of part of their power: that we meet them so rarely and yet with such amazing force each time we do. So, to return to our production, I interpolated the witches' first scene at the exit of the bloody sergeant for surgeons. The sergeant, who had been attended throughout by the three nurses trying to minister to his wounds, found himself alone with his angels not of mercy but of death. They killed him, his part in their story served, and then removed their surgical masks to ask when they would meet again. A manipulative revision, but *Macbeth* is such a well-known play and the opening scene such a familiar cliché that I hoped our surprise relocation would make an audience listen harder rather than sit back and listen to the familiar thunderclaps and cackling. The final bonus of the nurses idea was in the very British desire to see our hos-pital sisters as sexually provocative, and I'm sure Shakespeare had that in mind when he wrote the weyard sisters.

Just after the murder of Duncan is discovered, Macbeth makes a slip that almost implicates him, but attention is distracted by the line "Look to the lady"—what's happening here? Does Lady Mac-

beth faint or pretend to faint (how could an audience tell the difference?) or could she throw up or do something else?

Nunn: Unquestionably, Lady Macbeth is the better of the two at handling the immediate aftermath of the murder, and so we made it clear that her "fainting" was a vitally necessary device to prevent the questioning of her husband from going any further. However, something entirely unforeseen changes her ability to handle such situations; her husband begins to exclude her from his thoughts and plans, and so, at the very time when she feels they most need each other, he rejects her, one senses for the first time, in their intense marital relationship. So what we watch in the middle reaches of the play is not only the creation, step by step, of a tyrant dictator, but even more upsettingly, the breakup of a marriage.

Doran: I believe that Lady Macbeth faints. I don't think it's a ploy to distract from her husband. She doesn't really rescue him from his mistake because suspicion is still clearly focused towards him. It's the moment that the reality of what Lady Macbeth has done suddenly happens upon her, and she passes out. I think it is at that point that Macbeth ceases to trust her and begins to use her, and so it is a crucial point. I think the enormity of the crime as it is described brings back the image of her dead father and she isn't able to deal with it, or with the accumulated pressure from events around her.

Goold: As you say, the difference is impossible for the audience to detect, but we played it as a genuine faint. We went with the idea that Macbeth, as a soldier, would know how to kill Duncan—a quick stab or two to the vital organs—and that the "gashed stabs" he describes are inflicted by the bloodthirsty Lady Macbeth when she returns the daggers. So in our production he entered from the murder with only a few streaks of blood on his hands but when she returned she looked like she had been bathing in an abattoir. His speech then, which precipitates the faint, was played as an accusation in part to her for her violence, which he has only just witnessed with Lennox. That became the start of his active separation from her and precipitated the faint along with Lady Macbeth being forced to re-see the murder through his description. We also played the second of Ban-

6. and 7. Contrasting approaches to the weyard sisters: taking control of Ian McKellen in Trevor Nunn's 1976 production (top) and as sinister nurses with Patrick Stewart in Rupert Goold's 2007 production.

quo's "Look to the lady" as an aside and warning to Macduff. He is trying to tell the Thane of Fife that he suspects Lady Macbeth may be at the root of the crime.

The text seems to support the view that Lady Macbeth has lost a child in the past. Do you agree, and what implications did this have for her character and the relationship between the Macbeths in your production? Children and childlessness do keep recurring in the play, don't they?

Nunn: Duncan has children to inherit his crown. Banquo has a child who will be the progenitor of a line of kings. Macduff has children, who can be used to cause the ultimate suffering for the father's disloyalty. Macbeth, essential to Shakespeare's scheme, has no children. The glimpse that we are given of a past time of joy and sublimation for the Macbeths in the passing reference to "I have given suck" sets up unspoken reverberations which are vast, as we realize that childlessness is possibly the prime cause for Macbeth craving power in lieu of a future investment in the next generation. Clearly that backstory of the lost child is vital for developing the character of Lady Macbeth, and the use of the image of the baby at the breast, so painfully part of their shared marital history, in demanding action from her husband, shows how extreme she is prepared to be. But as with all offstage events, I think it would be a mistake to give that strand of the story a prominence that is never articulated in the text. Shakespeare provides us with a suggestion and I would recommend that therefore it's what he wants, the tip and not the iceberg.

Doran: Because Lady Macbeth says "I have given suck, and know / How tender 'tis to love the babe that milks me," she clearly has had a child before. It seemed to us to be most fruitful to decide that this was a child that the Macbeths have had and which has died, rather than being either a fantasy on her part or the child of another marriage. Also later on Macduff says "he has no children," after Macbeth has slain Macduff's entire family. We spent a lot of time with Antony Sher and Harriet Walter [who played the Macbeths] discussing what this meant, and we decided that this was a taboo subject for them, which they had suppressed; they had never talked about it. That is why it is at that crucial moment, as Macbeth decides while the king is banqueting that he can no longer go ahead with their proposed plan to murder him, that she brings up the subject. It focuses his mind and makes him realize how serious she is. That became crucial to the playing of the scene. Because they couldn't have children the Macbeths required something else in which to pour their energies, which they thought would be the crown. The dead child became a catalyst in their decision to go ahead with the plan. So from that point of view it was very important.

We also extended the idea. When Lady Macbeth welcomes Duncan to Dunsinane, we had Macduff there with his wife and their children. As Lady Macduff, this fecund woman with all her pretty children, passed Lady Macbeth, Harriet gave her a very wan smile, and you could tell that children were something she desperately wanted, but that now, somehow because of her dead child, was unable to have. This was a moment on which we were able to focus particularly in the filmed version. So the lack of children in Lady Macbeth's world became very important for us. She needed to replace that with some other ambition.

Goold: Is the child even Macbeth's? In the sources there is a suggestion she has been married before and Macbeth is the conqueror of her previous husband. We talked about the issue a lot in rehearsal but in playing it seemed to lose its significance, at least for Lady Macbeth, who never mentions it again; when in her sleepwalking she acknowledges the crimes against Macduff, it is more for the loss of his wife than his children. I think it haunts the childless Macbeth more, and I always found his fear that Banquo would come to the crown, "No son of mine succeeding," very moving. In our production we had a significant age gap between Macbeth and Lady Macbeth and so sex was more significant than children. Child-killers are, though, a recurrent theme from the murder attempt on Fleance, through to the Macduffs and by way of the sow "that hath eaten / Her nine farrow." We tried to accentuate the vulnerability of children by having Macduff and his wife and family arrive on the night of Duncan's murder, to put their family in the foreground prior to the Lady Macduff scene.

How did you stage the banquet scene where Macbeth is confronted by Banquo's ghost that only he can see?

Nunn: Staying true to the principle that everything must be entirely credible in our small space, I decided that the ghost of Banquo must be only in Macbeth's mind at the banquet, just as the dagger that he saw before him was no such thing. I remember we rehearsed the scene with Banquo there, before removing him, so that Ian McKellen could gauge precisely what he would do if he discovered a corpse accusing him at his dinner table. The impact in performance was truly upsetting, one might say sickening, as I think no lighting effect or ghostly makeup would have been.

Doran: Macbeth dismissed a servant to get some wine to fill up everybody's goblets so they could make a toast. When he turned around to see the servant return it was actually Banquo, who then disappeared amongst the guests. That was quite freaky for the audience. They knew the man coming back was the servant, but then suddenly when they looked he had turned into Banquo. It created quite a shock.

8. The Macbeths have only each other: Antony Sher and Harriet Walter in Gregory Doran's 1999 production.

Goold: For ages I wrestled with the twin academic positions: that one needs to see the ghost and so feel the full horror of the scene for Macbeth; and on the other hand, that we should never see him so we can focus on the scorpions in Macbeth's mind. Then I looked at the scene again and realized it was close to where the interval, if there is to be one, is usually taken (at the end of this scene). This gave me the idea of playing the scene twice—once where we see the ghost and then again when we don't. So we took the interval at a hugely intense moment as the blood-boltered Banquo strode down the table to challenge his king having descended in a lift bleeding all over the walls (in a shameless steal from *The Shining*!). We then returned, replayed the scene from the start with some minor changes (the dialogue between Macbeth and the murderer was inaudible the second time, so we focused on the guests and the excluded Lady Macbeth), and then at the moment the ghost arrived we saw nothing. We then stayed in Macbeth's world until we found another moment for a sudden and shocking arrival of the ghost at an unexpected moment later in the scene.

And what about the Porter?

Nunn: We were very fortunate in having the young Iain McDiarmid as the Porter, and we used his Scottishness to the full, not to mention his flamboyant comedic bravura. He was a very real, hungover, cussed Porter, but he spoke directly to the audience, involving them and almost forcing them to laugh in the midst of their distress and grief at what they had just witnessed. As he does in so many of the plays—like the Clown bringing the asp to Cleopatra—Shakespeare lightens the tone just before he darkens it to something even deeper than it was.

Doran: The Porter is a great moment; suddenly there is this unexpected, funny scene right at the height of the drama, the tragedy, and the tension. It's a brilliant device. The difficulty is to make it funny, because the jokes, about Henry Garnet and Jesuits, are very topical. We had a rather brilliant actor called Stephen Noonan who happened to be a very clever imitator, so I allowed him a bit of leeway. He did use the text but he would talk to the audience. When it came to the line "What are you?" occasionally some people replied, for example with "I'm a teacher," and that gave him license to say "Well, you're certainly going to hell," or whatever. There was one wonderful moment one night when he said, "What are you?" to a lady on the front row. She replied "Is this in the play?" and Steve said, "Well, *I'm* in the play." It was a great, sort of weird, Pirandellian moment! He also did impersonations of Tony Blair as the equivocator, which of course at the time, as any politician was saying white is black and black is white, seemed to be very appropriate. It caught the mood of the Porter scene. Mind you, our playing time was one hour fifty-eight, but it could stretch to two hours and seven minutes depending on how long the Porter went on! He crashed out of a trap on the stage, and he was a very violent, disgusting creature who was both intimidating and hilariously funny. What we tried to do was translate the topical allusions and the weird freshness of the wit while using as much of the text as possible to do that. I think in the film version he uses virtually all of the text.

Goold: The first speech is impenetrable and cursed because people expect it to be funny. We made the familiar double with Seyton and just tried to make him as scary and threatening as possible: the kind of morbid thug who would usually end up in prison in a well-balanced society but in times of strife and chaos finds himself working the gas chambers. It is indicative of Macbeth's employ that he has hired such a man—perhaps an old soldier. The comedy must have been electric in 1606 after the publicity surrounding the execution of the original equivocator Father Garnet, but unless one allows the actor to improvise—something we tried but that never seemed quite right—it's very hard. I have some truck with the idea that the comedy is necessary, not to lighten or change the mood in the play but to introduce the scabrous bleak humor that will eventually consume the nihilistically ironic Macbeth in Act 5.

The text is a lot shorter than is the case in Shakespeare's other tragedies, so you don't have to cut so much—and some productions have achieved great intensity by having no interval. By the same account, some of the most successful productions have

had the intimacy of chamber or black-box productions: were pace and claustrophobia among the qualities you looked for?

Doran: Absolutely they were. We really learned that from Trevor Nunn's 1976 production. We were able to play it in the Swan very fast without an interval. Shakespeare didn't have intervals, but of course he quite often gives the lead actor a big scene off in Act 4. Macbeth has the England scene when he can relax. I think the only cut we made was Hecate, because I'm sure that's a bit of Middleton; it seems to me to be inferior.

I think somebody once said that, in *Macbeth*, if anyone had time to think the events wouldn't happen. The furious pace of the text is crucial; things happen in this terrible whirlwind. The claustrophobia of the play is intensified by Shakespeare's lighting effects; he's brilliant at lighting his own plays. There isn't a single scene in *Macbeth* that takes place in daylight. At the beginning of the England scene Malcolm says, "Let us seek out some desolate shade, and there / Weep our sad bosoms empty." And there is one scene between the old man and Ross where "by th'clock, 'tis day, / And yet dark night strangles the travelling lamp." It's always dark and gloomy. The shadows Shakespeare creates we fill with our own fear, therefore the claustrophobia and the darkness of the play are crucial. It's famously a play that is often better when you read it than when you see it in the theater, because of that complicity of your imagination. If you can in performance suggest, allow the audience to engage their own fear, they will fill those shadows with their own dark imaginings. That contribution, the intensity of the audience's reaction, increases the tension of the play.

Goold: Claustrophobia is vital, at least in Acts 1, 2, and 5. Our production opened in the three-sided Minerva Studio in Chichester, and so from the start we knew we had to effectively stage the play on a single set—in our case, a space that was part-hospital, part-kitchen, and part-morgue. However, the claustrophobia must be unusual, and one of our greatest successes was in Howard Harrison's bright, hard lighting throughout the play that stopped the crepuscular gloom that many productions (and actors!) get lost in. Kubrick's *2001* is hugely claustrophobic but searingly bright, as is Ridley

Scott's *Alien*. Pace was something that I felt much more ambivalent about. I know that the received wisdom is to play *Macbeth* pell-mell but I guess you have to respond to your actors. Patrick Stewart, older than many Macbeths and exploring that sense of mortality throughout, brought to the role his own thoughtful and intense charisma—one that counterpointed well with Kate Fleetwood's quicksilver fury as Lady Macbeth. I always felt the play would fight back if we got too measured—and it often did, but almost always in Acts 3 and 5—but that we shouldn't set out to turn up the speed without letting the language out first. After all, we see gripping, pacy murder stories all the time; what distinguishes *Macbeth* into a league shared maybe only with *Crime and Punishment* is the depth of its interior psychology. These things shouldn't always be rushed.

The one scene where the pace seems to flag is that at the English court. But then this interlude is particularly important for the development of Malcolm and Macduff, isn't it?

Nunn: It was vital to the scheme of my production that full weight was given to the England scene, where an opposite set of beliefs, under the patrimony of a deeply religious king, is developed in necessary contradiction to the things that Macbeth in repeated soliloquy has been encouraging us to think. Nevertheless, I proposed cutting some elements of the scene, but much inspired by the arguments of Bob Peck as Macduff and Roger Rees as Malcolm, a number of my proposed cuts were restored. I had reduced the amount of testing of Macduff by Malcolm, but if there was any one individual who led the movement toward a less recited, more instant coinage of Shakespeare's language at Stratford at this time, it was the late and deeply lamented Bob Peck; it was his example that led to the scene having a centrality that only the requirements of television editing were able to compromise.

Doran: In the England scene I think Shakespeare allows you to debate what it is that we require our rulers to be. One of the difficult things about the early part of the play is that Scotland in Macbeth's time is not a country where kings succeed through primogeniture, so although Malcolm becomes the Prince of Cumberland, it isn't an automatic choice that Duncan would choose him or his son as the next king. Indeed at that point, because Macbeth has performed in such an extraordinary fashion in routing the enemy, everybody expects that he will be rewarded and perhaps nominated as the next king. So there is a slight sense that in a way he was robbed of the crown, which of course he then seizes through devious means. But then we are asked to consider whether Malcolm himself is appropriate to be leader of the country. The trick that Malcolm plays on Macduff of pretending he is a deeply flawed character forces Macduff to decide whether a man of such low morals should indeed accept the throne. That shift of perspective is important for the audience to see a larger canvas; not just to involve themselves in how Macbeth has hacked his way to the throne, but to inquire what it is that we want our monarch, our rulers, to be. It's about good government.

Goold: A brilliant scene and one that in any other play with less bravura theatricality would be celebrated. I've always felt it suffers from undercasting—particularly if the actor playing Malcolm is inexperienced. Because Patrick was an older Macbeth we had an older company than usual, and so in Scott Handy had an actor of huge experience and talent in classical theater. This is a scene that focuses on what was for me the thematic heart of the play—what it is to be a man. Questions of masculinity haunt the play—Lady Macbeth wishes she were a man, she mocks her husband's lack of manliness, he dares "do all that may become a man: / Who dares do more is none." Here, in the longest scene in the play, Malcolm explores for himself and in role-play what his own masculinity is and how it might be exposed as a king but also how inexperienced and unmanly he truly is. Then at the most heartbreaking moment in Shakespeare, when Macduff hears of his family's slaughter, Malcolm urges him to "Dispute it like a man" (what a martial and British sentiment! The fear of the unmanly tears of compassion!) and Macduff reminds us that true manliness lies at the margins of this brutal, sexualized, ferocious play when he declares "I shall do so / But I must also feel it as a man." It's a great scene. It will always struggle after the sensationalism of the apparitions and the Lady Macduff murder in terms of sheer theatricality, but good actors and being brave with the pacing will make it a rich and profound experience. Two particular moments in our production stood out for me: one was Malcolm's exploration of the princely virtues, which we played as an initial retort but that became a slow and terrified exploration of his own potential inadequacy. The other was a bold and almost two-minute pause we took after Macduff receives the news of his family's slaughter and Malcolm says "Merciful heaven!" After this agonizing awkward hiatus, Malcolm whispered: "What, man, ne'er pull your hat upon your brows: / Give sorrow words. The grief that does not speak / Whispers the o'er-fraught heart and bids it break." Beautiful transcendent lines in a transcendent scene at the heart of his greatest play.

How did you deal with the theatrical superstitions linked to this play—not mentioning its title, and all that? Why is this the one Shakespearean play to have such rituals surrounding it?

Nunn: The *Macbeth* "bad luck" superstition remains potent among actors and directors and almost certainly derives initially from the discomfort that surrounds any dabbling with the black arts. The word "Macbeth" or any quote from the play must never be uttered in a theater, other than in the course of doing that play. I love the alternative story, that this derives from the days when stock companies toured the country led by actor-managers. If business was really bad, those actor-managers, in the desperate knowledge that everyone would soon be unemployed, would have to resort to presenting the biggest crowd-pleaser . . . *Macbeth*. So understandably, "Don't say that word round here!" My experience in doing the production of the play with Ian McKellen and Judi Dench was completely the opposite. Rehearsals were a constant and exciting delight—often amidst bouts of laughter, we all remained close and caring friends through The Other Place in Stratford, then the main theater, then Newcastle, then the Warehouse, then the Young Vic, and then the television studio. That should have cured me of the superstition once and for all. But I still feel very distressed if somebody inadvertently says the "M" word in a theater.

Doran: Very straightforwardly. On the first day of rehearsals I said, "We are doing a play called *Macbeth*. *Macbeth*, *Macbeth*, *Macbeth*!" I think that the whole superstition thing is a total nonsense. There are delightful stories about the terrible things that have happened doing *Macbeth*, but if you have a group of actors together for as long as a year doing *Twelfth Night* then terrible things no doubt happen, but we never call it "The Illyrian Play"! Obviously it's a play with sword-fights, actors sometimes get tired and swordfights can go wrong, so that could be dangerous. I'm fascinated by the history of it but I think it's nonsense in terms of the actual production. I felt it was reductive. So we resolutely on the first day decided to banish those superstitions and just refer to it as *Macbeth*. It must have worked because we were very lucky in having a very successful production!

Goold: They say more about the theatrical community than the play, I fear. It is a difficult play, though; perhaps only *Romeo and Juliet* is harder, because, just as with *Romeo and Juliet* the play will not happen if you do not believe in the love of the lovers, *Macbeth* has to be scary, and if it doesn't chill you then it will never take flight. Perhaps the difficulty of getting terror right onstage has made it so cursed. All I can say is that we stared it hard in the eyes and it was the most fortunate career-changing moment of my and my family's life. We certainly got lucky with it, but even then I remember landing on the plane back from the Tony Awards a year after our journey had begun and feeling the most intense relief that we had touched ground safely—I kept thinking the play might bite back one day!

SHAKESPEARE'S CAREER
IN THE THEATER

BEGINNINGS

William Shakespeare was an extraordinarily intelligent man who was born and died in an ordinary market town in the English Midlands. He lived an uneventful life in an eventful age. Born in April 1564, he was the eldest son of John Shakespeare, a glove-maker who was prominent on the town council until he fell into financial difficulties. Young William was educated at the local grammar in Stratford-upon-Avon, Warwickshire, where he gained a thorough grounding in the Latin language, the art of rhetoric, and classical poetry. He married Ann Hathaway and had three children (Susanna, then the twins Hamnet and Judith) before his twenty-first birthday: an exceptionally young age for the period. We do not know how he supported his family in the mid-1580s.

Like many clever country boys, he moved to the city in order to make his way in the world. Like many creative people, he found a career in the entertainment business. Public playhouses and professional full-time acting companies reliant on the market for their income were born in Shakespeare's childhood. When he arrived in London as a man, sometime in the late 1580s, a new phenomenon was in the making: the actor who is so successful that he becomes a "star." The word did not exist in its modern sense, but the pattern is recognizable: audiences went to the theater not so much to see a particular show as to witness the comedian Richard Tarlton or the dramatic actor Edward Alleyn.

Shakespeare was an actor before he was a writer. It appears not to have been long before he realized that he was never going to grow into a great comedian like Tarlton or a great tragedian like Alleyn. Instead, he found a role within his company as the man who patched up old plays, breathing new life, new dramatic twists, into tired repertory pieces. He paid close attention to the work of the university-educated dramatists who were writing history plays and tragedies for the public stage in a style more ambitious, sweeping, and poetically grand than anything that had been seen before. But he may also have noted that what his friend and rival Ben Jonson would call "Marlowe's mighty line" sometimes faltered in the mode of comedy. Going to university, as Christopher Marlowe did, was all well and good for honing the arts of rhetorical elaboration and classical allusion, but it could lead to a loss of the common touch. To stay close to a large segment of the potential audience for public theater, it was necessary to write for clowns as well as kings and to intersperse the flights of poetry with the humor of the tavern, the privy, and the brothel: Shakespeare was the first to establish himself early in his career as an equal master of tragedy, comedy, and history. He realized that theater could be the medium to make the national past available to a wider audience than the elite who could afford to read large history books: his signature early works include not only the classical tragedy *Titus Andronicus* but also the sequence of English historical plays on the Wars of the Roses.

He also invented a new role for himself, that of in-house company dramatist. Where his peers and predecessors had to sell their plays to the theater managers on a poorly paid piecework basis, Shakespeare took a percentage of the box-office income. The Lord Chamberlain's Men constituted themselves in 1594 as a joint stock company, with the profits being distributed among the core actors who had invested as sharers. Shakespeare acted himself—he appears in the cast lists of some of Ben Jonson's plays as well as the list of actors' names at the beginning of his own collected works—but his principal duty was to write two or three plays a year for the company. By holding shares, he was effectively earning himself a royalty on his work, something no author had ever done before in England. When the Lord Chamberlain's Men collected their fee for performance at court in the Christmas season of 1594, three of them went along to the Treasurer of the Chamber: not just Richard Burbage the tragedian and Will Kempe the clown, but also Shakespeare the scriptwriter. That was something new.

The next four years were the golden period in Shakespeare's

career, though overshadowed by the death of his only son, Hamnet, aged eleven, in 1596. In his early thirties and in full command of both his poetic and his theatrical medium, he perfected his art of comedy, while also developing his tragic and historical writing in new ways. In 1598, Francis Meres, a Cambridge University graduate with his finger on the pulse of the London literary world, praised Shakespeare for his excellence across the genres:

> As Plautus and Seneca are accounted the best for comedy and tragedy among the Latins, so Shakespeare among the English is the most excellent in both kinds for the stage; for comedy, witness his *Gentlemen of Verona*, his *Errors*, his *Love Labours Lost*, his *Love Labours Won*, his *Midsummer Night Dream* and his *Merchant of Venice*: for tragedy his *Richard the 2*, *Richard the 3*, *Henry the 4*, *King John*, *Titus Andronicus* and his *Romeo and Juliet*.

For Meres, as for the many writers who praised the "honey-flowing vein" of *Venus and Adonis* and *Lucrece*, narrative poems written when the theaters were closed due to plague in 1593–94, Shakespeare was marked above all by his linguistic skill, by the gift of turning elegant poetic phrases.

PLAYHOUSES

Elizabethan playhouses were "thrust" or "one-room" theaters. To understand Shakespeare's original theatrical life, we have to forget about the indoor theater of later times, with its proscenium arch and curtain that would be opened at the beginning and closed at the end of each act. In the proscenium arch theater, stage and auditorium are effectively two separate rooms: the audience looks from one world into another as if through the imaginary "fourth wall" framed by the proscenium. The picture-frame stage, together with the elaborate scenic effects and backdrops beyond it, created the illusion of a self-contained world—especially once nineteenth-century developments in the control of artificial lighting meant that the auditorium could be darkened and the spectators made to focus on the lighted stage. Shakespeare, by contrast, wrote for a bare platform stage with a standing audience gathered around it in a courtyard in full daylight. The audience were always conscious of themselves and their fellow spectators, and they shared the same "room" as the actors. A sense of immediate presence and the creation of rapport with the audience were all-important. The actor could not afford to imagine he was in a closed world, with silent witnesses dutifully observing him from the darkness.

Shakespeare's theatrical career began at the Rose Theatre in Southwark. The stage was wide and shallow, trapezoid in shape, like a lozenge. This design had a great deal of potential for the theatrical equivalent of cinematic split-screen effects, whereby one group of characters would enter at the door at one end of the tiring-house wall at the back of the stage and another group through the door at the other end, thus creating two rival tableaux. Many of the battle-heavy and faction-filled plays that premiered at the Rose have scenes of just this sort.

At the rear of the Rose stage, there were three capacious exits, each over ten feet wide. Unfortunately, the very limited excavation of a fragmentary portion of the original Globe site, also in 1989, revealed nothing about the stage. The first Globe was built in 1599 with similar proportions to those of another theater, the Fortune, albeit that the former was polygonal and looked circular, whereas the latter was rectangular. The building contract for the Fortune survives and allows us to infer that the stage of the Globe was probably substantially wider than it was deep (perhaps forty-three feet wide and twenty-seven feet deep). It may well have been tapered at the front, like that of the Rose.

The capacity of the Globe was said to have been enormous, perhaps in excess of three thousand. It has been conjectured that about eight hundred people may have stood in the yard, with two thousand or more in the three layers of covered galleries. The other "public" playhouses were also of large capacity, whereas the indoor Blackfriars theater that Shakespeare's company began using in 1608—the former refectory of a monastery—had overall internal dimensions of a mere forty-six by sixty feet. It would have made for a much more intimate theatrical experience and had a much smaller capacity, probably of about six hundred people. Since they paid at least six-pence a head, the Blackfriars attracted a more select or "private" audience. The atmosphere would have been closer to that of an indoor performance before the court in the Whitehall Palace or at Richmond. That Shakespeare always wrote for indoor production at court as well as outdoor performance in the public theater should make us cautious about inferring, as some scholars have, that the opportunity provided by the intimacy of the Blackfriars led to a significant change toward a "chamber" style in his last plays—which, besides, were performed at both the Globe and the Blackfriars. After the occupation of the Blackfriars, a five-act structure seems to have become more important to Shakespeare. That was because of artificial lighting: there were musical interludes between the acts, while the candles were trimmed and replaced. Again, though, something similar must have been necessary for indoor court performances throughout his career.

Front of house there were the "gatherers" who collected the money from audience members: a penny to stand in the open-air yard, another penny for a place in the covered galleries, sixpence for the prominent "lord's rooms" to the side of the stage. In the indoor "private" theaters, gallants from the audience who fancied making themselves part of the spectacle sat on stools on the edge of the stage itself. Scholars debate as to how widespread this practice was in the public theaters such as the Globe. Once the audience were in place and the money counted, the gatherers were available to be extras onstage. That is one reason why battles and crowd scenes often come later rather than early in Shakespeare's plays. There was no formal prohibition upon performance by women, and there certainly were women among the gatherers, so it is not beyond the bounds of possibility that female crowd members were played by females.

The play began at two o'clock in the afternoon and the theater had to be cleared by five. After the main show, there would be a jig—which consisted not only of dancing, but also of knockabout comedy (it is the origin of the farcical "afterpiece" in the eighteenth-century theater). So the time available for a Shakespeare play was about two and a half hours, somewhere between the "two hours' traffic" mentioned in the prologue to *Romeo and Juliet* and the "three hours' spectacle" referred to in the preface to the 1647 Folio of Beaumont and Fletcher's plays. The prologue to a play by Thomas Middleton refers to a thousand lines as "one hour's words," so the likelihood is that about two and a half thousand, or a maximum of three thousand lines made up the performed text. This is indeed the length of most of Shakespeare's comedies, whereas many of his tragedies and histories are much longer, raising the possibility that he wrote full scripts, possibly with eventual publication in mind, in the full knowledge that the stage version would be heavily cut. The short Quarto texts published in his lifetime—they used to be called "Bad" Quartos—provide fascinating evidence as to the kind of cutting that probably took place. So, for instance, the First Quarto of *Hamlet* neatly merges two occasions when Hamlet is overheard, the "Fishmonger" and the "nunnery" scenes.

The social composition of the audience was mixed. The poet Sir John Davies wrote of "A thousand townsmen, gentlemen and whores, / Porters and servingmen" who would "together throng" at the public playhouses. Though moralists associated female playgoing with adultery and the sex trade, many perfectly respectable citizens' wives were regular attendees. Some, no doubt, resembled the modern groupie: a story attested in two different sources has one citizen's wife making a post-show assignation with Richard Burbage and ending up in bed with Shakespeare—supposedly eliciting from the latter the quip that William the Conqueror was before Richard III. Defenders of theater liked to say that by witnessing the comeuppance of villains on the stage, audience members would repent of their own wrongdoings, but the reality is that most people went to the theater then, as they do now, for entertainment more than moral edification. Besides, it would be foolish to suppose that audiences behaved in a homogeneous way: a pamphlet of the 1630s tells of how two men went to see *Pericles* and one of them laughed while the other wept. Bishop John Hall complained that people went to church for the same reasons that they went to the theater: "for company, for custom, for recreation . . . to feed his eyes or his ears . . . or perhaps for sleep."

Men-about-town and clever young lawyers went to be seen as much as to see. In the modern popular imagination, shaped not least by *Shakespeare in Love* and the opening sequence of Laurence Olivier's *Henry V* film, the penny-paying groundlings stand in the yard hurling abuse or encouragement and hazelnuts or orange peel at the actors, while the sophisticates in the covered galleries appreciate Shakespeare's soaring poetry. The reality was probably the other way around. A "groundling" was a kind of fish, so the nickname suggests the penny audience standing below the level of the stage and gazing in silent open-mouthed wonder at the spectacle unfolding above them. The more difficult audience members, who kept up a running commentary of clever remarks on the performance and who occasionally got into quarrels with players, were the gallants. Like Hollywood movies in modern times, Elizabethan and Jacobean plays exercised a powerful influence on the fashion and behavior of the young. John Marston mocks the lawyers who would open their lips, perhaps to court a girl, and out would "flow / Naught but pure Juliet and Romeo."

THE ENSEMBLE AT WORK

In the absence of typewriters and photocopying machines, reading aloud would have been the means by which the company got to know a new play. The tradition of the playwright reading his complete script to the assembled company endured for generations. A copy would then have been taken to the Master of the Revels for licensing. The theater book-holder or prompter would then have copied the parts for distribution to the actors. A partbook consisted of the character's lines, with each speech preceded by the last three or four words of the speech before, the so-called "cue." These would have been taken away and studied or "conned." During this period of learning the parts, an actor might have had some one-to-one instruction, perhaps from the dramatist, perhaps from a senior actor who had played the same part before, and, in the case of an apprentice, from his master. A high percentage of Desdemona's lines occur in dialogue with Othello, of Lady Macbeth's with Macbeth, Cleopatra's with Antony, and Volumnia's with Coriolanus. The roles would almost certainly have been taken by the apprentice of the lead actor, usually Burbage, who delivers the majority of the cues. Given that apprentices lodged with their masters, there would have been ample opportunity for personal instruction, which may be what made it possible for young men to play such demanding parts.

After the parts were learned, there may have been no more than a single rehearsal before the first performance. With six different plays to be put on every week, there was no time for more. Actors, then, would go into a show with a very limited sense of the whole. The notion of a collective rehearsal process that is itself a process of discovery for the actors is wholly modern and would have been incomprehensible to Shakespeare and his original ensemble. Given the number of parts an actor had to hold in his memory, the forgetting of lines was probably more frequent than in the modern theater. The book-holder was on hand to prompt.

Backstage personnel included the property man, the tire-man who oversaw the costumes, call boys, attendants, and the musicians, who might play at various times from the main stage, the rooms above and within the tiring-house. Scriptwriters sometimes made a nuisance of themselves backstage. There was often tension between the acting companies and the freelance playwrights from whom they purchased scripts: it was a smart move on the part of Shakespeare and the Lord Chamberlain's Men to bring the writing process in-house.

Scenery was limited, though sometimes set pieces were brought on (a bank of flowers, a bed, the mouth of hell). The trapdoor from below, the gallery stage above, and the curtained discovery-space at the back allowed for an array of special effects: the rising of ghosts and apparitions, the descent of gods, dialogue between a character at a window and another at ground level, the revelation of a statue or a pair of lovers playing at chess. Ingenious use could be made of props, as with the ass's head in *A Midsummer Night's Dream*. In a theater that does not clutter the stage with the material paraphernalia of everyday life, those objects that are deployed may take on powerful symbolic weight, as when Shylock bears his weighing scales in one hand and knife in the other, thus becoming a parody of the figure of Justice who traditionally bears a sword and a balance. Among the more significant items in the property cupboard of Shakespeare's company, there would have been a throne (the "chair of

9. Hypothetical reconstruction of the interior of an Elizabethan playhouse during a performance.

state"), joint stools, books, bottles, coins, purses, letters (which are brought onstage, read or referred to on about eighty occasions in the complete works), maps, gloves, a set of stocks (in which Kent is put in *King Lear*), rings, rapiers, daggers, broadswords, staves, pistols, masks and vizards, heads and skulls, torches and tapers and lanterns, which served to signal night scenes on the daylit stage, a buck's head, an ass's head, animal costumes. Live animals also put in appearances, most notably the dog Crab in *The Two Gentlemen of Verona* and possibly a young polar bear in *The Winter's Tale*.

The costumes were the most important visual dimension of the play. Playwrights were paid between £2 and £6 per script, whereas Alleyn was not averse to paying £20 for "a black velvet cloak with sleeves embroidered all with silver and gold." No matter the period of the play, actors always wore contemporary costume. The excitement for the audience came not from any impression of historical accuracy, but from the richness of the attire and perhaps the transgressive thrill of the knowledge that here were commoners like

themselves strutting in the costumes of courtiers in effective defi-
ance of the strict sumptuary laws whereby in real life people had to
wear the clothes that befitted their social station.

To an even greater degree than props, costumes could carry symbolic importance. Racial characteristics could be suggested: a breast-
plate and helmet for a Roman soldier, a turban for a Turk, long robes
for exotic characters such as Moors, a gabardine for a Jew. The figure
of Time, as in *The Winter's Tale*, would be equipped with hourglass,
scythe, and wings; Rumour, who speaks the prologue of *2 Henry IV*,
wore a costume adorned with a thousand tongues. The wardrobe in
the tiring-house of the Globe would have contained much of the
same stock as that of rival manager Philip Henslowe at the Rose:
green gowns for outlaws and foresters, black for melancholy men
such as Jaques and people in mourning such as the Countess in *All's
Well That Ends Well* (at the beginning of *Hamlet*, the prince is still in
mourning black when everyone else is in festive garb for the wedding
of the new king), a gown and hood for a friar (or a feigned friar like
the duke in *Measure for Measure*), blue coats and tawny to distinguish
the followers of rival factions, a leather apron and ruler for a carpenter (as in the opening scene of *Julius Caesar*—and in *A Midsummer
Night's Dream*, where this is the only sign that Peter Quince is a carpenter), a cockle hat with staff and a pair of sandals for a pilgrim or
palmer (the disguise assumed by Helen in *All's Well*), bodices and kir-
tles with farthingales beneath for the boys who are to be dressed as
girls. A gender switch such as that of Rosalind or Jessica seems to
have taken between fifty and eighty lines of dialogue—Viola does not
resume her "maiden weeds," but remains in her boy's costume to the
end of *Twelfth Night* because a change would have slowed down the
action at just the moment it was speeding to a climax. Henslowe's
inventory also included "a robe for to go invisible": Oberon, Puck,
and Ariel must have had something similar.

As the costumes appealed to the eyes, so there was music for the
ears. Comedies included many songs. Desdemona's willow song, perhaps a late addition to the text, is a rare and thus exceptionally
poignant example from tragedy. Trumpets and tuckets sounded for
ceremonial entrances, drums denoted an army on the march. Background music could create atmosphere, as at the beginning of

Twelfth Night, during the lovers' dialogue near the end of *The Merchant of Venice*, when the statue seemingly comes to life in *The Winter's Tale*, and for the revival of Pericles and of Lear (in the Quarto text, but not the Folio). The haunting sound of the hautboy suggested a realm beyond the human, as when the god Hercules is imagined deserting Mark Antony. Dances symbolized the harmony of the end of a comedy—though in Shakespeare's world of mingled joy and sorrow, someone is usually left out of the circle.

The most important resource was, of course, the actors themselves. They needed many skills: in the words of one contemporary commentator, "dancing, activity, music, song, elocution, ability of body, memory, skill of weapon, pregnancy of wit." Their bodies were as significant as their voices. Hamlet tells the player to "suit the action to the word, the word to the action": moments of strong emotion, known as "passions," relied on a repertoire of dramatic gestures as well as a modulation of the voice. When Titus Andronicus has had his hand chopped off, he asks "How can I grace my talk, / Wanting a hand to give it action?" A pen portrait of "The Character of an Excellent Actor" by the dramatist John Webster is almost certainly based on his impression of Shakespeare's leading man, Richard Burbage: "By a full and significant action of body, he charms our attention: sit in a full theater, and you will think you see so many lines drawn from the circumference of so many ears, whiles the actor is the centre. . . ."

Though Burbage was admired above all others, praise was also heaped upon the apprentice players whose alto voices fitted them for the parts of women. A spectator at Oxford in 1610 records how the audience were reduced to tears by the pathos of Desdemona's death. The puritans who fumed about the biblical prohibition upon cross-dressing and the encouragement to sodomy constituted by the sight of an adult male kissing a teenage boy onstage were a small minority. Little is known, however, about the characteristics of the leading apprentices in Shakespeare's company. It may perhaps be inferred that one was a lot taller than the other, since Shakespeare often wrote for a pair of female friends, one tall and fair, the other short and dark (Helena and Hermia, Rosalind and Celia, Beatrice and Hero).

We know little about Shakespeare's own acting roles—an early allusion indicates that he often took royal parts, and a venerable tradition gives him old Adam in *As You Like It* and the ghost of old King Hamlet. Save for Burbage's lead roles and the generic part of the clown, all such castings are mere speculation. We do not even know for sure whether the original Falstaff was Will Kempe or another actor who specialized in comic roles, Thomas Pope.

Kempe left the company in early 1599. Tradition has it that he fell out with Shakespeare over the matter of excessive improvisation. He was replaced by Robert Armin, who was less of a clown and more of a cerebral wit: this explains the difference between such parts as Lancelet Gobbo and Dogberry, which were written for Kempe, and the more verbally sophisticated Feste and Lear's Fool, which were written for Armin.

One thing that is clear from surviving "plots" or storyboards of plays from the period is that a degree of doubling was necessary. *2 Henry VI* has over sixty speaking parts, but more than half of the characters only appear in a single scene and most scenes have only six to eight speakers. At a stretch, the play could be performed by thirteen actors. When Thomas Platter saw *Julius Caesar* at the Globe in 1599, he noted that there were about fifteen. Why doesn't Paris go to the Capulet ball in *Romeo and Juliet*? Perhaps because he was doubled with Mercutio, who does. In *The Winter's Tale*, Mamillius might have come back as Perdita and Antigonus been doubled by Camillo, making the partnership with Paulina at the end a very neat touch. Titania and Oberon are often played by the same pair as Hippolyta and Theseus, suggesting a symbolic matching of the rulers of the worlds of night and day, but it is questionable whether there would have been time for the necessary costume changes. As so often, one is left in a realm of tantalizing speculation.

THE KING'S MAN

The new king, James I, who had held the Scottish throne as James VI since he had been an infant, immediately took the Lord Chamberlain's Men under his direct patronage. Henceforth they would be the King's Men, and for the rest of Shakespeare's career they were favored with far more court performances than any of their rivals.

There even seem to have been rumors early in the reign that Shakespeare and Burbage were being considered for knighthoods, an unprecedented honor for mere actors—and one that in the event was not accorded to a member of the profession for nearly three hundred years, when the title was bestowed upon Henry Irving, the leading Shakespearean actor of Queen Victoria's reign.

Shakespeare's productivity rate slowed in the Jacobean years, not because of age or some personal trauma, but because there were frequent outbreaks of plague, causing the theaters to be closed for long periods. The King's Men were forced to spend many months on the road. Between November 1603 and 1608, they were to be found at various towns in the south and Midlands, though Shakespeare probably did not tour with them by this time. He had bought a large house back home in Stratford and was accumulating other property. He may indeed have stopped acting soon after the new king took the throne. With the London theaters closed so much of the time and a large repertoire on the stocks, Shakespeare seems to have focused his energies on writing a few long and complex tragedies that could have been played on demand at court: *Othello*, *King Lear*, *Antony and Cleopatra*, *Coriolanus*, and *Cymbeline* are among his longest and poetically grandest plays. *Macbeth* only survives in a shorter text, which shows signs of adaptation after Shakespeare's death. The bitterly satirical *Timon of Athens*, apparently a collaboration with Thomas Middleton that may have failed on the stage, also belongs to this period. In comedy, too, he wrote longer and morally darker works than in the Elizabethan period, pushing at the very bounds of the form in *Measure for Measure* and *All's Well That Ends Well*.

From 1608 onward, when the King's Men began occupying the indoor Blackfriars playhouse (as a winter house, meaning that they only used the outdoor Globe in summer?), Shakespeare turned to a more romantic style. His company had a great success with a revived and altered version of an old pastoral play called *Mucedorus*. It even featured a bear. The younger dramatist John Fletcher, meanwhile, sometimes working in collaboration with Francis Beaumont, was pioneering a new style of tragicomedy, a mix of romance and royalism laced with intrigue and pastoral excursions. Shakespeare experimented with this idiom in *Cymbeline* and it was presumably with his blessing that Fletcher eventually took over as the King's Men's company dramatist. The two writers apparently collaborated on three plays in the years 1612–14: a lost romance called *Cardenio* (based on the love-madness of a character in Cervantes' *Don Quixote*), *Henry VIII* (originally staged with the title "All Is True"), and *The Two Noble Kinsmen*, a dramatization of Chaucer's "Knight's Tale." These were written after Shakespeare's two final solo-authored plays, *The Winter's Tale*, a self-consciously old-fashioned work dramatizing the pastoral romance of his old enemy Robert Greene, and *The Tempest*, which at one and the same time drew together multiple theatrical traditions, diverse reading, and contemporary interest in the fate of a ship that had been wrecked on the way to the New World.

The collaborations with Fletcher suggest that Shakespeare's career ended with a slow fade rather than the sudden retirement supposed by the nineteenth-century Romantic critics who read Prospero's epilogue to *The Tempest* as Shakespeare's personal farewell to his art. In the last few years of his life Shakespeare certainly spent more of his time in Stratford-upon-Avon, where he became further involved in property dealing and litigation. But his London life also continued. In 1613 he made his first major London property purchase: a freehold house in the Blackfriars district, close to his company's indoor theater. *The Two Noble Kinsmen* may have been written as late as 1614, and Shakespeare was in London on business a little over a year before he died of an unknown cause at home in Stratford-upon-Avon in 1616, probably on his fifty-second birthday.

About half the sum of his works were published in his lifetime, in texts of variable quality. A few years after his death, his fellow actors began putting together an authorized edition of his complete *Comedies, Histories and Tragedies*. It appeared in 1623, in large "Folio" format. This collection of thirty-six plays gave Shakespeare his immortality. In the words of his fellow dramatist Ben Jonson, who contributed two poems of praise at the start of the Folio, the body of his work made him "a monument without a tomb":

> And art alive still while thy book doth live
> And we have wits to read and praise to give . . .
> He was not of an age, but for all time!

SHAKESPEARE'S WORKS: A CHRONOLOGY

1589–91	? *Arden of Faversham* (possible part authorship)
1589–92	*The Taming of the Shrew*
1589–92	? *Edward the Third* (possible part authorship)
1591	*The Second Part of Henry the Sixth*, originally called *The First Part of the Contention betwixt the Two Famous Houses of York and Lancaster* (element of co-authorship possible)
1591	*The Third Part of Henry the Sixth*, originally called *The True Tragedy of Richard Duke of York* (element of co-authorship probable)
1591–92	*The Two Gentlemen of Verona*
1591–92; perhaps revised 1594	*The Lamentable Tragedy of Titus Andronicus* (probably co-written with, or revising an earlier version by, George Peele)
1592	*The First Part of Henry the Sixth*, probably with Thomas Nashe and others
1592/94	*King Richard the Third*
1593	*Venus and Adonis* (poem)
1593–94	*The Rape of Lucrece* (poem)
1593–1608	*Sonnets* (154 poems, published 1609 with *A Lover's Complaint*, a poem of disputed authorship)
1592–94/ 1600–03	*Sir Thomas More* (a single scene for a play originally by Anthony Munday, with other revisions by Henry Chettle, Thomas Dekker, and Thomas Heywood)
1594	*The Comedy of Errors*
1595	*Love's Labour's Lost*

1595–97	*Love's Labour's Won* (a lost play, unless the original title for another comedy)
1595–96	*A Midsummer Night's Dream*
1595–96	*The Tragedy of Romeo and Juliet*
1595–96	*King Richard the Second*
1595–97	*The Life and Death of King John* (possibly earlier)
1596–97	*The Merchant of Venice*
1596–97	*The First Part of Henry the Fourth*
1597–98	*The Second Part of Henry the Fourth*
1598	*Much Ado About Nothing*
1598–99	*The Passionate Pilgrim* (20 poems, some not by Shakespeare)
1599	*The Life of Henry the Fifth*
1599	"To the Queen" (epilogue for a court performance)
1599	*As You Like It*
1599	*The Tragedy of Julius Caesar*
1600–01	*The Tragedy of Hamlet, Prince of Denmark* (perhaps revising an earlier version)
1600–01	*The Merry Wives of Windsor* (perhaps revising version of 1597–99)
1601	"Let the Bird of Loudest Lay" (poem, known since 1807 as "The Phoenix and Turtle" [turtledove])
1601	*Twelfth Night, or What You Will*
1601–02	*The Tragedy of Troilus and Cressida*
1604	*The Tragedy of Othello, the Moor of Venice*
1604	*Measure for Measure*
1605	*All's Well That Ends Well*
1605	*The Life of Timon of Athens*, with Thomas Middleton
1605–06	*The Tragedy of King Lear*
1605–08	? contribution to *The Four Plays in One* (lost, except for *A Yorkshire Tragedy*, mostly by Thomas Middleton)

1606	*The Tragedy of Macbeth* (surviving text has additional scenes by Thomas Middleton)
1606–07	*The Tragedy of Antony and Cleopatra*
1608	*The Tragedy of Coriolanus*
1608	*Pericles, Prince of Tyre*, with George Wilkins
1610	*The Tragedy of Cymbeline*
1611	*The Winter's Tale*
1611	*The Tempest*
1612–13	*Cardenio*, with John Fletcher (survives only in later adaptation called *Double Falsehood* by Lewis Theobald)
1613	*Henry VIII (All Is True)*, with John Fletcher
1613–14	*The Two Noble Kinsmen*, with John Fletcher

THE HISTORY BEHIND THE TRAGEDIES: A CHRONOLOGY

Era/Date	Event	Location	Play
Greek myth	Trojan War	Troy	*Troilus and Cressida*
Greek myth	Theseus King of Athens	Athens	*The Two Noble Kinsmen*
c. tenth–ninth century BC?	Leir King of Britain (legendary)	Britain	*King Lear*
535–510 BC	Tarquin II King of Rome	Rome	*The Rape of Lucrece*
493 BC	Caius Martius captures Corioli	Italy	*Coriolanus*
431–404 BC	Peloponnesian War	Greece	*Timon of Athens*
17 Mar 45 BC	Battle of Munda: Caesar's victory over Pompey's sons	Munda, Spain	*Julius Caesar*
Oct 45 BC	Caesar returns to Rome for triumph	Rome	*Julius Caesar*
15 Mar 44 BC	Assassination of Caesar	Rome	*Julius Caesar*
27 Nov 43 BC	Formation of Second Triumvirate	Rome	*Julius Caesar*
Oct 42 BC	Battle of Philippi	Philippi, Macedonia	*Julius Caesar*
Winter 41–40 BC	Antony visits Cleopatra	Egypt	*Antony and Cleopatra*
Oct 40 BC	Pact of Brundisium; marriage of Antony and Octavia	Italy	*Antony and Cleopatra*
39 BC	Pact of Misenum between Pompey and the triumvirs	Campania, Italy	*Antony and Cleopatra*

39–38 BC	Ventidius defeats the Parthians in a series of engagements	Syria	*Antony and Cleopatra*
34 BC	Cleopatra and her children proclaimed rulers of the eastern Mediterranean	Alexandria	*Antony and Cleopatra*
2 Sep 31 BC	Battle of Actium	On the coast of western Greece	*Antony and Cleopatra*
Aug 30 BC	Death of Antony	Alexandria	*Antony and Cleopatra*
12 Aug 30 BC	Death of Cleopatra	Alexandria	*Antony and Cleopatra*
Early first century AD	Cunobelinus/ Cymbeline rules Britain (and dies before AD 43)	Britain	*Cymbeline*
During the reign of a fictional (late?) Roman emperor		Rome	*Titus Andronicus*
c. ninth–tenth century AD	Existence of legendary Amleth?	Denmark	*Hamlet*
15 Aug 1040	Death of Duncan I of Scotland	Bothnguane, Scotland	*Macbeth*
1053	Malcolm invades Scotland	Scotland	*Macbeth*
15 Aug 1057	Death of Macbeth	Lumphanan, Scotland	*Macbeth*
7 Oct 1571	Naval battle of Lepanto between Christians and Turks	The Mediterranean off the coast of Greece	A context for *Othello*

FURTHER READING
AND VIEWING

CRITICAL APPROACHES

Adelman, Janet, *Suffocating Mothers: Fantasies of Maternal Origin in Shakespeare's Plays, Hamlet to The Tempest* (1992). Strong psychoanalytical reading.

Bayley, John, *Shakespeare and Tragedy* (1981). Subtle reading.

Booth, Stephen, *King Lear, Macbeth, Indefinition and Tragedy* (1983). Not for beginners, but very penetrating.

Bradley, A. C., *Shakespearean Tragedy* (1904). Classic interpretation that is still valuable.

Calderwood, James L., *If It Were Done: Macbeth and Tragic Action* (1986). Good on tragedy as performance.

Norbrook, David, "*Macbeth* and the Politics of Historiography," in *Politics of Discourse: The Literature and History of Seventeenth-Century England*, ed. Kevin Sharpe and Steven N. Zwicker (1987), pp. 78–116. Important historical contextualization.

O'Toole, Fintan, *Shakespeare Is Hard, but So Is Life: A Radical Guide to Shakespearian Tragedy* (2002, originally published in 1990 with the title *No More Heroes*). Ideal for beginners, especially in exposing the uselessness of the idea of "the tragic flaw."

Wills, Garry, *Witches and Jesuits: Shakespeare's Macbeth* (1995). Detailed reading in the light of the Gunpowder Plot.

THE PLAY IN PERFORMANCE

Bartholomeusz, Dennis, *Macbeth and the Players* (1969). Exemplary stage history, with much critical insight.

Brooke, Michael, "*Macbeth* on Screen," www.screenonline.org.uk/tv/id/566363/. Excellent brief overview of very wide range of film and television versions.

Brown, John Russell, *Focus on Macbeth* (1982). Fine blend of criticism and dramaturgy.

Granville-Barker, Harley, *Prefaces to Shakespeare: Macbeth* (1930, repr. 1993). Enduring insights from a great man of the theater.

Kliman, Bernice, *Macbeth*, Shakespeare in Performance (1992). The best of the guides to the play via modern performances.

Macbeth, Shakespeare in Production, ed. John Wilders (2004). Overview of modern productions.

Players of Shakespeare 4: Further Essays in Shakespearian Performance by Players with the Royal Shakespeare Company, ed. Robert Smallwood (1998). Includes Derek Jacobi on playing Macbeth.

Rosenberg, Marvin, *The Masks of Macbeth* (1978). Much fascinating detail on actors' interpretations down the ages.

Rutter, Carol Chillington, *Clamorous Voices: Shakespeare's Women Today* (1988). Includes Sinead Cusack on playing Lady Macbeth.

Williams, Gordon, *Macbeth*, Text and Performance (1985). Useful guide.

For a more detailed Shakespeare bibliography and selections from a wide range of critical accounts of the play, with linking commentary, visit the edition website, www.rscshakespeare.co.uk.

AVAILABLE ON DVD

Kumonosu jô, variously known in English as *Throne of Blood* and *The Castle of the Spider's Web* (1957, DVD 2001), directed by Akira Kurosawa. Superlative translation to Samurai Japan.

Macbeth, directed by Roman Polanski (1971, DVD 2002). With Jon Finch and Francesca Annis. Bloody and controversial, but has stood the test of time well.

Macbeth, directed by Trevor Nunn (1978, DVD 2004). Film of Nunn's RSC production with Ian McKellen and Judi Dench: though unable to reproduce the intensity of live theater, especially in a case such as this, it does give continuing life to a masterly production.

Macbeth, directed by Jack Gold (1983, DVD 2004). Low-key production in the BBC television Complete Shakespeare series, but with a thoughtful performance from Nicol Williamson as Macbeth and Jane Lapotaire strong as Lady Macbeth.

Macbeth, directed by Gregory Doran (Channel 4 television 2001, DVD 2003). Film of Doran's RSC production with Antony Sher and Harriet Walter: though unable to reproduce the intensity of live theater, especially in a case such as this, it does give continuing life to an immensely powerful production.

Orson Welles' Macbeth, directed by Orson Welles (1948, DVD 2003). Facinating version by one of cinema's greats.

Shakespeare Retold: Macbeth (BBC television and DVD, 2005), directed by Mark Brozel. Ingenious updating to the kitchen of a celebrity chef, with excellent performances by James McAvoy and Keeley Hawes. Plot and themes, but not language, of the original.

Verdi's Macbeth, conducted by James Levine (DVD 2008). New York Metropolitan Opera production.

REFERENCES

1. Francis Gentleman, "Macbeth," in his *The Dramatic Censor: or, Critical Companion* (1770, repr. 1975), pp. 79–113.
2. *The Universal Museum*, review of 9 January 1762, in *Shakespeare: The Critical Heritage* Vol. 4, 1753–1765, ed. Brian Vickers (1976), pp. 460–62.
3. Thomas Campbell, *Life of Mrs Siddons* (1834), pp. 10–11.
4. Roger Manvell, *Sarah Siddons: Portrait of an Actress* (1970), p. 119.
5. Manvell, *Sarah Siddons*, p. 122.
6. Fanny Kemble, *Journal*, 18 February 1833.
7. *Macbeth*, Shakespeare in Production, ed. John Wilders (2004), p. 27.
8. *Macbeth*, Shakespeare in Production, p. 27.
9. William Hazlitt, "Mr Kean's Macbeth" in his *Collected Works* (1903), vol. 8, pp. 204–7.
10. Review of *Macbeth* in *The Athenaeum*, 1 June 1844.
11. Review in *The Times* (London), 28 September 1847.
12. Review of *Macbeth* in the *Illustrated London News*, 23 March 1850.
13. George Henry Lewes, *Dramatic Essays* (1896), p. 238.
14. See *Macbeth*, Shakespeare in Production, p. 42.
15. *Macbeth: New Variorum Edition of Shakespeare*, ed. H. H. Furness (1873, repr. 1963), p. 470.
16. *The Athenaeum*, 5 January 1889.
17. Quoted in Sandra Richards, "Lady Macbeth in Performance," *The English Review*, 1 (1990), pp. 2–5.
18. *The Athenaeum*, 5 January 1889.
19. *Academy*, 15 April 1876, quoted in *Macbeth*, Shakespeare in Production, p. 47.
20. *The Times* (London), 5 July 1884.
21. *The Times* (London), 5 July 1884.
22. Review in *Blackwood's Edinburgh Magazine*, September 1911.
23. J. L. Styan, *The Shakespeare Revolution: Criticism and Performance in the Twentieth Century* (1977), p. 150.
24. Michael Mullin, *Macbeth Onstage: An Annotated Facsimile of Glen Byam Shaw's 1955 Prompt-book* (1976), p. 184.
25. Mullin, *Macbeth Onstage*, p. 185.

26. James Agate, "Macbeth" in his *Brief Chronicles: A Survey of the Plays of Shakespeare and the Elizabethans in Actual Performance* (1943, repr. 1971), pp. 225–28.

27. Audrey Williamson, "Shakespeare and the Elizabethans," in her *Theatre of Two Decades* (1951), pp. 264–89.

28. J. C. Trewin, *Observer*, 15 June 1952.

29. Joseph Thorp, *Punch*, 10 May 1933.

30. *The Times* (London), 8 June 1955.

31. Irena R. Makaryk, "Shakespeare Right and Wrong," *Theatre Journal*, 50 (1998), pp. 153–63.

32. Stanley Wells, *Shakespeare: A Dramatic Life* (1994), p. 213.

33. *Macbeth*, Shakespeare in Production, p. 133.

34. Gareth Lloyd Evans, "Macbeth: 1946–80 at Stratford-upon-Avon," in *Focus on Macbeth*, ed. John Russell Brown (1982), p. 76.

35. Stephen Wall, *Times Literary Supplement*, 16 April 1982.

36. Roger Warren, *Shakespeare Quarterly*, 34 (1983).

37. Wall, *Times Literary Supplement*, 16 April 1982.

38. Warren, *Shakespeare Quarterly*, 34 (1983).

39. Suzanne Harris, "Macbeth," in *Shakespeare in Performance*, ed. Keith Parsons and Pamela Mason (1995).

40. *Macbeth*, Shakespeare in Production, p. 133.

41. Jonathan Pryce in interview with Matt Wolf, *City Limits*, 1–13 November 1986.

42. Sinead Cusack, "Lady Macbeth's Barren Sceptre," in Carol Rutter, *Clamorous Voices: Shakespeare's Women Today* (1988).

43. Michael Billington, *Guardian*, 13 November 1986.

44. Irving Wardle, *The Times* (London), 12 November 1986.

45. *Macbeth*, RSC Education Pack, 1993.

46. *Macbeth*, RSC Education Pack, 1993.

47. Charles Spencer, *Daily Telegraph*, 17 November 1999.

48. Susannah Clapp, *Observer*, 21 November 1999.

49. Fergal Keane, "Where violent sorrow seems a modern ecstasy," RSC program, *Macbeth*, 1999.

50. Gordon Williams, *Macbeth*, Text and Performance (1985), p. 77.

51. Quoted, Joanna Bourke, "Shell Shock during World War One," www.bbc.co.uk/history/worldwars/wwone/shellshock_03.shtml.

52. Jonathan Pryce in interview with Lesley Thornton, *Observer*, 9 November 1986.

53. Wardle, *The Times*, 12 November 1986.

54. Eric Shorter, *Daily Telegraph*, 13 November 1986.

55. Cusack, "Lady Macbeth's Barren Sceptre."
56. Billington, *Guardian*, 13 November 1986.
57. Wardle, *The Times*, 12 November 1986.
58. Cusack, "Lady Macbeth's Barren Sceptre."
59. Interview with Peter Lewis, *The Times* (London), 16 December 1993.
60. Derek Jacobi, "Macbeth," in *Players of Shakespeare* 4, ed. Robert Smallwood (1998).
61. Irving Wardle, *Independent on Sunday*, 19 December 1993.
62. Jacobi, "Macbeth."
63. Jacobi, "Macbeth."
64. Jacobi, "Macbeth."
65. Williams, *Macbeth:* Text and Performance (1985), p. 119.
66. Michael Billington, *Guardian*, 18 December 1993.
67. Cusack, "Lady Macbeth's Barren Sceptre."
68. Cusack, "Lady Macbeth's Barren Sceptre."
69. Paul Taylor, *Independent*, 18 December 1993.
70. John Gross, *Sunday Telegraph*, 21 November 1999.
71. Paul Taylor, *Independent*, 18 November 1999.
72. Michael Billington, *Guardian*, 17 November 1999.

ACKNOWLEDGMENTS AND PICTURE CREDITS

Preparation of "*Macbeth* in Performance" was assisted by a generous grant from the CAPITAL Centre (Creativity and Performance in Teaching and Learning) of the University of Warwick for research in the RSC archive at the Shakespeare Birthplace Trust. The Arts and Humanities Research Council (AHRC) funded a term's research leave that enabled Jonathan Bate to work on "The Director's Cut."

Picture research by Michelle Morton. Grateful acknowledgment is made to the Shakespeare Birthplace Trust for assistance with reproduction fees and picture research (special thanks to Helen Hargest).

Images of RSC productions are supplied by the Shakespeare Centre Library and Archive, Stratford-upon-Avon. This library, maintained by the Shakespeare Birthplace Trust, holds the most important collection of Shakespeare material in the UK, including the Royal Shakespeare Company's official archives. It is open to the public free of charge.

For more information see www.shakespeare.org.uk.

1. "Macbeth and Banquo" in private collection © Bardbiz Limited
2. Ellen Terry (1888). Reproduced by permission of the Shakespeare Birthplace Trust
3. Directed by Glen Byam Shaw (1955). Angus McBean © Royal Shakespeare Company
4. Directed by Peter Hall (1967). Tom Holte © Shakespeare Birthplace Trust
5. Directed by Adrian Noble (1986). Joe Cocks Studio Collection © Shakespeare Birthplace Trust

6. Directed by Trevor Nunn (1976). Joe Cocks Studio Collection © Shakespeare Birthplace Trust

7. Directed by Rupert Goold (2007). © Donald Cooper/Photostage

8. Directed by Gregory Doran (1999). Jonathan Dockar Drysdale © Royal Shakespeare Company

9. Reconstructed Elizabethan playhouse © Charcoalblue

With new commentary, as well as definitive
text and cutting-edge notes from the RSC's
William Shakespeare: Complete Works,
the first authoritative, modernized edition of
Shakespeare's First Folio in more than 300 years.

Hamlet

Love's Labour's
Lost

A Midsummer
Night's Dream

Richard III

The Tempest

Also available in hardcover
William Shakespeare: Complete Works

**"Timely, original, and beautifully
conceived . . . a remarkable edition."**
—James Shapiro, professor, Columbia
University, bestselling author of *A Year in the
Life of Shakespeare: 1599*